RELIGION AND CULTURE SERIES

Joseph Husslein, S.J., Ph.D., General Editor

THE CHRISTIAN CHURCHES OF THE EAST

POPE PIUS X, PATRIARCH OF THE WEST AND SUPREME PONTIFF,
with Lord Cyril VIII, Patriarch of Antioch, and other members
of the Melkite hierarchy

THE CHRISTIAN CHURCHES OF THE EAST

VOLUME I: CHURCHES IN COMMUNION WITH ROME

By DONALD ATTWATER

The Church of Jesus Christ is neither Latin nor Greek nor Slav but Catholic; accordingly she makes no difference between her children, and Greeks, Latins, Slavs, and members of all other nations are equal in the eyes of the Apostolic See. — POPE BENEDICT XV

THE BRUCE PUBLISHING COMPANY
MILWAUKEE

Nihil obstat: JOHN A. SCHULIEN, S.T.D., Censor librorum
Imprimatur: ✠ MOYSES E. KILEY, Archiepiscopus Milwaukiensis
Die 18 Septembris, 1946

TO

G. B. AND O. B.

WITH

GRATITUDE AND AFFECTION

(Second Printing — 1948)

INTRODUCTION TO VOLUME I

THIS book was first published in 1935 under the title of *The Catholic Eastern Churches*. It has now been stringently revised and, so far as difficult times allow, brought up to date, and is re-published with its fellow on the Dissident or Separated Eastern Churches. The two books are intended as a modest and elementary contribution for English-speaking people to the wider spreading of knowledge about the Christian East; familiarity with whose history, religious life, and present state was so often urged on Catholics (and by implication on other Christians) of the West by the late Pope Pius XI.

Though the expression "Eastern church" is often met, bearing various meanings, there is not in fact, and never has been, a single unified Eastern church corresponding to the Western church over which the Bishop of Rome presides as patriarch as well as supreme pontiff. The "Eastern church" now consists of four unrelated divisions, of which the first two (*Nestorians* and *Monophysites*) are esteemed heretical and consist of six separate churches; the third also is separated from Rome (the *Orthodox*) and consists of some fifteen self-governing churches, most of which are national and all in communion one with another; and the fourth division consists of nine fully organized churches and a number of groups, one in Catholic faith and morals and the communion of the Holy See, known as the *Catholics of Eastern rite*. It is with the last-named division that this book is concerned. Charity begins at home; and until we of the West learn more about the Orientals of our own communion and (I regret to have to add) realize that they are every bit as fully and unequivocally Catholic as ourselves, and act accordingly, it is in vain that we consider all the millions of non-Catholic Orientals, work toward

whose reconciliation with the Holy See was such an outstanding activity of Pius XI's pontificate.

Successfully to present Catholicism to others needs that we should first ourselves realize Catholicism at its best and most authentic. A study, however slight, of the Catholic East contributes to this by emphasizing the variousness and all-embracing-ness of the Church, and helps powerfully to break down that exclusive occidentalism and Europeanism of which we Western Catholics are so often, and not always unjustly, accused: a narrow particularism that is not compatible with Catholicity and is a formidable barrier for non-Catholics of other ancient civilizations, the more so since they themselves are frequently corrupted with particularism, especially in its nationalist form.

I also hope that in a modest way this book may serve another purpose. "So far from being an obstacle," says that distinguished scholar and monk, Dom Fernand Cabrol, "the exact knowledge of facts is, on the contrary, of the greatest assistance to true piety." I include in these pages a considerable number of facts (which I have done my best to make exact) about the various aspects of Eastern religious life, and especially about its public worship. There is no need to apologize for and explain the amount of space given to this last to those who appreciate the fundamental identity of true Christian life with the life of common worship, and who know how strongly the recent Roman pontiffs have encouraged a "liturgical movement" in the Western church. The religious life of Eastern Catholics is notably centred ✓ in the Mass as a communal sacrificial meal and in the daily observances of the Church's year; we may therefore profit by a consideration of their example, and "be moved to a yet warmer love for the true Bride of Christ" by looking upon her "entrancing beauty in the diversity of her various rites" (Pope Pius XI).

This book makes no claim to be anything more than a popular work, an *oeuvre de vulgarisation*. The writer has had some personal experience of Christian life in the Near East; but for the historical parts and accounts of more remote churches he has had to rely on the works and information of others, and has done no original research of his own. Some of the numerous books consulted are noted in the bibliographies that follow each section and further information about each of the churches concerned can be found in the general reference books mentioned at the end. These bibliographies are meant mostly for the general reader and so, except here and there, do not include technical works or those in more esoteric languages than English, German, and French.

It may well appear fantastic that no more than a dozen or so pages is given to the relations between East and West during the first fourteen hundred years of the Church's history. But on that subject many volumes have been written, and this writer's concern is with more recent times and contemporary conditions. Nevertheless the earlier centuries must on no account be ignored by anyone who wants to get a good general grasp of the present-day situation; of no subject is it more true that "The roots of the present are in the past." As Professor A. D. Ritchie has observed, "You cannot expect to understand what a living thing is except by seeing how it has come to be what it is, and considering all the relevant data. That is just the trouble: there are too many data. Writing history consists principally in leaving things out, and the shorter the history the more you leave out."

The perhaps rather daunting schematic arrangement of Chapters IV to VIII was imperatively necessary for the clear and orderly treatment of a very complex subject; for the same reason I gave up any attempt to treat the various groups in chronological order or according to ethnic or geographical affinities: to have done so would have resulted in the most complete confusion. I have instead primarily taken them in alphabetical order of liturgical families, and secondarily in the chronological order of the renewed adherence of the different bodies to the Holy See. But on account of their importance the churches of the Byzantine rite are dealt with first, and for convenience their liturgical rite is considered before the people instead of afterwards as elsewhere; and it was found convenient for historical reasons to treat the ("pure") Syrians before the Maronites.

I have not attempted to be consistent in the transliteration or translation of foreign names — it seems impossible in all but erudite works. With practically no knowledge of tongues at my disposal, I have endeavoured to make respectable words out of them, without doing outrageous violence to any forms that are well known in English. To save constant repetitions, I may say here that, except in those cases where I have been able to get later official information, all statistics are taken from the *Statistica con Cenni Storici . . . di Rito Orientale,* published by the Sacred Eastern Congregation at Rome in 1932. I cannot say how much I owe to this book, and must record my grateful thanks to its anonymous compiler: an anonymity easily pierced, and covering one to whom everybody interested in Eastern ecclesiastical affairs owes an incalculable debt.

As regards customs, ritual, etc., I have concerned myself only with typical Catholic usages, which do not necessarily hold good for non-Catholics of the same rite, though to a very large extent they are identical. Only occasionally do I note divergences under this head, though they are often implied by the context (e.g., when a Catholic body uses a Roman office translated into its own liturgical tongue).

The names used for the different groups of Catholic Easterners are those found in the above-mentioned official *Statistica.* They have the advantage of being clear and in accordance with past history and present fact; they have the disadvantage of often being different from what the people concerned call themselves or are called locally, especially in North America. The commonest colloquial name is "Greek Catholic," for any Catholic of the Byzantine rite; apart from the scientific inadmissibility of such a usage, it is unsuitable in a book like this because of the difficulty of distinguishing between Rumanian and Melkite and Greek and other "Greek Catholics." I suppose that within limits people are entitled to call themselves what they like; but a writer on the subject can hardly be expected to grapple with such atrocities as "Ruthenian-Greek-Roman Catholic" — which I have seen in an American paper.

Catholic Orientals are sometimes called "Uniates." This word is derived from Latin *unio*, "union," through the Polish *unia* (Russian *unija*, Greek *ounia*), whereas the word for "union" is ordinarily *jednosc, soedinenie*, and *enosis* in those languages respectively. It was coined as a term of contempt by the opponents of the Union of Brest (p. 69), and for that reason alone its use by Catholics is to be deplored. It is often used in a hostile sense by non-Catholics and it is repudiated by those of whom it is used;[1] moreover, it is never found in official ecclesiastical acts at Rome or in such publications as the *Annuario Pontificio*. "Catholic of such and such a rite" is more trouble to say and write, but it is strictly accurate and void of offence or regrettable association.[2]

A word, too, about "rite." This term primarily means the words to be said and actions to be done in performing a given act of religion; e.g., the rite of Baptism. By extension it means a complete system of ritual and prayer to be used in the worship of God and the administration of the sacraments; so we have the Antiochene rite, the whole complex of prayers and ceremonies originating at or associated with the city and patriarchate of Antioch. In time this gets modified, on the one hand into what we call the "Syrian rite" and on the other into the "Maronite rite." (The English technical word "use" ["ad usum ecclesiae Sarum"] is obviously fitted for the sub-rites, e.g., the Maronite and the Ethiopic. Unfortunately it has become almost obsolete.) Counting the several variations of the Latin rite as only one, there are ten rites in this last sense, and each one is represented by a body of Catholics using it today (and, with the exception of the Latins and Maronites, by much larger non-Catholic bodies as well). Each of these bodies is also called a rite, which in this sense is equivalent to "church" and includes the manner of organization, proper canon law, customs, etc., appertaining thereto.

---

[1] It is rather as if an Eastern Catholic should insist on calling English-speaking Catholics "Romanists" — a term forever associated by us with the attacks of Protestantism.

[2] "United Rumanians," "United Syrians," and so on, is a convenient and harmless expression, very popular in French.

Every child of Catholic parents belongs to one or other of these rites. If his parents differ in rite, he belongs to that of the father; if only one parent is a Catholic, the child belongs to that parent's rite. The word *rite* constantly occurs in these pages in one or other of all these senses: which one is meant should be clear from the context.

Throughout this volume I have had time and again to refer to and emphasize differences of one sort or another between the Catholic churches of the East and of the West. This was necessitated by the nature and object of the work. But I must say, once and for all, that the differences, striking as they are, are less important than the likenesses which underlie them. I refer, of course, to accidentals. In its faith, its religious doctrines and canons of conduct, there is complete oneness in all parts of the Catholic Church: there is no room for either likeness or dissimilarity — there is simply identity. But even in accidental matters — of worship, discipline, usage, mental habit — study and examination show how often the same or similar ideas, framework, origin, are behind the differing practices of East and West. And above all and in all is the same enlightening Spirit.

My grateful thanks for help generously given are due to many people in many lands, too numerous to name individually. All the illustrations, unless otherwise noted, are reproduced by kind permission of the editor of the *Eastern Churches Quarterly*.

DONALD ATTWATER

CONTENTS

LIST OF ILLUSTRATIONS

THE CHRISTIAN CHURCHES OF THE EAST

CHAPTER I

EAST AND WEST BEFORE THE SCHISM

ONE of the most common misunderstandings about the Catholic Church is that it is uniform in all respects throughout the world. That is not true. The Church has unity, that is, there is only one true church and she is one in herself, and she has uniformity of faith in things divinely revealed, whether touching dogma or the principles of right conduct: these things are matters of absolute truth and therefore necessarily uniform. But beyond that, no. There is not and never has been any principle of uniformity in Catholicism that requires all Catholics to worship with the same liturgical forms, in the same language, to be subject to an identical canon law, to have the same customs and usages. And, in fact, they do not.

It is easy to see how the misunderstanding has arisen. Most American and western European Catholics never assist at any Mass but the Roman Mass in the Latin tongue, or come across usages with which they are not more or less familiar, or hear of discipline that differs from their own; pulpit, press, and private conversation all seem to assume (sometimes definitely say) that these things are and must be the same for all Catholics everywhere. And yet we have not to look very far to see that this seeming uniformity is fallacious. To mention only one thing, but the most important of all, the Mass: the prayers and ceremonies of the Mass as celebrated by a Dominican or Calced Carmelite friar are not exactly the same as those in the Roman Missal; nor are those of the Carthusian monks, nor those used in the archdioceses of Milan and Braga and Lyons, or at Toledo; while in many churches in Yugoslavia the Roman Mass is celebrated in Slavonic.

1

The Mass is always and everywhere *one* considered as the Eucharistic Sacrifice: the true sacrifice of the body and blood of Christ made present on the altar by the words of consecration, the representation and renewal of the offering made once for all on the cross of Calvary, the doing of that which our Lord at the Last Supper told us, through His apostles, to do; and that is what matters, and all that matters, essentially. But to say that in every Catholic church Mass is celebrated with the same prayers and ceremonies is not true. The Eucharistic Sacrifice is one, the ways of offering it are many.

The varieties of the Latin Mass mentioned above are more or less closely related to and resemble the usual Roman form. But there are other Catholics, eight millions of them, distinguished as the Catholics of the Eastern rites, whose Mass is altogether different in its prayers and externals from those with which we are familiar, who are subject to different canon law, who differ from us in almost every conceivable thing — always excepting faith and morals.

For some time after all the Apostles were dead the organization and liturgy of the Church were fluid. The unit was the local church, the community of Christians in one place, whose bishop, assisted by priests and deacons, "presided in the place of God," as St. Ignatius the Godbearer says, over the faithful of that locality. It was not long before certain important bishops were exercising jurisdiction over other bishops, especially those whom they had themselves ordained and set over some new Christian community.[1] This was the beginning of "metropolitans" or "archbishops" and led later to the very important office of "patriarch" and the accompanying territorial division. The forms of worship

---

[1] The principle that a bishop has jurisdiction over the bishop whom he consecrates is a very important one in ecclesiastical history, especially in the East. The pope as Patriarch of the West has the right to consecrate all bishops of the Western church (a right which for obvious reasons he does not exercise in person); the same with the other patriarchs.

and offering the Holy Sacrifice differed from church to church and were in the vernacular of the local faithful (e.g., Aramaic at first in Jerusalem, Greek at Antioch and Rome); gradually these forms solidified into types or "families," those of the most important churches becoming the norms for the lesser ones associated with or dependent on them.[2]

From the earliest times a primacy of the see of St. Peter in Rome was recognized by all other sees, and the next most important bishops were those of Alexandria (whose church may have been founded by St. Mark) and Antioch, where also St. Peter had presided, and these were also the three chief cities of the Roman Empire. After Constantine the Great had transferred his capital to the east, Constantinople soon climbed to the second place of ecclesiastical honour. These four cities give their names to the four chief types of Christian liturgy, which with their variants are in use today. In the early centuries the East played a preponderating part in Christian history and thought (Greek was the language of the Roman church until about the middle of the third century: Latin was first used for liturgical purposes in Africa); the Greek fathers and doctors not merely left an ineffaceable mark but were the fundamental formative influences in the post-apostolic Church; the first eight oecumenical councils were all held in the East and were predominantly Oriental in their constitution. For seventy-five years in the sixth and seventh centuries almost every one of the popes of Rome was a Greek or Syrian: and there were others; over twenty Oriental popes in all.

Though, of course, the great heresies of the early days of Christianity, Arianism, Pelagianism, etc., did not disappear without leaving a trace, only two of them are still represented by existing churches, whose origins were in the Christological controversies of the fifth century which are known respectively as Nestorianism and Monophysism.

---

[2] In the middle of the third century Firmilian, bishop of Caesarea in Cappadocia, remarks that the liturgical variety then existing made no difference to unity.

The heresy which takes its name from Nestorius, bishop of Constantinople, maintains that in our Lord there are *two* persons, God the Son and the man Jesus, and that Jesus alone was born of our Lady and died on the cross. The controversy raged round the representative word *theotokos*, Mother of God, a title which the Nestorians, of course, refused to recognize. Diodoros, bishop of Tarsus, and Theodore, bishop of Mopsuestia, rather than Nestorius, were the originators of the heresy, which was condemned in the year 431 by the oecumenical Council of Ephesus. Refusal to accept this condemnation gave rise to the separate heretical *Nestorian Church*, those members of which who have returned to Catholicity are called Chaldeans (see p. 198).

Twenty years later there was an even worse schism. The patriarch of Alexandria supported the false doctrine of a monk called Eutyches (d. *c.* 455), who taught that in Jesus Christ there is only one nature, His humanity being completely absorbed in and identified with His divinity and His body not of one substance with ours, which means that He was not really a man at all and His earthly life only an appearance. It arose from the opposition to Nestorianism, which was led by St. Cyril, Patriarch of Alexandria, upon whose death in 444 his successor Dioscoros hotly and unscrupulously took up the cause of the innovators. After six years of controversy and violence the Emperor Marcian convened a council, at which Pope St. Leo I's legates presided. It met at Chalcedon and, after deposing Dioscoros who refused to submit to the "dogmatic letter" in which, two years earlier, the pope had defined the truth about the disputed matters, the bishops on October 22, 451, declared the Catholic faith to be that in the one person of Jesus Christ there are two real, perfect, and complete natures, the divine and the human. Thus the Council of Ephesus was confirmed against Nestorianism, and Eutychianism solemnly condemned. Many in Egypt and Syria refused to accept the findings of the council, and so gave rise to several schismatic churches, namely, the *Coptic* in Egypt, the *Syrian Jacobite*, the *Armenian*, the *Ethiopic*, and (indirectly and centuries later) the *Malabar Jacobite*

Churches; minorities from all of these have since come back to Catholic unity (see pp. 132, 142, 152, 181, 210).

These bodies are known historically as the "monophysite churches," because they are supposed to uphold the doctrine of our Lord's "one nature." But it is not so simple as that. Apart from some extremists, the so-called monophysites in fact repudiated (and repudiate) the teaching of Eutyches. What exactly they did profess, and why (apart from very powerful political and "nationalist" considerations) they rejected the Council of Chalcedon, are extremely difficult questions to which no satisfactory answers have yet been found.[3] Such problems are not the concern of this book, and so herein the usual historical terms "Monophysism" and "monophysite" are used, without the intention of begging any questions. The important point here is that the churches mentioned above have for the past fifteen hundred years been out of communion with both Catholics and Orthodox.

For six hundred years after the Council of Chalcedon the Universal Church remained organized in five distinct parts, the patriarchates of Rome (or the West), Constantinople, Alexandria, Antioch, and Jerusalem. The West included roughly everything west of a line from the eastern end of Crete to Danzig (though the borders, especially Illyricum, were disputed with Constantinople), with the north coast of Africa; Constantinople had Thrace, most of Asia Minor and, at the very end of the period, Russia; Alexandria was reduced to the few Catholics left in Egypt and the lands south of it who were faithful to Chalcedon; Antioch ruled the similar but much larger Catholic remnant in Syria; Jerusalem had the small territory of Palestine and the Sinai peninsula. Each of these divisions was administratively independent of the other and appointed its own patriarch locally, and each had its own liturgy, discipline, and customs,[4] though ultimately what was left of the last three patriarchates

---

[3] The best treatment of the subject is by Maspero, *Historie des Patriarches d'Alexandrie* (Paris, 1930). Monophysite theologians have often accused the Chalcedonian fathers of Nestorianism.

[4] But a man did not necessarily have the same liturgy as his patriarch, e.g., the pope ruled over Byzantines in *Magna Graecia* and Illyricum.

became uniform with Constantinople, the imperial city. (In those days there was more liturgical and disciplinary uniformity in the Catholic East than in the West; Constantinople much more than Rome has always tried to impose her own observances as a matter of principle.) The four Eastern patriarchs recognized in the Bishop of Rome, as successor of St. Peter, a primacy of jurisdiction of uncertain extent, and a final court of appeal in doctrinal matters, although the dogma of papal infallibility was not yet distinctly formulated and defined.

At that time one could speak of an Eastern and a Western part of the Church with more definiteness than now, and the difference was much more than geographical and ritual (as it still is). It was temperamental, and there was a strong cultural division. Surprising as it may seem to us, Constantinople looked on western Europe as a land of barbarians — and not without reason. She, "the New Rome," was the heir of the glories both of Greece and Rome and, with all her glaring faults, a not unworthy one; she was, too, the bulwark of Christendom, staving off to the best of her ability the Arabs, Turks, and Mongols while the western countries were painfully hammering out a new order from the ruins of the western empire and the new barbarian peoples that occupied its lands.

Nevertheless, despite the unhappy rivalry that emerged, there was fundamentally less cultural cleavage between the western Europeans centred at Rome and the eastern Europeans centred at Constantinople (for they all had roots in Old Rome) than there was between both and the Asiatic Christians in Syria and farther east. From some aspects the more or less arbitrary line of division between Christian east and west should be drawn north and south through Antioch rather than through Constantinople. But as ecclesiastical history, closely bound up with secular history, developed, it is an irregular course roughly from Riga through Constantinople to Alexandria that the line takes.

Constantinople (Byzantium) is the critical point, for that was the imperial city, where there developed the idea of the Church as a civil institution in which the sacred Emperor had in practice a controlling function — the phenomenon of Caesaro-papism, which meant the subjection of religion to the state. Herein perhaps was the tap-root of Byzantine particularism, and so of the separatist tendency of the Byzantine church.

Friction and ill feeling between East and West were thus manifest at an early date. It was aggravated by Constantinople's rise to ecclesiastical power, and her ambition was increased after the Arabs had overrun the other Eastern patriarchates and made them powerless. On the other hand, it is admitted that Rome did not always act with discretion and in a spirit of conciliation, though it was a perfectly legitimate political action that deepened and made critical the historical background of tension and rivalry: this was the crowning by Pope St. Leo III on Christmas Day in the year 800 of the Frankish Charlemagne as Emperor of the West. Constantinople, both civil and religious, was deeply wounded by what she interpreted as the transference to the West of the age-long *imperium* of the Byzantine *basileus*.

Little by little she allowed herself to be led away by the idea of setting up a Byzantine universality in opposition to Roman universality and, when opportunity offered, at its expense.[5] The first stakes in this struggle were the southern Slavs and the slavonized Tartars of Bulgaria, who were established on the borders of the two powers, and the duel, though its most important consequences did not come till later, was fought out chiefly during the ninth century. It was with a letter written at the patriarch's order by Leo, the metropolitan of the Bulgars, that the schism of Cerularius began.

Meanwhile, temporary formal ruptures of communion became more and more frequent, until in the year 858 there began the "affair of Photios," who had been made patriarch of Constantinople by the emperor Michael III the Drunkard and his uncle Bardas Caesar: serious difficulties between him and Pope St. Nicholas I followed. There is no need to go into all that here, but this much must be said: For centuries Photios has been re-

---

[5] As early as 586 John IV the Faster assumed the title of Oecumenical Patriarch, still borne by the patriarch of Constantinople.

garded by Catholics as a great man whose insatiable ambition betrayed him into becoming the arch-schismatic and opponent of the primacy of the Holy See, and by the Orthodox (who keep his feast as a saint on February 6) as the great champion of Eastern independence against the encroachments of Rome. But in our own time the historical records on which these judgments were based have received new and intensive study from Catholic scholars, of which the result has been — not indeed entirely to rehabilitate Photios — but to produce a picture of what actually occurred quite different from the one hitherto rather uncritically accepted. Pope St. Nicholas himself called Photios "a man of great virtue and world-wide knowledge," and it has always been recognized in the West that he "was one of the greatest men of the Middle Ages, one of the most remarkable characters in all church history. . . . The greatest scholar of his time . . . [with] no shadow of suspicion against his private life" (Fortescue). We now know that he was not as well the unscrupulous ecclesiastic we had hitherto supposed, even though he did quarrel with the pope (and the Bulgarian question just referred to was involved in that) and make charges against practices of the Western church. All the same, the Photian troubles unquestionably did harm, and helped to bring Greeks and Latins, East and West, into formal opposition.[6]

Mutual distrust and jealousy grew, and one hundred and eighty-six years later, when the churches were enjoying, as the patriarch John XI Bekkos says, "complete peace," the patriarch of Constantinople, Michael Cerularius, suddenly attacked Pope St. Leo IX. He impugned certain Western customs as unchristian, and without provocation closed all the Latin churches in Constantinople.

The principal customs which Cerularius, borrowing from Photius, objected to were celibacy of the clergy (never the rule

---

[6] A summary, with pertinent bibliography, of the findings in this matter of Fathers Amann, Laurent, Grumel, and Dvornik can be found in the *Clergy Review* (London) for November, 1938, by Father Andrew Beck, called "Propaganda in History: the Greek Schism." See also Fliche & Martin, *Histoire de l'Eglise,* tome VI (Paris, 1938).

in the East), fasting on Saturdays as well as Fridays (then usual in the West), and the use of unleavened bread (*azyme*) in the Eucharist. It must be clearly understood that neither the pope nor anybody else had asked Constantinople to adopt any of these practices. There was no mention at first of the *Filioque*, but that trouble, too, was in its origins more disciplinary and liturgical than dogmatic. The East has always attached more importance to matters of discipline and ritual than the West has. At this time all their traditional usages were esteemed of directly apostolic origin and were given a textual support from Holy Scripture (e.g., for fasting, Luke 5:33–35). Also they had a great aversion for "judaizing," hence their objection to *azyme* and the Sabbatine fast.[7]

Cerularius had not the support of the emperor Constantine IX, but he was a man of ambition, unscrupulous and forceful, and ready to defy emperor as well as pope; and in the course of the resulting controversy he struck Leo IX's name from the commemoration in the liturgy. After vain negotiations the legates sent from Rome solemnly excommunicated Cerularius and two of his prelates in the church of the Holy Wisdom on July 16, 1054. Just as the liturgy was about to begin, Cardinal Humbert of Silva Candida, Cardinal Frederick Gozelon, and Peter, archbishop of Amalfi, passed through the crowded church, entered the sanctuary, and laid the act of excommunication upon the altar. "*Videat Deus et judicet*," they exclaimed, and departed.

It was a regrettably theatrical gesture, and recent scholarship has criticized it heavily (*e.g.* Jugie, in *Echos d'Orient*, No. 188, 1937). At the moment of the excommunication St. Leo IX, the pope from whom the legates received their powers, was dead, and it is arguable that those powers had accordingly lapsed; it is also arguable that Leo would not have approved their violent action; it is certain that Cardinal Humbert was extremely ill-informed about the East and the matters in dispute. In any case,

---

[7] In our own times Eastern Catholics received without demur the definitions of the Immaculate Conception and papal infallibility, but raised endless trouble about the Gregorian kalendar and the election of bishops (Melkites in 1857–60, Armenians and Chaldeans in 1867–79).

though this event is commonly taken to be the definitive separation of East from West, it was long before the schism was everywhere consummated, set, and accepted as permanent; Rome's practice today is rather to date it from 1472, when Constantinople formally repudiated the Union of Florence.[8] Nevertheless, July 16, 1054, may well be regarded as the most calamitous date in Christian history. It marks the beginning of the complete parting of East and West, and no subsequent reconciliation has been lasting or widespread enough to make any substantial difference.

The Great Church of Constantinople itself was not (and has never been) excommunicated by the Holy See, who accused her of no heresy; but she separated from Rome, and the other Byzantine patriarchates followed, thus forming what is now known as the *Orthodox Eastern Church*.[9]

Today the Eastern Catholics again form a considerable, if heterogeneous body; but the non-Catholic Easterns, hardly less heterogeneous, outnumber them very many times. Truth does not depend on a counting of heads and the unity of the Catholic Church is indefectible, it remains formally resplendent; but materially she is maimed and weakened, lacking these wandering children: the unhealed breach between Rome and the East is the biggest, saddest, and most significant among the divisions of Christendom.

After Cerularius there were no continuously and unambiguously Catholic Orientals at all except the Greeks in southern Italy and Sicily (*Magna Graecia*), whose wavering loyalty to the Holy See was consolidated and strengthened at the Council

---

[8] An example of this is the permission given to Russian Catholics to observe the feast of St. Sergius of Radonezh (d. 1392) and of other mediaeval Russian saints.

[9] It would appear that historically the epithet "Orthodox" in this connection distinguishes those Christians who accepted the Council of Chalcedon: see P. de la Taille in *Orientalia Christiana*, Vol. V, no. 21, p. 281. Some Byzantines in communion with Rome call themselves "Catholic-Orthodox," quite reasonably. In the *berat* which the sultan formerly gave to a newly elected Catholic Melkite patriarch he was called head of the *Rûm kathulik milleti*, of which the English equivalent is "Catholic Orthodox nation."

of Bari in 1098, largely through the efforts of St. Anselm, archbishop of Canterbury, and, after the First Crusade, the Maronites
in Syria and some Armenians. There were for long theologians
on both sides who appreciated the wickedness and folly of the
situation and did their best to mend it, but the schism gradually
hardened, ecclesiastical intercourse between East and West grew
less and less, and the churches drifted further apart.[10] One of the
biggest factors against reconciliation was, unhappily, provided
by the Westerners themselves in the way they conducted the
Crusades, especially the fourth. Indeed, it can be cogently argued
that the Crusades did far more to produce a spirit of separatism
between ordinary Christians of East and West than the actions
of bishops such as Cerularius and Humbert could ever have done.
It is, as Dr. Fortescue says, "an abominable story," and the Greeks
did not forgive and never have forgiven the Latins for sacking
Constantinople in 1204, driving out their bishops, stealing their
churches, murdering their emperor, and setting a Frank in his
place for fifty-seven years; they resented and feared the haughty
arrogance and domineering efficiency of Normans and English-
men, and wanted to have nothing to do with either them or their
church. In particular, the playing fast and loose with Eastern
sees and their holders made the name of Crusader — and consequently of Catholic — stink in the nostrils of pious Orientals.
What Pope Innocent III himself thought of the heroes of the
Fourth Crusade can be read in his letter to Cardinal Peter of
Capua: "The Latins have given an example only of perversity
and works of darkness. It is natural that (the Greeks) should
regard them as curs. These soldiers of Christ . . . are drenched
in Christian blood." Unfortunately the pope himself adopted a
policy that was the very reverse of pacifying. Furthermore, the
Greeks looked time and again to their fellow Christians in the
West for help in their struggle against the oncoming tide of Islam;
but it was rarely forthcoming and never effective. This was not
always the Westerners' fault. But the only western "powers" help-

---

[10] One Greek bishop was present at the eleventh oecumenical council
(Lateran III) in 1179.

ing the Greeks at the last defence of Constantinople, the city that
had conserved European culture through the barbarian dark
ages, were a handful of men sent by the pope and five ships and
seven hundred men from the republic of Genoa. When, after the
Council of Florence, the news reached Constantinople that the
Greek bishops Bessarion and Isidore had been made cardinals,
"Better," said Duke Luke Notaras, remembering the fourth crusade, "better the turban in Constantinople than a Roman cardinal's hat." The people of the city were to learn whether it was
so or not.

There were, nevertheless, two attempts at complete reunion
during the Middle Ages, both originating on the Eastern side and
both prompted fundamentally by political considerations —
though very worthy ones. The emperors at Constantinople hoped
by recognizing the pope to encourage him to send a crusade
that would draw off the Franks from their capital and drive the
Saracens into the desert. The patriarch Joseph I was not so willing, so the emperor Michael VIII Palailogos shut him up in a
monastery, set up John Bekkos, who was favourable, in his stead,
and sent representatives in 1274 to the Second Council of Lyons,
who concluded a union with the Roman Church. There was no
difficulty about it, because the emperor said that his representatives were to make the union and not argue. But the people and
clergy of Constantinople did not want it, it was never effective,
and was formally repudiated by the emperor Andronikos II eight
years later. The story of the Union of Florence in 1439 is very
similar, though with more important results. John VII Palailogos
wanted help against the Ottoman Turks, who were at his very
gates. This time the patriarch of Constantinople, Joseph II, himself attended the council,[11] as well as representatives from other
churches, and, after much discussion, acts of reunion were effected on behalf of the four Orthodox patriarchs, the katholikos
of the Armenians, the Coptic patriarch, some Syrian Jacobites,
and one Nestorian bishop. In the case of the last four the union

---

[11] He died in Florence. His tomb may be seen in Santa Maria Novella.

was never effective, though it had important repercussions in the non-Byzantine East.

The "four points of the Council of Florence" which formed the basis of agreement with the Orthodox were their acceptance of the supreme primacy of the pope, of the validity of the use of unleavened bread in the Eucharist, of the existence of purgatory, and of the procession of the Holy Ghost from the Father and the Son.[12] In Russia the Great-Prince Basil II refused the union at once, but it was the remote cause of the reconciliation of the Kievan eparchies at Brest in 1595. In the patriarchates of Alexandria, Antioch, and Jerusalem it subsisted for a time, and indeed never completely died out in the second of them. At Constantinople it was not well received; but at the taking of the city by the Turks in 1453 the last Liturgy was celebrated in the church of the Holy Wisdom ("St. Sophia") and the last Roman emperor, Constantine XII, died in battle, in communion with the Holy See.

These efforts at reuniting Christendom failed primarily because they were not undertaken from pure motives of love of God and concern for the good of religion.[13] Moreover, despite the interest of Roman church authorities, much of the West was indifferent to the matter, while in the East people and clergy as a whole were strongly against union with Rome. For the rest, the Crusades were instrumental in regularizing the Maronites of Syria in communion with the Holy See, from which they have never since swerved, and in organizing a church of Armenian Catholics

---

[12] These four points were made the basis of the Rumanian reunion at Alba Julia in 1698.

[13] A Catholic has so often to disagree with Canon J. A. Douglas, one of the leaders of the Anglican-Orthodox *rapprochement*, that it is a special pleasure to quote him with approval when he writes: "As the story is told in our text-books Christian disunion is presented as the evil fruit simply of theological perversity. That story needs to be rewritten. Threatening to the vital truths of the gospel as undoubtedly they were, heresies have rarely done more than provide battle flags for national and social quarrels. All the historic schisms which have endured have been far more the work of the politician and the statesman than of the theologian. No one can understand the Orthodox Church today without grasping that fact."

in Asia Minor, most of whom afterwards fell away. From time to time Dominican and Franciscan friars were active in Armenia, Syria, Egypt, and Ethiopia, and among the Nestorians, but with no solid results; obscure groups were reconciled here or there and came to an end; sometimes influential individuals were convinced but found few to follow their example. Such, for instance, were the Greek theologian Barlaam, whom Pope Clement VI made bishop of the Byzantine diocese of Gerace in Calabria, and his disciple Demetrios Kydones, secretary to the emperor John Kantakuzena, who was reconciled in 1350 and translated the *Summa contra Gentiles* and other works of St. Thomas Aquinas into Greek. In connection with these events Clement's successor, Innocent VI, sent the Carmelite bishop Peter Thomas to Constantinople with the style of "Legate to the Eastern Church," in 1359.

Twenty years after the end of the Byzantine empire, the Church of Constantinople formally repudiated the Union of Florence, in part under pressure from Constantinople's new Turkish masters, and the other Orthodox patriarchates drifted in her wake. That date, 1472, as much as, and in some ways more than, 1054, marks the real break between Eastern and Western Christendom. Between those two dates the state of schism had not yet hardened and become completely set: the Orthodox, in the nature of things never so conscious of Old Rome as the West, had not noticed much practical difference; the Catholics for long had looked on the Orthodox, not as a "different church," but as part of the One Church temporarily out of communion — a state of affairs that had been known at times before. But now, in addition to the ecclesiastical disagreements, the Christian people of the Byzantine East (except the Russians) were under the civil rule of a great foreign and non-Christian power which aimed at further conquests in Europe: the Turks would not tolerate the association of the Christian church in their dominions with the Christian church of their "Frankish" enemies — that is an important aspect of the Greek schism that is often overlooked.

So in 1472 the separation became as it were definitive: Catholics and Orthodox have since looked on one another, not simply as erring brethren, but as members of, so to speak, quite different and separate Christian families.

It was not till the sixteenth century that permanent reunions of Orientals in notable numbers began to take place, beginning with some Nestorians in 1551. The more important of these were of the Ruthenian dioceses of southwest Russia in 1595, of the Rumanians in Transylvania in 1698, and of the Melkites in 1724, all from the Orthodox. But these and other like movements were not of sufficient weight to alter substantially the non-Catholic churches of the East, and except for the continual subdivision of the Orthodox and other internal results of history, they remain as bodies today what they were five hundred years ago.

CHAPTER II

THE EASTERN CATHOLICS TODAY

WHAT would have been the position today had the schism never happened or had the brief reunion patched up at the Council of Florence in 1439 been permanent? Other things being equal, there would now be some 482 million Catholics in the world (instead of about 335 million), of whom one third would be using the liturgy of Constantinople, in numerous languages, with communion in both kinds, a married parochial clergy, and all other their own customs, under their own patriarchs, subject to the pope as supreme pontiff. But the schism *did* take place, and those who had separated from Rome looked upon the Catholic Church as a West-European institution, "Latin" in its outlook, worship, and usages: as if Catholicism were synonymous with the Western church. And after the Council of Trent there was a greater and ever increasing uniformity of worship, discipline, and administration. Throughout the later Middle Ages it was almost true to say that in every Catholic church the Mass was the Latin, western Mass. Almost, but not quite. There remained faithful to Rome a body of Christians of Greek blood in southern Italy and Sicily who kept their Greek liturgy and customs; there was in the Lebanon the larger body of Maronite Catholics, with their Syrian liturgy and customs; and after the First Crusade there was in Cilicia a number of Catholics of the Armenian rite who had returned to communion with the Holy See. This tiny minority of Catholic Easterners served providentially to preserve the material catholicity, the all-embracingness, the diversity-in-union of the Church of Christ.

Up to the time of the schism there had never been any idea of uniformity in the Universal Church outside the necessary uniformity in faith and morals: such a notion would have been regarded as superfluous, impracticable, improper, and more than a little laughable. The rites of the East Syrian monk who gave communion to Edward I of England in France early in the fourteenth century must have been as unfamiliar to the king as they would be to us: but they did not cause him to question the stranger's catholicity and orthodoxy. After the schism, as I have said, the Church quite accidentally took on to all intents and purposes an entirely Western, Latin, and more uniform complexion (though it must not be forgotten that in those days the Latin Mass varied in details almost from diocese to diocese).[1] This was greatly extended by the missionary activities of the sixteenth and seventeenth centuries. But at the very time when Spanish, Portuguese, and French missionaries were carrying Catholic faith and Western practices to the heathen of the New World and the Far East, bodies of Eastern Christians nearer home began to return to the pope's obedience. The first of these was led by the Nestorian katholikos John Sulaka in 1551. From that time onward there has been a continuous movement of Orientals back to Catholic unity, generally a dribble of individuals but sometimes amounting to the small wave of an "hierarchical reunion," down to the reconciliation of Mar Ivanios and Mar Theophilos in India in 1930. It is with these Catholics and their few predecessors that this book is concerned.

When these people submitted themselves to the Holy See they kept their own forms of worship, church law, and religious customs. It must be clearly understood that this is not a matter of *concession* but of *right:* they as Catholics have as much right to their traditional and immemorial usages as we Latins have to ours.[2] To attempt to produce a universal uniformity in these

---

[1] During the latter Middle Ages there were in England and Wales alone the "uses" of Sarum, York, Hereford, and Bangor, to say nothing of those of the religious orders.

[2] No doubt in the abstract the Holy See could impose the Latin rite on, say, Byzantines — and could impose the Byzantine rite on Latins. It is as likely to do the one as the other.

things would be artificial, unnatural, untraditional, un-Catholic; and it would not succeed. Moreover, their orders being, in general, valid, their prelates and priests were usually reinstated in the offices which they had held as schismatics. There were only two exceptions to this on a large scale, the Ethiopians and the Malabarese in the seventeenth century: both were disastrous and resulted in the loss of several million people to the Church. Both these tragedies were due to too close a dependence of missionary clergy on a "Catholic power" (Portugal) and to the disregard by European prelates (who were ignorant and frightened of Oriental ways) of the instructions of Rome that these people's lawful customs were not to be interfered with.

Since then the Holy See has made it perfectly clear time and again that the Church is Catholic and not specifically Latin or European. In his bull "Etsi pastoralis" in 1742 for the Italo-Greeks, Pope Benedict XIV declared that they were to keep to their own rites, recognized the ordination of the married, and ordered that no precedence was to be based on rite; certain provisions that implied privileges for the Western rite were abrogated subsequently. In the following year he addressed a decree, "Demandatam caelitus," to the Melkites, in which he forbade them to alter their liturgy or to become Latins without Rome's express permission. In 1755 the same pope issued an encyclical letter, "Allatae sunt," to the missionaries in the Near East. Herein he traced the consistent attitude of the Holy See in this matter from the eleventh century onwards, and set out legislation based on the text "We desire most intensely that all people should be Catholics but not all Latins," reminding those whom he addressed that their function was to support and help the local indigenous Catholic clergy and not to boss them. Pope Pius IX emphasized the same things in his appeal to the separated Orientals, the encyclical "In suprema" of 1848.

In 1893 the international eucharistic congress was held in Jerusalem and at it the Eastern element predominated. It marks a new era in the history of the Catholic East, of which the first important fruit was Pope Leo XIII's constitution "Orientalium *dignitas"* in 1894.[3] Among other things, this emphasized that all rites are on exactly the same footing religiously and canonically; moreover, it decreed that any Western priest who should persuade an Eastern Christian to adopt the Latin rite should by that very fact incur suspension from his sacerdotal functions. Any Eastern non-Catholic who becomes a Catholic is strongly encouraged to adhere to the rite which he has hitherto followed, though it seems he is not bound to;[4] without a rescript from the Holy See, no Catholic can change his canonical status from Eastern to Western, or vice-versa (Canon 98, § 3).

That is the law, but it is well known that it is not everywhere administered in its full rigour,[5] and that is one of the reasons why non-Catholic Easterners insist that "Rome wants to turn them all into Latins." The relative insignificance of some of the Eastern churches and the obscurity of the individuals who compose them, right and proper soil wherein Christianity may flourish, produce a result very marked among the smaller ones and apparent in its degree in all of the Eastern churches — some dissidents who wish to return to Catholic unity, especially if they be persons of some culture or position, or if, on the other hand, they be extremely poor and downtrodden, ask to be, and are, allowed to join the Latin rite. Numbers of Orientals, whether Catholic or to be reconciled, and even bodies of non-Christians living among Catholics of Eastern rite (e.g., Alauite villages in Syria) do this. Why? Spiritual reasons? Undoubtedly, sometimes

---

[3] This pope did a pleasing thing toward our separated Eastern brethren in 1882. He substituted the title "titular bishop" for "bishop *in partibus infidelium*" because some of the sees *i.p.i.* again had Christian populations, though not in communion with Rome.

[4] In 1933 a Japanese convert was received into the Church in Poland as a Byzantine.

[5] Even still one meets and hears of cases of most improper pressure being applied to induce Orientals to "turn Latin." The Russian exarch Leonid Feodorov (see p. 125) had to report to Rome that the Latin Catholics of Petersburg acted on their allegation that the papal directions contained in *"Orientalium dignitas"* were intended only for the churches of the Levant. The present writer has been assured by a very high ecclesiastic in the Levant that *"Orientalium dignitas"* applies only to Europe. And to my certain knowledge his clergy were so instructed in the local seminary.

and in part. But there are other reasons, the existence of which the Western missionaries admit but do not enlarge upon: material reasons. The Latin rite stands for European civilization and influence, for its attractive ideas of progress, for prestige, education, commerce, pseudo-Parisian clothes, for being "in" with the Franks; Eastern rites are looked down on as being for mere peasants; too often, nay, ordinarily, Latins accept rather than oppose such wrong views. I have shown that all rites and those who belong to them are equal in the Church: but in practice they are often, accidentally but inevitably, nothing of the sort — and it is the Latin rite that always gains from the misfortunes of its brethren; and European missionaries accept and encourage, not always overtly or even consciously, that situation. It is an appalling sight to see little Syrian children marching through the streets, dressed in immaculate little French suits, each with a tricolour in his hand, and singing "Je suis chrétien" (it would be no less appalling were the suits, flags, and words English). "But," it is often asked, "can't an Oriental save his soul in the Latin rite?" That is the crux, and when one answers "Of course he can, and does" the objector thinks there is no more to be said. But there is, a whole lot of things, and one is, over and above "saving souls" and the perfectly clear mind of the Holy See on the matter: What about the quality of the souls to be saved?

The perfection of a man resides in this, that he lives in accordance with the laws, general and particular, of human *being*. And the Church as Church, and especially the Holy See of Rome itself, has never lost sight of the fact that a particular law of an Eastern Christian is that he practises an Eastern rite: otherwise he may be to that extent an oriental *manqué*. There is an analogous state of affairs in the country where I used to live, where people give up their own Welsh language because it has not the social prestige or commercial value of English. A Welshman who does that runs the risk of spoiling his perfection as a Welsh human being, as a soul to be saved. Just so, only more so, a Syrian or a Copt who turns Latin. *Inglese italianato, diavolo incarnato* expresses the same idea in more forcible terms. The italianized Englishman, the Welshman who loses his Welsh, the Oriental westernized, whether in ecclesiastical rite or in manners, can get to heaven all right: but surely when they get there they may have to begin with shame (if there were shame in heaven) to take the lower place — below plain Harry Brown, below the Merioneth shepherd, below the illiterate Maronite peasant. I need hardly add that this consideration has nothing to do with the virtue of patriotism or the disorder of political nationalism. Of late years Rome has become more strict in her insistence that people shall stick to their own rite, and the adequacy of the reasons of those who desire a dispensation to change it be more strictly examined. Increasing numbers of Latins are allowed to do so in order that they may work as priests or nuns among their Eastern brethren.

It is one thing to "belong" to a rite and quite another to "frequent" it. Western Catholics are not only at liberty but strongly recommended by the Holy See to frequent the churches of Eastern Catholics, and vice versa, so that they may learn more about one another and strengthen the bond of mutual charity. Not only that, but the Code of Canon Law expressly lays down (canon 866) that a Latin Catholic may receive communion in a Catholic Eastern church out of devotion (and not merely in case of necessity), even if to do so involves receiving in both kinds. The only restriction in this matter is that "Easter duties" and the last sacraments should be received if possible in one's own rite. Marriages should be according to the rite of the groom, and the bride is free to adopt her husband's rite either permanently or until widowhood. Children follow the rite of their father (unless he be a non-Catholic), even if through error or in emergency they have been baptized by a priest and with the ceremonies of another rite.

Several popes from Gregory XIII onwards made tentative efforts to establish at Rome some sort of congregation or permanent commission to deal with Oriental affairs. Eventually, in 1862, Pius IX erected a congregation "for Eastern Rite business," as a department of the Sacred Congregation for the Spreading of the Faith. This was found inconvenient and the association with the

Propaganda, whose concern is primarily with the heathen, recognized to be unfortunate, and in 1917 Benedict XV set up a new and independent Sacred Congregation for the Eastern Church (whose name has apparently been altered to "the Sacred Eastern Congregation").[6] Of this congregation the prefect is always the reigning pope in person, and its personnel consists of a cardinal secretary and sixteen other cardinals, an assessor, a *sostituto,* and a body of expert consultors (a number of whom are, of course, Orientals), together with the usual officials. This congregation is competent in all matters arising out of the Eastern rites whether persons, discipline, or divine worship are in question. Later legislation has extended its jurisdiction to Latin Catholics also in Egypt, Eritrea and northern Ethiopia, southern Albania, Bulgaria, Cyprus, Greece, Irak, Palestine, Persia, Syria, and Turkey, where formerly there was a double jurisdiction with the Congregation *de Propaganda Fide.*

There is also since 1929 a commission to deal with the codification of Eastern canon law; fourteen of the Eastern churches have delegates on this body. The very first canon of the Roman *Codex Juris Canonici* says that it does not bind the Eastern churches except when it deals with matters which from the nature of the case affect them also (viz., canons 1, 98, 106, 542, 622, 756, 782, 804, 816, 819, 864, 866, 881, 905, 955, 1004, 1099).

In 1917 Benedict XV created the Pontifical Institute for Eastern Studies ("The Oriental Institute"), which is now one of the autonomous institutions of the Pontifical Gregorian University and is under the direction of the Society of Jesus. Its ordinary course is of two years, and it is open to all Eastern clergy (whether Catholic or not) and to Westerners, especially those who are going to work in the East. Its professorial body is extraordinarily strong (twelve nationalities are represented on it) and includes eight professors of Eastern languages, that of Turkish and of Islamic religion being Msgr. Paul Mulla, an Ottoman convert from Islam.

---

[6] In the *motu proprio* of erection the Pope made use of the words printed on the title page of this book.

The position today of the former Eastern church, then, is that the overwhelming majority of Christians belong to the separated Orthodox churches; a minority belong to the old heretical Nestorian and monophysite churches (their originating heresies seem now to be material only); and another minority is Catholic. These are divided into Catholics of the Byzantine rite, subdivided into ten separate groups, chiefly ethnological; of the Alexandrian rite, in two independent bodies (Copts and Ethiops); of the Antiochene rite, in three bodies (Syrians, Maronites, Malankarese); of the Armenian rite; and of the Chaldean rite, in two churches (Chaldeans proper and Malabarese). They together represent a proportion of twenty-six non-Latin Catholics to every thousand Latin Catholics, and of about fifty-six Catholic Easterns to every thousand non-Catholic Easterns.

After all that has been said there should be no need to emphasize that these Eastern Catholics are as fully and completely members of the Church as are we Westerners: they are not an inferior kind or sort of halfway house to Rome, but just plain Catholics, as were St. Athanasius, St. John Chrysostom, St. Basil, St. Gregory Nazianzen, St. Gregory of Nyssa, St. Ignatius of Antioch, St. Cyril of Jerusalem, St. Cyril of Alexandria, St. John the Damascene, St. Ephrem the Syrian, St. James of Nisibis, St. Gregory the Wonderworker, St. Gregory the Enlightener, St. Theodore the Studite, St. Antony the Abbot — none of whom celebrated the Roman Mass or said their prayers in Latin.

It is sometimes said that Catholics of Eastern rite have a horrid tendency to go into schism when they can't have their own way. Before making such a judgement it is desirable to acquaint oneself with the Eastern point of view and to study the traditional relationship between Rome and the East. From the very fact that they are Orientals they have never been, and are not even now, in such close touch historically and juridically with Rome as we of the West. We do not realize how many of *our* relations with the Holy See are in its patriarchal and not its papal capacity; the pope is our patriarch as well as supreme pontiff and so is bound to mean more in practice to an American or a

Frenchman than to a Syrian or Russian. Some people have tried to make capital out of the fact that the Eastern bishops at the Vatican Council supported the party who regarded a definition of the pope's infallibility as inopportune. That proves nothing; a loyal Catholic was perfectly entitled to think it inopportune; thousands did. Those bishops had solid reasons for fearing the effect of such a definition on the non-Catholic Christians of the East. Time has proved that they were right; just as time has proved that the reasons in favour of defining the pope's infallibility were right too. And what was the upshot of the council? Papal infallibility was defined to be an article of faith and was at once accepted throughout the Catholic East; it was in the West, especially in Germany, that some Catholics went into schism rather than accept the decree of the oecumenical council.[7] And as a matter of sober history some of the Eastern Catholic bodies, e.g., the Melkites, have loyally suffered as much during the past three hundred years for their allegiance to the Holy See as any one of the Western churches has been called on to do. I am not concerned to deny that there has been a number of schisms among the Orientals[8] — some of them are referred to elsewhere in this book — but they were rarely, if ever, concerned with any matter fundamental to Catholic Christianity. And, though nothing can justify the sin of schism, it can sometimes be explained, and we do well to bear in mind that these little, oppressed bodies of Eastern Catholics have centuries of neglect, persecution, and inculpable separation from the center of unity behind them; and that, to a small, depressed, and sometimes ignorant people who, rightly or wrongly, think they have a legitimate cause of complaint, schism must often oppear to be the only weapon of defence against a powerful and well-equipped

---

[7] In our own day we have seen a schism among the Latin Czechs — to name no others. In this matter of schism we cannot afford to take a "superior attitude."

[8] I do not refer to such common incidents as ecclesiastics and others becoming Catholic and then returning to schism soon after. These are easily explained by their grossly inadequate "reasons" for reconciliation in the first instance. It is on sound historical grounds that the submission of dissident prelates to Rome is often regarded with a prudent scepticism.

authority. In his splendid book on the Italo-Greeks and Melkites Dr. Adrian Fortescue, after pointing out what irritations and injustices have been suffered by Catholics of Eastern rite through the disregard by local Latins of the instructions of the Holy See, says, "The really wonderful thing about them is . . . their magnificent loyalty to the Catholic ideal. It is the right sort of loyalty, to an ideal, not to a person. They have no more personal devotion toward Italian cardinals and the monsignori of the Roman congregation than we have in the North. What they care for is the one united Church of Christ throughout the world, and the Holy See as guarding that unity . . ." (*The Uniate Eastern Churches*, p. 23). The Eastern Catholics are neither favourers of schism, as their Catholic critics assert, nor yet groaning under the yoke of Rome, as so many non-Catholics fondly imagine.

Of all the matters for discussion arising out of the Eastern Catholics and their customs, none are more frequently debated than those of clerical marriage and the "hybridization" of rites.

The custom of a celibate clergy has become so firmly rooted in Western Catholic consciousness, its economic, administrative, and social advantages have been so amply demonstrated, and the spiritual qualities accruing from this willing asceticism are so resplendent, that we are prone to forget that it is not an evangelical precept and that it took a thousand years for it to become general in the West. In the East, whether before or after the schism, clerical celibacy was never the rule for the lower clergy. There the normal law is that a married man may be ordained to the diaconate and priesthood and retain his wife; he may not be married after receiving the diaconate or, if his wife dies, marry again; bishops must be single or widowers, and for that reason were formerly invariably chosen from among the monks. Of all the so-called peculiarities of the Easterns this is the one that seems most troublesome to Westerners — this and communion in both kinds, which was the practice in the West too until the twelfth century. Once I had to read a paper on the Eastern rites to a Catholic audience, and afterwards the wife to a well-known Irish man of letters came up and told me that, as I had spoken without disapproval of married priests, I could not possibly be a Catholic. I protested that I was. Not a *Roman* Catholic, then. Yes, a Roman Catholic. At last my chairman, who happened to be a bishop, persuaded her that I really was in communion with the pope of Rome and the bishop of Cork, so she said as a parting shot that "nothing would induce *her* to go to confession to a married priest." I could think of no more devastating reply than that she was not likely to be asked to.[9] Another woman of my acquaintance, of a quite different class, simple but intelligent, who had heard that there were married Catholic priests somewhere in the world, was quite distressed: that none of our clergy were under any circumstances allowed to have wives was for her apparently an ultimate proof of the truth of Catholicism. A well-known Catholic "intellectual" once admitted to me that he could not reconcile himself to the idea of a married priest; he was conscious that his attitude was unreasonable and all against his own instincts, and he must try and get over it. I think those three examples about cover the average Western reaction to this subject.

Now, we must do better than that, and help others to do better than that, if we are to produce a more sympathetic atmosphere and state of mind where Orientals are concerned. An unmarried clergy is one of the great achievements of Western Christianity and there is not the remotest chance of the Latin church altering its law in this matter; nor, for an indefinitely long period, will the Eastern churches to any considerable extent alter theirs. Without doubt the ultimate ideal aimed at is general clerical celibacy among the Orientals as well, but only one Eastern body (the Malabarese) as yet has the full Western discipline,[10] and the Church is not likely to favour any *strict* application of that discipline to the East at large, for the simple reason that it would

[9] I may note here that a Syrian priest told me that in parts of his country people would not go to confession to an *unmarried* priest.

[10] The disciplines in force among Catholics of various Eastern rites are noted in the following chapters. About 50 per cent of the 8000 secular priests are married. As a general thing, all non-Catholic secular priests are married before ordination.

be a further barrier raised against reunion of the dissidents. We Latin Catholics must make up our minds that any and every mass reunion of Orientals will bring more and more married priests into the Church and we must face the fact that there is no *essential* inconsistency between holy orders and marriage. We must, however, admire the austerity involved in the voluntary renunciation of marriage and appreciate the heightened spirituality which this asceticism for God's sake has brought to the Western clergy; we know what an advantage celibacy has been in spreading the Gospel in foreign missions and in many aspects of parochial work at home; we realize how much this selfless renunciation has done to raise the priesthood in the eyes of the faithful. But on the other hand, whatever accidental difficulties may be involved, the fact that a priest has received one more sacrament than usual does nothing to derogate from his sacerdotal dignity. The popular Western attitude is not only unreasonable — it may easily become uncharitable. In places where there are married Eastern Catholic clergy, America, for example, this attitude of their Latin brethren is extremely distressing and embarrassing to those priests — and to their wives and children.[11] If we can do something to modify that attitude of mind among people in our own country we shall have done a work of charity and something that will help to encourage non-Catholic Eastern clergy toward reunion. Pope Pius XI spoke quite unambiguously in his encyclical letter *"Ad Catholici sacerdotii"*: "What we have said in commendation of clerical celibacy must not be interpreted as though it were Our mind in any way to cast reflection on or as it were disapprove the different discipline legitimately prevailing in the Eastern church."

"Hybridization" is the modification of Eastern liturgies, customs, and modes of thought by undiscriminating adoption of foreign practices and submission to foreign influences; as these practices and influences mostly come from the West it is also

---

[11] A Byzantine priest who had to minister to his people in a European city told me with tears in his eyes that his neighbours, clerical and lay, made him feel like a criminal because he had a wife and children. "And," he added, "the Holy Father himself has blessed my family."

called "latinization," but occasional examples of small hybridisms
from one Eastern rite to another are to be met with. Another
term, "uniatism," has come into use to designate this process by
which Catholics of Eastern rites tend to become de-orientalized,
neglecting the study of the Eastern Fathers and the early councils, adopting Western disciplinary customs, forms of popular
devotion, and ascetical treatises to the exclusion of their own,
adapting themselves to a European or alien outlook, and accepting liturgical hybridism. In spite of the fact that the Church is
opposed to this process, especially since the constitution "Orientalium dignitas" of Leo XIII, most of the Catholic Eastern
churches have suffered more or less from it, some of them very
badly. Sometimes it is due to what can only be called "aggression," as when in 1636 the bishop of Paphos in Cyprus descended
upon the Maronite colonies in his diocese and arbitrarily insisted
that they should give up using wooden altar "stones" and
administering communion in both kinds, that they should put
holy-water stoups in their churches and kneel throughout the
Liturgy, and other things entirely foreign to their customs. Quite
often it is due to the Orientals themselves, many of whom, long
subject to the Turks or other tyrants, have a sense of inferiority
and think that anything from the West is essentially superior, or
else they want to flatter and please their European benefactors.
And much of it is due to the well-meaning efforts of Western, but
particularly French, missionaries and nuns, who sincerely believe
that a more or less tactful process of latinization is in the best
interests of the Orientals: some of them apparently could not
imagine that pure Eastern customs were best fitted to the needs
of Easterners, that they were really as legitimate as those of
Rome, and they seem to have thought that the popes were
inadequately informed about Eastern affairs. There has been
in our day a strong, but not complete, reaction against
hybridization.[12]

---

[12] An example of how strong it is at Rome: In 1934 the administrator
apostolic of the Copts asked the Sacred Eastern Congregation for permission to translate into Arabic for use in his rite the Latin formula for

And this is well, for such innovations make the most noticeable external difference between dissidents and Catholics of the same rite and so come to be improperly identified with Catholicism itself, which becomes in consequence in worse odour than ever among the dissidents, who are greatly attached to their own legitimate customs and fear to lose them if they submit to the Holy See.[13] Hybridization, so often condemned at Rome,[14] is a grave stumbling-block to reunion, and it is in effect a practical identification of Catholicism solely with the Western church — the false idea that Eastern Catholicism is essentially an inferior or only half authentic article, and that the more it is made to resemble the Latin church the more "really Catholic" it will be. Moreover, the ancient Christian liturgies are works of art, the supreme works of art, manifestations of the religious, social, and cultural life of Christian communities over long centuries, and to tinker with them, to spoil their integrity by borrowing from alien cultures, is unworthy of the Catholic mind: it is not in accordance with that variety, inclusiveness, and local perfection and fitting-ness which are marks of the Church as the universal ark of salvation.[15]

blessing the five-fold scapular. It was refused, the Holy See having directed that if the Copts wanted to use scapulars they must be blessed in a way more conformable with their own rite. The prayers and works required to gain the jubilee of the Redemption indulgence varied in every rite (S. C. O. April 3, 1934).

[13] Among cultured non-Christians as well as among the Christians of the East the greatest obstacle to the acceptance of Catholicism nowadays is its apparent exclusive occidentalism and Europeanism. What the Hindu refuses is not the Christian faith but its European trappings and civilization and modes of thought, says Dr. H. C. E. Zacharias in Renascent India, and he relates the horrified indignation of an Indian Catholic at "the impious alliance between the missionaries and the foreign powers in China." It is a small but significant step that Pope Pius XI forbade the building of churches in gothic or other European styles in China.

[14] Those occasional papal pronouncements that seem to approve "latin-izing" are either due to special local circumstances (e.g., the Italo-Greeks in the sixteenth century, Kholm in 1874), or, if compared with earlier and later decrees, are seen to be advancing stages in the recovery and keeping of integral orientalism.

[15] From this point of view a case can be made out for the long-established modifications of the Italo-Greeks (and in a lesser degree of the Ruthenians), as being now assimilated and historically proper to them. Cf. the 800-year-old "latinisms" of the Armenian rite.

What these external differences between West and East in worship and discipline are, will be found set out in some detail in the chapters which follow, but a few general observations may usefully be made here, especially as regards that which matters most — the Mass. And first of all, Orientals do not, in their own languages, call it "Mass." That word in its primary and original sense means the complex of prayers and ceremonies, words and actions, *as used in the Western church*, which, said and done with the requisite intention by a minister validly ordained to that end, effects the Eucharistic Sacrifice. Orientals call it "the Divine Liturgy" or "the Offering."[16] Things should be called by their proper names, and so in this book "the Liturgy" means the Eucharistic Sacrifice in one or other of its Eastern forms, unless the context obviously requires the more extended meaning of the word.

Eastern Liturgies are on the whole more primitive in type than the Roman Mass, which underwent a good deal of alteration during the fifth–sixth century: they are longer, their *tempo* is slower, their material expression more ample and their atmosphere more "mysterious" than in the Latin Mass; their language is more artless, less refined and scholarly (but not less theologically accurate); a later but very notable characteristic is a tendency to ritual purely for the sake of its symbolism; they lack the straightforward simplicity to which we are accustomed. In them the deacon has an important part, and is the only sacred minister necessary to the celebrant at a solemn Liturgy; particularly is it his business to form a link between celebrant and people by means of litanies and, especially in the Byzantine and Armenian rites, in a sense to direct the proceedings as a sort of glorified master of ceremonies for both priest and people, so perpetuating the primitive diaconal charge of the congregation.

What we call "low Mass" is a comparatively late development

---

[16] Cf. the Celtic languages, which have no word for *Missa*. Irish *An t-Aifreann*, Welsh *yr Offeren*, Cornish *an offeren*, Scots *an aifrionn*, are all equivalent to the Greek *Anaphora* and Syrian *Kurbana*, "Offering" or "Sacrifice." Arabic-speaking people in common speech call the Litury of any rite *Kuddas*, "hallowing."

of Christian worship; in the Western church solemn Mass is the normal Mass still (though we often forget this). In the East it is not only the normal but a sung Liturgy is the usual and ordinary way of celebration. All Catholic Eastern rites now provide for "low Mass" on week days, but in only some of them is the form systematized.[17] The scriptural lessons and certain chants and verses are variable, according to the feast or time, and the Gospels, Epistles, and Acts are read through progressively in the course of the year. On the other hand, all of them (except the Armenian and Malabarese) have a number of alternative *anaphoras*, that is to say, different "canons of the Mass,"[18] which are used interchangeably on certain occasions, somewhat after the manner of our proper prefaces. The celebrant's voice can be heard by all throughout the church, *especially* at the words of consecration, except, of course, that when the deacon or choir are chanting he speaks in a low voice. "Low Masses" are supposed likewise to be said aloud, but this is one of the matters in which admiration for Roman prestige has often led to an unreasoning and unnecessary adoption of Roman customs.[19] Organs are not customary in Eastern churches, though unhappily they are now sometimes heard.[20] The *"Glory to God in the Highest"* does not figure in any Eastern Mass, and the Creed of Nicaea-Constantinople is the only one used liturgically.

Orientals have to a large extent conserved the true Christian tradition of *standing* at public prayer (kneeling is proper only to penitential seasons, and sitting, to them, a sign of laziness or even disrespect), and in general there are few or no seats in their churches (except in Western countries); women, too, are very

---

[17] Some time ago I assisted at an unsung Byzantine Liturgy twice within a short period: one celebrated by a Melkite, the other by a Russian. If I had not known beforehand, I could hardly have told what Liturgy the Melkite was celebrating, and it was not recognizably the same as that of the Russian, who even as it was chanted certain parts of it, notably the words of consecration.

[18] Strictly speaking, the part of the Roman Mass from the beginning of the preface to the postcommunion corresponds to the Eastern *anaphora*.

[19] There is nothing intrinsically sacred about an inaudible canon of the Mass. It has been general in the West since the tenth century.

[20] It is doubtful if organs are really more than *tolerated* in the Latin rite.

often accommodated apart from men.[21] There is no principle against vernacular liturgical languages in the Catholic Church and many Easterns assist at the Liturgy in their daily tongue; others understand the language used rather better, I suppose, than we understand the English of Chaucer, and a minority make use of a quite dead language.[22] Unless "latinized," Orientals do not genuflect but bow profoundly (as in the West until relatively lately, and still liturgically among Carthusians, Dominicans, and Calced Carmelites), and all Byzantines, Catholic or not, make the sign of the cross with the thumb and first two fingers *from right to left,* as all Christians probably did in earlier times.

Other notable customs normal to the East are the use of leavened bread for the altar (as for centuries in the West), the reception of communion in both kinds together (as at Rome till the fourteenth century), Baptism by immersion and Confirmation given immediately after by the priest, and the forbiddance of statues in the churches — except under Western influence, only pictures, wall-paintings, and mosaics are allowed. This appears to be a backwash of the Iconoclasm controversy of the eighth and ninth centuries. On the other hand, the great veneration accorded to these *eikons* is a most notable characteristic of Eastern religious life.

Oriental Catholics have retained far more than ourselves the notion of religious worship as a social and corporate act centred in the Holy Sacrifice, but they had no extra-liturgical *cultus* of

---

[21] The Code of Canon Law considers that desirable for us, too. See canon 1262, § I.

[22] Articles are often written to explain to Protestants why the Western church continues to use a dead language for her services, in which great stress is laid on the practical advantages that accrue, such as uniformity of celebration and fixity of meaning. This is quite right, but must not be over-emphasized, because the Church has never insisted on a uniform or non-vernacular language. The ultimate reason for having a special liturgical language is its consonance with the nature of Christian worship: the Mass is a sacrifice, in the first place an act to be done (*actio*), as well as a prayer to be said, and it is done in and with the proper hieratic forms, of which the hieratic language is one. The vestments are another; they are simply the proper clothes for the purpose, handed down through the ages: symbolical meanings attached to them are a mediaeval addition.

THE CHURCH OF ST. BARBARA, VIENNA
(*Byzantine Rite*)

Beginning of the Liturgy

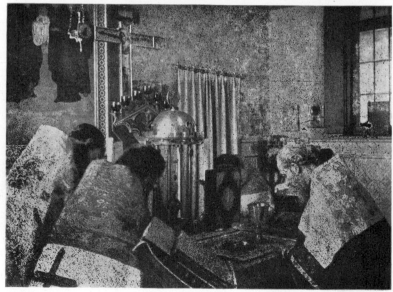

The Consecration

THE BYZANTINE LITURGY

BYZANTINE BISHOP GIVING A SOLEMN BLESSING
(The late Gregory Hajjar, Bishop of Akka)

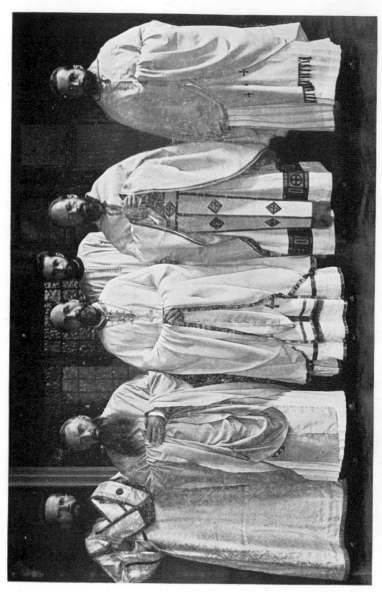

CONCELEBRANTS OF SLAV-BYZANTINE LITURGY IN WESTMINSTER
CATHEDRAL, ENGLAND
On the extreme left, the Deacon

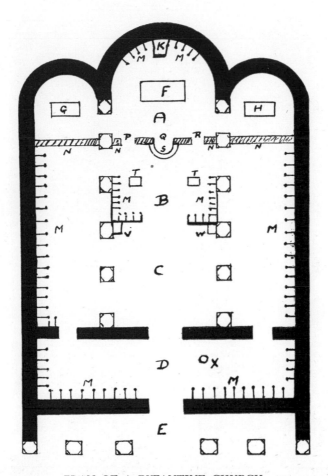

PLAN OF A BYZANTINE CHURCH

A, Sanctuary (*bema*). B, Choir (*khoros*). C, Nave (*naos*). D, Narthex.
E, Vestibule. F, Altar. G, *Prothesis*. H, *Diakonikon*. K, Bishop's throne
(*kathedra*), MMMM, Stalls (*stasidia*). NN, Eikonostasis. P, North door.
Q, Holy doors. R, South door. S, Step (*solea*). TT, Lecterns (*analogia*).
V. Pulpit (*ambon*). W, Eikon-stand (*proskynetarion*). X, Baptismal font.

BYZANTINE ALTAR VESSELS
(Asterisk, paten, lance, spoon)

MELKITE CHURCH AT ALEXANDRIA
(On the right a parekklesia)

A BYZANTINE BISHOP ENTHRONED

Mgr. Cyril Kurtev at his consecration as Titular Bishop of Briula
at San Clemente in Rome, 1926

RUSIN CHURCH
in the Hucul district of Podkarpatska Rus

the Blessed Sacrament until it was introduced from the West, and the degree of it varies from rite to rite and even within the same rite. Latins are naturally surprised, even shocked, by the apparent indifference sometimes shown by Orientals in the presence of the Blessed Sacrament. The surprise is not all on one side; their veneration is directed rather toward the whole sanctuary as the holy place of God, for the Host in the Tabernacle is very far away, "on the throne of the Lord, surrounded by all the holy ministers, by all the angels, and by all the saints." They sometimes remind us that the efficacy of the Eucharist as a sacrifice is bound up with the act of the Mass, and as a sacrament with the act of eating with faith. We excite devotion by displaying the Blessed Sacrament, theirs is aroused by its very hiddenness. Both attitudes are permissible, both true, both Catholic; and so with other divergences that we continually meet.

While all Liturgies are identical theologically and are fundamentally identical in structure, there are nevertheless differences between the celebration of the Mass of the West and of the Eucharistic Liturgies of the East that go deeper than accidental differences of languages, of forms of words, of actions, of music, of ceremonial dress. But, like many deeper things, they are more easily "felt" (I do not mean merely by a comparison of resulting emotions; the mind, too, can "feel") than understood and expressed in words. One deep difference has been illustrated thus by Dr. Andrew de Ivanka (*Irenikon*, Vol. IX, No. 5, p. 420): "Whoever has had occasion to assist at an Eastern Liturgy, even if only in the little church of some Ukranian country parish, and has been struck by the intimate participation and inspired collaboration of even the most simple peasants in the wonders of the Liturgy, that perfect *ensemble* of teaching, prayer, and sacred action, he alone is able to estimate the treasure of doctrine, lived faith, and encouragement to religion of which Catholics in the West are deprived." "Intimate participation" and "inspired collaboration" in the teaching, prayer, and sacred action of the Liturgy certainly hardly describe the usual relation between western Catholics and the Mass.

It is undoubtedly true that the disposition and temperament of peoples have profoundly affected the spirit and form of their Liturgies. We commonly take it for granted that lay people do not in any degree influence such matters. It is a mistake. Their influence is not expressed corporately or juridically, that is all. The Holy Spirit of God, concentrated in the bishops of His Church, is also diffused among *all* her members; and that Spirit is not gainsaid or without effect merely because we are unconscious or forgetful of it. For instance, the definition of the conception of our Lady free from the state of original sin was not the work of a body of theologians; it was the expression by proper authority of what the *whole* Church knew by faith to be true. And so the needs and natures and graces of the people at large, clergy and laity, help to mould our forms of corporate worship, even within the limits of the same technical "rite." Nobody present at a Russian Liturgy could suppose himself to be in a Greek church, or would mistake a Maronite for a Roman Mass (though their vestments and church appointments are both alike); nay, one assisting at Mass in Brittany or Naples could be forgiven did he not recognize the same act and form of worship he had seen in a Catholic church in a London suburb. Some Orientals, without external necessity and for purely spiritual reasons, habitually frequent Latin churches, and the reverse process is far from unknown. Such exceptions serve to emphasize the part of temperament in determining liturgy. On the other hand, liturgy also influences people, and thus there is produced a continual action, interaction, and tension — and without tension there is no human life.

The variousness of human temperament has had its profound and legitimate effect on religious life and worship no less in the East than in the West. The Oriental, for instance, in general prefers an interior process before, often at the expense of, external discipline, juridicism in all its forms is foreign to him, his note is "passivity" rather than "activity." It is significant that the sacraments may be administered by deprecatory forms, "The servant of God N., is baptized . . . ," "May God, through me, a sinner, forgive thee. . . ." Confirmation is received passively by babes, there is sometimes no explicit contract between the parties to a marriage, the monk does not "make his profession" but "receives the habit." Western man has his mystics and contemplatives, but in general prides himself on being a "practical fellow"; among the Slavs, on the contrary, preoccupation with efficiency and order is little esteemed, and mysticism, in a broad sense, is the heritage of all. Holiness to them definitely means contemplation, and the complete recluse is the practical as well as the abstract ideal of a holy man. Orientals have been accustomed in a large measure to leave the obligations of religion and morality to the individual conscience, rather than to make them the subjects of positive law. For example, the obligation of public worship. All that Eastern canon law has to say about it is that a Christian living in a town who absents himself from church for three Sundays running shall be deprived of communion (canon 80 of the Council *in Trullo,* canon 11 of Sardica). Most Catholics have now adopted some form of the Western legislation, together with the general principle of dispensation, which again is quite foreign to the East. The lack of a system of recognized dispensation does not necessarily operate in favour of the individual supplying a lax one for himself, as the following anecdote, related to me by a French priest who had worked among Byzantines, shows. An old Catholic woman of that rite found the Lenten fast very trying and her parish priest (trained under Western influence) offered to dispense her. "You cannot dispense me from the law of God," said she. "Then the bishop can." "No. He cannot." "Then I will go to the pope for you." "His Holiness would be better employed fasting himself than by releasing an old woman from it," was the reply, not intended disrespectfully. In this connection it is to be noted that, whatever the practice may be, the theoretical standard of physical asceticism is far more exacting in the East than in the West (except in the matter of clerical marriage).

The Eastern religious temperament is indeed radically different from the Western, but is not therefore in itself at variance with Catholicism, which is not tied to any one temperament or mentality. It is true that Western prestige and the Roman genius for centralization, acting involuntarily (and contrarily to official legislation) on relatively small bodies, have tended to make of the Catholics of Eastern rite a religious and cultural hybrid. Nevertheless, these Catholics continue to display the spiritual and religous characteristics proper to them as Orientals, and among the more recent groups there is a strong consciousness of the need to maintain their orientalism integrally for the Church's sake as well as their own. The Christians of both West and East have suffered and tended to develop one-sidedly through being deprived, for hundreds of years, of each other's contribution to philosophy, theology, general culture, and Christian life, and the balance can never be redressed from one side only. It was "as a member of the true and venerable Orthodox Eastern or Greco-Russian church" that the great philosopher and theologian Vladimir Solovyev on February 18, 1896, declared that he recognized "as the supreme judge in matters of religion . . . the apostle Peter, who lives in his successors and who did not hear our Lord's words in vain."

Catholicism, universality, is not a matter of numbers, and the whole body of Eastern Catholics, relatively small though it be, is a very important part of the Catholic economy. Without them, the Universal Church would appear perilously like what so many of its opponents assert it to be — a product solely West-European in religious culture, disposition, and history. Of all people we Catholics of the Latin rite should glory in these Catholics of Eastern rite, as the late Dr. Adrian Fortescue said, for "they are an exceedingly important factor in our concept of the universal Church; they are our great palpable argument that the primacy of Rome is more than patriarchal rights over part of the Church. Indeed, in some ways, it is just they who save the whole situation, from our point of view. . . . The fact that vast numbers of the members of the Eastern patriarchates have gone out of the

Church altogether, distressing as it is, does not affect the legal position. . . . In spite of the many heresies and schisms which at various times have robbed each patriarchate of its members, the constitution of the Catholic Church remains what it has always been, not one patriarchate with one rite, but the union of East and West, differing in rites, having in many cases different details of canon law, but united in the profession of the same faith and in conscious inter-communion" (*op. cit.*, pp. 27, 28). That position is safeguarded by the Eastern Catholics.

There is another thing. It is a charge often made against the Church, and it is a charge to which intelligent people today are very sensitive, and rightly so, that she stretches the necessary uniformity of revealed truth, faith, and morals, to cover other things; that she has no real regard for the variations in human mentality, temperament, and culture. The words and actions of many individual Catholics give colour to this accusation; even a great and learned publicist like Mr. Belloc, when he reiterates that "the Faith is Europe and Europe is the Faith" is saying something which, if taken at the foot of the letter (as all ordinary people take such sayings), would make of the Church a large European sect: on this showing, Ireland, for instance, must be imperfectly Catholic and imperfectly civilized, for she was never submitted to the rule of the Roman Empire or bathed herself in the waters of the Mediterranean basin. If this charge of desiring, or even tending, to impose an unhuman, unnatural uniformity on the human people whom God has made diverse were true, it would be a very serious, nay, a fundamental fault in the Church (which is impossible). On every page of this book it is demonstrated that this charge is false. "The Church," wrote Pope Pius XII in his encyclical letter "*Summi pontificatus,*" "the Church aims at unity, a unity determined and kept alive by that supernatural love which should be actuating everybody; she does not aim at a uniformity which would only be external in its effects and would cramp the natural tendencies of the peoples concerned. Every nation has its own genius, its own qualities, springing from the hidden roots of its being." And again Benedict XV, "The Church is not Latin or Greek or Slavonic; it is Catholic," oecumenical: and Catholicism includes *everything* that is not in any way sinful or in any way erroneous. Just as there is nothing secular but sin, so there is nothing foreign to Catholicism but error, ugliness, and disaccord with right reason. The prevailing Latin uniformity of the Church today is simply the result of historical events: it might just as well have been Greek; in another two thousand years it may be Chinese. Catholicism is the religion of variety, the variety displayed by seventeen hundred million people (or however many there may be in the world), and the best and simplest proof of this is the variousness of divine worship as used by Catholics, the fact that the Mass is one but the ways of celebrating it are many.

Many of the things referred to above are externals, matters of outward observance, and to them it is fatally easy to give too much importance. But the opposite mistake also must be avoided: it must not be forgotten that the sacramental principle — that which is inward and invisible signified and effected by that which is outward and visible — goes through the whole of Christian life, and is not confined to the seven great sacraments that have a special place in that life. The "inner life," asceticism, worship in spirit and in truth, the quality of religion, inevitably expresses itself in outward worship, just as it inevitably expresses itself in the ordinary affairs and relations of life, "how we behave." As a man believes, really believes, so he does or tries to do; and as a man does or tries to do, so he *is*. When we say there are differences of rite between East and West, we are saying that there are all sorts of other, objectively more important, differences. And it is this inner life, this religious quality, of the Orientals that we of the West have to try to grasp and understand and learn from — for it is all part of that grand synthesis of divine truth and love and human needs and duties that is called the Catholic Christian faith. And in like manner the

Orientals, whether Catholic or separated, can learn from the West.[23]

As a footnote to this chapter I quote the impression of a great English bishop, William Bernard Ullathorne of Birmingham, on first coming into contact with his Eastern brethren at the Vatican Council. It is quoted from his letters by Abbot Butler in his book on the council.

The orientals have sweet and clear voices, with a certain richness, especially the young and middle-aged, the older voices growing thinner. Their movements and gestures are quiet and gentle, full of dignity and self-possession. For instance, there is an Armenian archbishop, with grave but youthful features, very regular and sweet, with his coal-black hair parted *à la Nazarène*, and peaked beard, who has been twice in the ambo; and his entire presence, front face, profile, gentle gesture, and sweet full voice, earnest without effort — his whole man, in short, so irresistably strikes me as exactly like our idea of our Lord . . . even to the very costume, that I have been wonderfully captivated with this type from the plains from which the Hebrews sprang.

---

[23] There is an admirable essay on Eastern worship and asceticism by Father John LaFarge, S.J., in *The Eastern Branches of the Catholic Church* (see General Bibliography). And a book by an Orthodox monk called *Orthodox Spirituality* (London, 1945) tells us much that is true of Eastern Catholics as well, while underlining the fundamental identity of Eastern and Western Christianity.

CHAPTER III

THE BYZANTINE RITE:
LITURGY AND CUSTOMS

THE Byzantine rite[1] is the name given to the system and forms of worship and administration of the sacraments proper at first to the Church of Constantinople (Byzantium) and her dependencies. After the defection of the monophysites Constantinople gradually imposed her own liturgy on the faithful of the other patriarchates, and by the end of the thirteenth century the Melkites of Alexandria, Antioch, and Jerusalem had abandoned their own ancient usages in its favour. The Byzantine rite is therefore now used by the whole of the Orthodox Eastern Church and by many Catholics, and is the most widely spread rite after the Latin; it is followed by (nominally) 150 million Christians, of whom seven millions are Catholics.

The Byzantine rite has not the uniformity of the Roman use of the Latin rite, even among the dissidents. Catholics observe it with varying degrees of uniformity, whose deviations from the Constantinopolitan or Russian norms seem to be in corresponding ratio to the size of their body: e.g., the Greeks, Russians, and Bulgars preserve exact liturgical purity while the Ruthenians have all sorts of modifications, many of them from Western sources. The account given here follows in general the typical Greek or Russian observances, the principal modifications being noted later when dealing with the people concerned.

Church buildings. The system of building whose characteristic and essential feature is a dome covering a space which is square, and whose prototype is the great church (now a museum) of the

---

[1] It is often called the "Greek rite." See page 46.

Holy Wisdom ("St. Sophia") at Constantinople, spread all over the Byzantine religious world, much modified from place to place by local and national characteristics. The interior appearance of a Byzantine church is sufficiently well known. Its chief characteristic is a solid screen, covered with pictures (*eikons*, and therefore called the *eikonostasis*), before the altar and hiding the sanctuary (*bema*); this is pierced by lateral and middle ("holy") doors. Greek screens are usually lower than Russian ones. Among the Ruthenians these doors often are never shut and the screen is sometimes of openwork (I have seen it so in several Melkite churches).[2] The holy doors are closed and covered with curtains at certain parts of the liturgy. The *eikonostasis* or *templon* is not in its present form an ancient institution. From the earliest times there was a barrier of some sort between the sanctuary and the nave, first a low railing, then a row of columns or arches of stone, or even of wood, but still low, open, and without pictures; such screens still existed in Greece in the fourteenth century. The origin of the solid wooden screen covered with eikons seems to have been in the fourteenth to fifteenth century in Russia, and specifically in the region of Novgorod, and was due to the accumulation of eikons in the churches and to the abundance of wood for building found in Russia: thence the custom spread throughout the East.

The stone altar stands away from the east wall (apsidal), beneath a canopy on four columns (*ciborium*); it is square, flat, and plain, with a flat crucifix, two or more candlesticks, and the gospel-book upon it; the Blessed Sacrament is reserved in a small tabernacle or hanging pyx, but is not the subject of exterior *cultus* to anything like the same degree as in the West. To the north and south respectively, sometimes in separate apses, are altarlike tables, the *prothesis* and *diakonikon*. In the nave there are normally no seats, except around the walls, or statues,

---

[2] Some Byzantine churches in North America have no screen, as some in south Italy and Syria have not. I suppose this is temporary, due to lack of funds, for the *eikonostasis* is really now a liturgical necessity of the rite. The times at which the holy doors are open or shut vary; e.g., the Greeks open them at the priest's blessings, Russians do not.

but *eikons*, each with its lamp, are numerous. Men and women should properly be separated. The stalls for the choir are in front of the *eikonostasis*, though there is often a mixed choir occupying a decently screened gallery. There is sometimes an ambo on the north side in front of the screen and there is always one or more *proskynetaria*, small sloping desks on which the *eikon* of the saint or mystery of the day is exposed for veneration: the faithful cross themselves and bow three times and kiss it. In cathedrals the bishop's throne is in the apse behind the altar and there is another as well as an episcopal stall on the south side of the choir. Open "side altars" are an innovation; strictly speaking, if there is more than one altar each should have its own *eikonostasis*, etc., forming as it were a separate church (*parekklesia*). Larger churches have a closed porch (*narthex*) extending the whole width of the west end, with three ("royal") doors into the nave, containing the baptismal font.

Vestments correspond more or less to the Roman ones and have the same origins, but they have evolved into quite different shapes. The deacon wears a long, ungirdled, wide-sleeved tunic (*stikharion*), white or dark red and often embroidered; over it, his stole (*orarion*) is a long narrow strip of silk, worn over the left shoulder with the back end hanging to the ground and the front carried under the right arm and over the left shoulder (Greek) or hanging down back and front over the left shoulder (Russian). A priest puts on first a *stikharion*, plainer than the deacon's and with narrow sleeves; then the *epitrakhelion* or stole, in one piece with a loop at the top to go over the head, the *zone* (girdle), like a belt, the *epimanikia*, oversleeves or cuffs (unconnected with our maniple), and lastly the *phelonion* or chasuble, a long, full, bell-shaped garment, sometimes cut away up to the chest in front. In Catholic churches lace albs are now seen as often as *stikharia*, and among the Ruthenians the deacon's *stikharion* has usually become a dalmatic (under the *orarion*), worn over an alb. The vestments are usually white; there is no regular sequence of liturgical colours, except among the Ruthenians. A bishop wears the *sakkos* (rather like a

dalmatic) instead of the *phelonion* and a diamond-shaped ornament (*epigonation*) depending at his right side (cf. the pope's
subcinctorium). He also wears the crown (*mitra*) instead of the
priests *kalemaukion* (see below), the *omophorion*, like a long,
wide *pallium*, the pectoral cross, and two *enkolpia* or *panagia*,
round or oval medallions suspended from the neck bearing
images of our Lord and His all-holy Mother. The episcopal
crown or mitre is rather like the papal tiara, derived in shape
from the imperial crown, and the pastoral staff, shorter than
the Western crozier, ends in the form of two serpents facing one
another. Other episcopal insignia are the *khazranion*, a straight
ebony walking-staff,[3] and the *mandyas*, a processional garment
not unlike a blue or purple cope but longer and fastened at the
lower hem as well as at the neck.

The principal articles of clerical ordinary dress are the black
rason, a loose, wide-sleeved gown, and the *kalemaukion*, a
cylindrical hat about six inches high with a flat brim at the top,
rather like an inverted top-hat. Minor clerics and Russian priests
wear it without a brim, bishops and monks cover it with a black
veil falling on to the shoulders (a few bishops have this veil
white).[4] Russian priests often wear a pectoral cross. Byzantine
bishops do not normally wear rings, but all the Catholic hierarchs do so. The beard and long hair were formerly most
strictly *de rigueur* for all Byzantine clergy, but the latter is
going quickly out of fashion in many places and even clean-
shaven bishops and priests are now not unknown.

Liturgical books. In most Eastern rites the offices are arranged
in a number of separate books, each containing only those parts
required by individuals, e.g., celebrant, deacon, choir, as in the
West before about the eleventh century. The chief Byzantine
books (by no means uniform in arrangement) are the *Typikon*,

---

[3] A similar staff is carried by the bishops of Spain.
[4] The dissident patriarch of Moscow and the metropolitans of Kiev and
Petrograd were formerly the only ones to wear a white veil, but now it is
common with Slav bishops who exercise any sort of primatial jurisdiction.
The *rason* of monks is always black; that of other clergy may be any dark
colour.

a perpetual kalendar with full instructions for carrying out the office; the *Eukhologion* which is, roughly, a compendium of Mass-book, Office-book and, among the Greeks, pontifical and ritual; the books of the Gospels and Epistles; the *Horologion,* containing the common parts of the daily offices and certain proper hymns, etc., of the eucharistic liturgy; the *Triodion, Pentecostarion,* and *Parakletike* or *Oktoekhos,* choir-books forming a sort of "proper of the season" of both Mass and Office; the *Menaia,* one volume for each month, have the proper parts of the Divine Office for all fixed feasts, including the "historical lessons" for saints' days; and the psalter.

Numerous Catholic editions of these books have been published in various places according to local requirements, the typical Greek editions by the Propaganda Press at Rome. The best Orthodox editions were for long those of the Phoenix Press at Venice. The Orthodox books differ from ours practically not at all and in fact are used by some Catholics, e.g., the Russians, with such necessary modifications as the addition of the pope's name to the diptychs. A very fine edition of these books according to Melkite usages is being published by the Fathers of St. Paul at Harissa in the Lebanon. The *Horologion* appeared in 1928. A typical Slavonic edition is being undertaken at Rome, of which the *Sluzebnik* (*Eukhologion*) appeared in several formats between 1940 and 1945. It is in two separate and distinct editions, according to Russian ("vulgate") and Ruthenian usages respectively. This is being followed by the *Trebnik* (Ritual of the Sacraments). A definitive edition of the Greek *Horologion* was published at Rome in 1937. All these magnificent books were printed by the monks of the abbey of Grottaferrata (see p. 62).[5]

Altar-vessels and bread. These are the chalice (*poterion*); the paten (*diskos*), larger and deeper than the Western paten, with a rim and sometimes a foot; the *asteriskos,* made of two pieces

[5] During the war in Italy the press had to transfer its work to the Vatican Press. A bomb fell right into the printing-shop at the abbey, but did not explode.

of metal crossed and bent into two semicircles, sometimes with a small star hanging at the intersection, and put over the paten to prevent the veil touching the holy Bread;[6] the lance, a knife for cutting the altar-bread; the spoon, often with two small prongs projecting from the bowl, for giving Communion; and a small piece of sponge (*mousa*) sewn up in red silk, used for several purposes, including that of the Western "purificator." There is a small silk veil each for chalice and paten and a larger one (*aer*) to cover them both.

During celebration of the Liturgy the altar table is covered by an *antimension*, a piece of linen or silk about eighteen inches square on which are embroidered or painted instruments of the Passion, etc.; sewn into it is a tiny bag containing relics. It must be consecrated by a bishop.[7] Strictly speaking it is not required on a consecrated altar but is now always used, sometimes together with a "corporal" (*eileton*) of linen. The ordinary altar coverings are a linen cloth which hangs down on all sides, a silk or velvet one above it which may be coloured and embroidered, and a smaller brocade one on top.

The Eastern thurible has shorter chains than in the West and incense is offered by swinging these chains from their ends, with one hand. The *ripidion* or *hexapterygon* is a flat metal disk, representing a cherub's head surrounded by six wings, mounted on a shaft in such a way that it can be made to revolve on its axis. These are carried in processions and on pontifical occasions; their original use was to keep flies from the holy things during the *anaphora*, but the deacon now generally waves a veil instead.[8]

Bishops make use of a hand-cross to give certain blessings, as do Ruthenian and Russian priests, and some episcopal benedictions are given with a two-branched candlestick (*dikerion*) in the

---

[6] A similar thing is used to cover the paten when Communion is brought to the pope when he celebrates pontifically.

[7] During World War II American chaplains of the Latin rite were authorized to celebrate Mass on an *antimension*, as being more convenient than the portable altar-stone. Large numbers of *antimensia* were consecrated for their use by the three Byzantine bishops of North America.

[8] They were formerly used also in the West and have survived in the papal *flabella*.

left hand and a three-branched one (*trikerion*) in the right.

The Byzantine altar-bread (*prosphora*) is a flat round cake of leavened bread about 1½ inches thick, stamped in the middle with one or more square "seals" containing a cross between the letters I C X C N I K A ("Jesus Christ conquers"); on the left is a square with a triangle, called "the all-holy" because it is set aside as a commemoration of our Lady; and on the right three rows of three triangles for the choirs of angels and the saints. The portions of the Host that are to be reserved are all "anointed" with a drop of the sacred Blood; before administration to the sick or from the tabernacle (*artophorion*) it is dipped into unconsecrated wine.

Music. The music of the Byzantine rite varies from country to country, and in some large churches polyphony of a bad Western type is now heard, sometimes with the additional innovation of an organ. The traditional Greek liturgical chant is enharmonic with varying intervals between the notes, and as the modes are continually changing even in the same melody there is a singer appointed to sing the dominant (*ison*) throughout, changing it as the mode changes. This music requires an incredible skill of voice and accuracy of ear, for it abounds in quarter-tones and other strange intervals, but the result to Western ears is a barbarous and arbitrary wailing until one learns to recognize its strange beauty.

In Slav churches, on the other hand, the singing is immediately attractive to Westerners. Russia is the land of harmonized church music par excellence. After a varied and complex history Russian church music came into its own during the nineteenth century. Rimsky-Korsakov solved the problem of how best to harmonize the old Muscovite chants and his work was taken up by A. T. Gretchaninov, Rachmaninov, P. P. Chesnokov, and A. D. Kastalsky, with results in which some people find a far more religiously satisfying quality than in the musically greatest efforts of the classical polyphonists of the West.

Liturgical languages. The Byzantine is sometimes called the "Greek rite," because that was its original language, but it is characteristic of it that linguistic uniformity is not required and the numbers who use it in ancient Greek are relatively few; among Catholics, very few, only the "pure" Greeks and Italo-Greeks in fact. Church Slavonic ("*Staroslav*") is now its principal language, and it is also celebrated in Old Georgian and modern Rumanian, Magyar, and Arabic.[9]

THE EUCHARISTIC LITURGY

The Byzantine rite has two *anaphoras,* or rather, Liturgies, that of St. John Chrysostom for ordinary use and that of St. Basil for Sundays of Lent (except Palm Sunday), Maundy Thursday, Holy Saturday, the vigils of Christmas and the Epiphany, and St. Basil's feast, and a Liturgy of the Presanctified Gifts (called "of St. Gregory the Dialogue Writer," i.e., Pope St. Gregory the Great) for every day in Lent except Saturdays and Sundays; in practice this last is often sung only on Wednesdays and Fridays, the other weekdays of Lent (except Saturday) then having no celebration. The Liturgy of St. Chrysostom is simply a modification of the Liturgy of St. Basil, which in turn is a shortened edition of the early Liturgy of the Church of Constantinople, derived through Caesarea from the primitive uses of Antioch and Jerusalem; in the opinion of Dom Moreau they together form the most authentic expression of the Church's original liturgical tradition. Unlike practically all other Eastern *anaphoras,* those of Basil and Chrysostom have probably some association with the saints whose names they bear. St. Basil is said to have shortened and "edited" the liturgy of Caesarea, and his version was further modified (only slightly in the pre-anaphoral part: the ceremonies are identical) by St. John Chrysostom.

Concelebration by several celebrants together, all consecrating the same bread and wine, is very common among Byzantines. The senior in dignity officiates aloud at the altar, the others all saying the prayers in a low voice. Any number of priests, of

---

[9] And by the Orthodox in many tongues, including Japanese, Chinese, and, in some American churches, English. A Byzantine priest may celebrate in any of the approved liturgical languages he chooses, subject to local legislation.

priests and bishops, or of bishops alone, may thus celebrate together; each one so doing offers the holy sacrifice really and truly and may accept an offering therefor.[10]

Catholic Byzantine clergy celebrate "low Mass" on weekdays but there is no uniform version of the Liturgy adapted for this purpose, except to a certain extent among the Ruthenians.

There are many English translations of the text of the Liturgy of St. John Chrysostom, two of which are noted in the bibliography below. The following general points may be mentioned.

The deacon's normal place is in front of the screen, his function being precisely to be a link between the celebrant and the people. If there be no deacon, the priest has to sing or say everything, with the help of a lay cantor. Among the Orthodox a priest (other than as just mentioned) never acts as deacon.

The common ending to inaudible prayers throughout the service is by a raising of the voice, to which the singers respond "Amen." This is called an *ekphonesis;* cf. the conclusion to the "secret" in the Roman Mass.

No Catholics of Byzantine rite need sing "and from the Son" in the creed, unless its omission would cause scandal. In fact, most of them do sing it; but the words do not appear in the official Greek and Russian books printed at Rome. This need cause no surprise; the function of the liturgical creed is not to give a list of all our articles of faith.

It is Slavonic usage for the deacon (or priest) to lift up the chalice and paten (with his hands crossed) after the consecration. But the real "elevation," common to all Eastern liturgies, comes later, at the words "Holy things to the holy!" This has nothing essentially in common with the elevations at the consecration in the Roman Mass — it is rather the "little elevation" at

---

[10] This practice has gone out in the Western church since about the thirteenth century, but survives at the ordination of priests and consecration of bishops. In commemoration of the Council of Nicaea Pope Pius XI presided at a concelebration of the Byzantine Liturgy in St. Peter's on November 15, 1925. The concelebrants were six bishops (two Rumanian, one Italo-Greek, one Melkite, one Yugoslav) and a dozen priests. The creed of Nicaea was sung in Greek, Slavonic, Rumanian, and Latin, the last by the Pope himself.

A CHARACTERISTIC WOODEN UKRAINIAN CHURCH IN GALICIA

THE LATE ANDREW SZEPTICKY
Archbishop of Lvov and Metropolitan of Galich

UKRAINIAN CHURCH OF ST. NICHOLAS,
CHICAGO, ILLINOIS

CATHEDRAL OF ORADEA MARE, RUMANIA
(*Byzantine Rite*)

the end of the Roman canon. The mediaeval errors whose propagation made the Western elevations desirable were not known in the East.

The Lord's Prayer ends with the words "For thine is the kingdom and the power and the glory, Father, Son, and Holy Ghost, now and forever, world without end. Amen." They are not a Protestant innovation as is so often supposed.

At the end of the Liturgy blessed bread (*antidoron*) is distributed. It is Greek usage to bless it formally; in most churches it is what remains of the *prosphora* after the preparation, simply hallowed by its original use. The French *pain bénit* is a similar custom but not exactly equivalent. The custom may be regarded as a reminiscence of the primitive Christian love-feast.

THE DIVINE OFFICE

The Byzantine divine office (*Akolouthia*) has eight "hours," corresponding to those of the Roman breviary, but its composition is entirely different. The psalter is sung through every week and there is a large number of rhythmic hymns. The office is exceedingly long, and when sung takes about eight hours altogether; Catholic priests are bound to recite privately only as much as they conveniently can, and this by custom rather than by law.

Mesonyktikon (midnight-office) in its ordinary form consists of the *Trisagion*, Our Father, Nicene Creed, with psalms, prayers, and *troparia* (hymns), and a final litany. It is not sung on certain days. *Orthros* (Matins and Lauds) has in addition to psalms and hymns a litany, the *Magnificat*, the day's reading from the *Menaion*, and a gospel on Sundays and feasts, when an amplified form of *Gloria in excelsis Deo* is sung. After this office on a great feast those present are anointed with oil from the lamp burning before the *eikon* of the day. The offices of the First, Third, Sixth, and Ninth Hours each have three psalms, prayers, and hymns, and sometimes short additions called *mesoria*. *Hesperinos* (Vespers) begins the liturgical day, as with us. It is divided into three parts, of which the second contains the "hymn at the lighting of lamps," *Phos hilaron*,[11] which is the centre to which all parts of the office converge; it ends with the Song of Simeon, *Trisagion*, Our Father, the *troparion* of the day, and a prayer to our Lady. Normally *Hesperinos* is sung in every Byzantine church on Saturday evening. *Apodeipnon* (Compline; literally "after supper") is extra long during Lent and is joined to the night-office to form the vigil service of Christmas and Epiphany. Ordinarily it consists of three psalms, Nicene creed, *Trisagion*, Our Father, and a hymn for the day.

The short hymns of this rite are generally called *troparia*, and are composed of syllabic lines, based on the tonic accent; they are of frequent occurrence throughout the offices. Each strophe is properly a *troparion*, of which several make up an *ode*, the rhythm and melody following that of the first *troparion* (the *hirmos*). Nine odes, having reference to the scriptural canticles, make a *kanon* (three in Lent, *triodion*). There are numerous classes of *troparia*, e.g., a *theotokion* is in honour of our Lady, a *kontakion* refers to the feast of the day, an *apolytikion* precedes the dismissal, etc.

THE SACRAMENTS[12]

Baptism. After three exorcisms, renunciation of Satan is made and the Nicene creed said by the sponsor, the effect of which is to make the child a catechumen. Then the priest incenses the baptistery, the deacon says a litany, and after several prayers the priest blesses the water and oil. Then he anoints the child on the forehead, chest, back (each twice), ears, hands, and feet, and afterwards plunges it three times into the font, saying, "The servant of God N., is baptized in the name of the Father. Amen. And of the Son. Amen. And of the Holy Ghost. Amen." Psalm 31 is sung three times and a hymn, while the priest puts the baptismal garment on the child. He then proceeds to confirm it.

Confirmation. The child is anointed with holy chrism on the

---

[11] There is a good translation by Keble of this lovely hymn in *Hymns Ancient and Modern*, No. 18. The tune given to it there is good, too.

[12] The word "mystery" is used for "sacrament" throughout the East.

forehead, eyes, nostrils, mouth, ears, chest, hands, and feet with
the words "The seal of the gift of the Holy Ghost. Amen" at
each anointing. Priest and sponsor with the child then walk
around the baptistery, singing, "Thou who hast been baptized in
Christ hast put on the vesture of Christ. Amen." An epistle
(Rom. 6:3–11) and gospel (Matt. 28:16–20) are read, and the
rite ends with a short litany.

Penance. The penitent and confessor stand before an *eikon* of
our Lord, and after certain prayers (including the psalm
Miserere) the penitent confesses his sins. Then he kneels and the
priest prays for the penitent's pardon and gives him absolution
in a deprecative form, "May God, through me, a sinner, forgive
thee. . . ." But among the Slavs the form is "May our Lord and
God Jesus Christ through the goodness and depth of his love
for men forgive thee all thy sins, my child N. And I, an unworthy
priest, by the power that he has given me forgive thee and
absolve thee from all thy sins in the name of the Father. . . .
Amen." A penance is then imposed. Many Catholic Byzantines
have approximated this office more closely to the Roman usage,
and administer the sacrament in a confessional-box. The new
Slavonic books print an alternative shorter version of the rite.

Eucharist. After the Communion of the celebrant and ministers
the holy doors are opened and the deacon, standing thereat, lifts
up the chalice covered with its veil, exclaiming, "Draw nigh with
fear of God, with faith and with love!" Each lay communicant,
standing before the priest with hands crossed on the breast, receives a particle of the holy Body steeped in the precious Blood,
drawn from the chalice in the spoon, which is put into his
mouth. The words of administration are: "The servant (hand-
maid) of God, N., receives the precious and all-holy body and
blood of our Lord God and Saviour Jesus Christ for the forgiveness of his (her) sins and life everlasting. Amen." At solemn
celebrations each communicant sometimes at once receives a
draught of ordinary wine and a piece of blessed bread (cf. newly
made priests in the Roman rite of ordination). See also pages
85, 113.

Anointing[18] theoretically requires the ministration of seven priests, one for each anointing, but the sick must usually be content with one, who gives them all. Seven candles are lit, the priest incenses the room and those present, and blesses the oil. The sick person is anointed on forehead, eyes, nostrils, mouth, ears, chest, hands, and feet, a passage from the gospels being read before each anointing. The words of administration are: "O holy Father, physician of souls and bodies, who has sent us thine only Son, our Lord Jesus Christ, who cureth every sickness and saveth from death, heal thy servant N., from every bodily and spiritual ill that afflicts him and fill him with healthy life by the grace of thy Christ." A shorter version of this rite has been approved for the Slavs and Rumanians.

Orders. The orders of the Byzantine rite are reader, subdeacon ("minor"), deacon, priest, bishop ("major"). For the ordination of a deacon the candidate is led to the altar before the communion during the Liturgy. The bishop blesses him; then he kneels down, and the bishop lays his right hand on the candidate's head, invoking the Holy Ghost: "The grace of God, that always strengthens the weak and fills the empty, appoints the most religious subdeacon N., to be deacon. Let us then pray for him that the grace of the Holy Ghost may come upon him." He then vests him with the *orarion* and hands him the *ripidion*, exclaiming *Axios!*, "He is worthy!" which the assistants repeat, three times. The ordination of a priest is similar, he being vested in the *phelonion* and given the chalice; this takes place after the "great entrance." After the consecration the bishop gives a particle of the sacred Host to the new priest, who holds it in his hand until "Holy things to the holy" is sung. The episcopate is likewise conferred by laying on one hand and invoking the Holy Ghost; two co-consecrators are, of course, required. It is to be noted that there are no anointings in any of these ordinations.

---

[18] This is the Eastern name for what we call Extreme Unction. Our name is misleading. *Extreme* here means the *last* anointing we receive (i.e., after those at Baptism and Confirmation), not one to be received when *in extremis:* it is supposed to be administered before that. Dissident Orientals sometimes err the other way, by giving it to those who are not sick at all.

Some deacons remain in that order all their lives, and Eastern archdeacons are properly deacons, not priests.

Marriage. This office varies but little from country to country and has strongly influenced the corresponding services in non-Byzantine churches of the East.

Before they leave their house, bride and groom are blessed by their parents with *eikons* of our Lord and his all-holy Mother. The wedding ceremony itself consists of two parts, the betrothal and the blessing. The groom waits near a small table set before the *eikonostasis* and the bride comes to him up the church, preceded by a small boy carrying an *eikon*, while the choir sings a hymn, "Come, O Dove, from Zion." The priest gives each party a lighted candle, incenses them, and blesses them three times. Then, after prayers for conjugal fidelity and with further blessings, rings are mutually exchanged three times: "The servant of God N., joints him (her) self with the servant of God M." This ends the betrothal.

While the choir sings Psalm 127, the priest leads the couple to the table, before which a silken carpet is spread. Then, having ascertained the free consent of each, he brings two crowns of metal and precious stones from the sanctuary. With these he blesses groom and bride twice, and puts them on their heads, saying, "The servant of God N., is crowned with the servant of God M., in the name of the Father," etc. A passage from St. Paul's letter to the Ephesians (cap. v; cf. the Roman nuptial Mass) is read and the gospel of the wedding at Cana, and the choir sings the Lord's Prayer while the married couple drink thrice from a cup of blessed wine. The priest joins their hands, which he covers with his stole, and leads them in procession three times round the cross and gospel-book on the table while the choir sings three hymns. The ceremony ends with a prayer that invokes the memory and virtues of Abraham and Sara, Isaac and Rebecca, Jacob and Rachel. Some Eastern marriage rites require an explicit declaration of contract from the parties, others do not.

Kalendar. The reformed annual kalendar put forward by Pope Gregory XIII in 1582, and at once adopted by most of western

Europe except England and Wales, Scotland and Ireland, took a long time to get any foothold in the East. None of the dissident Orthodox churches began to accept it before 1924, and few Eastern Catholics before the beginning of the nineteenth century. Even now, though most of the different Catholic bodies have received it, a majority of the individuals are following the old Julian kalendar because that is the custom of the numerically superior Ruthenians. According to the Julian reckoning, fixed feasts fall thirteen days after the corresponding day by the Gregorian reckoning, and the two Easters and feasts depending thereon coincide about one year in every three.

The Byzantines have no liturgical cycles corresponding to those of the Roman church year, but the period from the Sunday "before Septuagesima" to the Saturday after Whitsunday (*triodion* of Lent and *triodion* of Easter) stands apart from all the rest in importance. Many Sundays are named after the gospel which is read: Sunday "of the Prodigal Son" (Septuagesima), "of the Paralytic" (third after Easter), etc. Certain feasts are preceded by vigils, of which the "greater vigils" extend over several days (e.g., five before Christmas), and there are likewise periods corresponding to the Western octave, which last from three (e.g., Sunday "of the Man Born Blind" — fifth after Easter) to nine days (e.g., Epiphany). An interesting observance is the feast called a *synaxis*, assembly, when the people meet together to honour those saints connected with the mystery celebrated on the previous day, e.g., of SS. Simeon and Anne on the day after the Purification of our Lady. The ecclesiastical year begins on September 1.

Feasts. These may be divided into "great," "lesser," "little," and what we should call "commemoration." Easter stands all by itself, and the two Sundays and three weekdays before and the Sunday after are all in the class of "great" (Greek usage). The feasts of saints celebrated naturally vary from country to country; e.g., the kalendar used by the Melkites has about 100 ancient feasts of all sorts in common with the Roman church, some of them on different dates. The traditional Slavonic kalendar naturally has a number of Russian and other saints little known elsewhere (the feasts of about thirty early ones have been admitted to Catholic observance), but also includes such great Western names as Irenaeus, Ambrose, Augustine, Benedict, Leo, Gregory, Jerome, Martin of Tours. To these, Catholic usage adds Francis of Assisi (deeply venerated among some Russian Orthodox), and, of course, the more recently recognized Eastern martyrs, St. Josephat Kuntsevich (see p. 69, and note), the Armenian Blessed Gomidas Keumurgian (June 5), the Maronites BB. Francis, Abdulmuti and Raphael Masabki (July 10), and the Ethiopian Blessed Gabra Michael (August 28). The chief more recent modifications among most Catholics are the addition of Corpus Christi and the Sacred Heart, and increased solemnity given to St. Joseph (on the Sunday after Christmas) and to the Child-begetting of the Mother of the Mother of God, i.e., the Immaculate Conception, on December 9.

Among the special Byzantine observances are the feast of Orthodoxy (first Sunday in Lent), celebrating the triumph of orthodox veneration for holy images over Iconoclasm in 842; the Three Holy Hierarchs (SS. Basil, Gregory Nazianzen, and John Chrysostom), on January 30; the foundation of Constantinople (May 11); our Lady of Kazan (July 8); the Miracle of our Lady at Miasene (September 1); and many feasts of the just of the Old Dispensation (Joseph, David, Elias, Josue, the Three Children, Job the Great Athlete, the Ancestors of the Messias, etc., and a general feast which includes Adam and Eve). The Exaltation of the Cross on September 14 is a specially solemn day. The number of "holydays of obligation" varies; the Melkites have 30 (in addition to Sundays), including St. Nicholas, St. George, and St. Elias.

Penitential seasons. Eastern fasting, like many other of their religious usages, is the observance proper to monks gradually extended to the people at large (but by custom more than by law), and it is notoriously severe. For centuries the pious faithful made it a point of honour to keep the fasts, and many still do; but conditions of modern life (to say nothing of religious cooling) make it increasingly difficult to do so. Among Catholics, the new conditions have been met in some places by canonical legislation, generally approximating to Western observances; in others, local customs are in process of evolution.

There is only one word, *nesteia*, to designate both fasting and abstinence and it is rather difficult to distinguish between them. Among the Greeks, fasting involves one meal only and that after sunset; strict abstinence forbids meat, milk, eggs, fish, oil, and wine; mitigated abstinence allows oil and wine, and sometimes fish; this is according to the old canons and customs, which envisaged strict fasting every Wednesday and Friday and in Lent, and abstinence on from 50 to 90 other days. But for the Catholic Melkites, for example, the second synod of Ain Traz in 1835 directed that fasting should consist of complete abstinence from food, drink, and tobacco until noon; afterwards anything may be eaten without limit of quantity, except meat, eggs, and milk. Their fasting days are five before Christmas, four before Epiphany, all Lent except Saturdays and Sundays and the Annunciation, and three other days. The same synod defined abstinence to extend to meat, eggs, and milk. It is obligatory for ten days before the fast of Christmas, twelve days before SS. Peter and Paul, fourteen days before the Assumption, on the solemnities of the Beheading of St. John Baptist and Holy Cross, and every Wednesday and Friday. But there is no fasting or abstinence during paschal-time and at certain other seasons, and even the above regulations are modified from place to place, apparently with no particular authority.

General observations. The Catholic Byzantines have taken up the use of Western "devotions," rosary, stations of the cross, etc., in varying degrees. Among their own observances is the Akathistos Hymn, an office in honour of our Lady which is sung publicly at certain times and much used privately as well. Holy water (*hagiasma*) is in use to a limited extent and it is solemnly blessed in the baptismal font (and sometimes in rivers or the sea) at the Epiphany, in commemoration of our Lord's baptism. Houses are blessed on the first day of every month, grapes or apples on the Transfiguration, and flowers, especially sweet basil, on the two feasts of the cross. The custom of blessing and eating corn-cakes (*kolybes*) in memory of the dead is unquestionably a pagan survival. On Good Friday a figure of our Lord is laid on an ornamental bier (*epitaphion*) with flowers, spices, and grave-clothes (the "Burial of Christ"). In the evening it is carried in procession round and out of the church, sometimes through the streets (the "Funeral of Christ"); and then laid on the altar or in the middle of the church while *troparia* modeled on the last five verses of Matthew 17 are sung. On a dozen chief feasts there is at the end of Vespers a procession (*Litia*) during which the Song of Simeon is sung, and five loaves of bread, wheat, wine, and oil are blessed (*Artoklasia*). The bread is distributed to the faithful, who are anointed on the forehead with the oil. This blessing of food, being associated with a vigil, may be the remnant of an evening meal.

It has been wittily observed that "visitors from the West commonly find Byzantine services interminable for the simple reason that they never stay to the end."

BIBLIOGRAPHY

de Meester, *The Divine Liturgy of . . . John Chrysostom.* Greek and English texts (London, 1926).

Sembratovich, *The Divine Liturgy of . . . John Chrysostom.* Translated from the Slavonic (Detroit, 1932). Translations of other Byzantine offices are published by Williams & Norgate of London.

Ordo Celebrationis Vesperarum, Matutini et Divinae Liturgiae iuxta Recensionem Ruthenorum (Rome, 1944).

Moreau, *Les Liturgies Eucharistiques* (Brussels, 1924).

Holloway, *A Study of the Byzantine Liturgy* (London, 1934).

Couturier, *Course de Liturgie Grecque-Melkite,* 3 vols. (Paris, 1912–1930).

Mercenier, *La Prière des Eglises de Rite Byzantin,* 2 vols. (Amay, 1939).

Stoelen, *L'Année Liturgique Byzantine* (Amay, 1928), Russian usage.

McNabb, *The Akathistos Hymn* (Ditchling, 1934).

Hamilton, *Byzantine Architecture and Decoration* (London, 1933).

Bréhier, *L'Art byzantine* (Paris, 1924).

Couturier, *Syllitourgikon*. Responses of the choir and other music in European notation (Paris, 1925).

Tillyard, *Byzantine Music and Hymnography* (London, 1930).

Schwarz, *Le chant ecclésiastique byzantin de nos jours* (In *Irénikon*, X, pp. 225, 235; XI, p. 168. Amay, 1933–1934).

Music for the Liturgy of St. John Chrysostom (Tournai, 1937), Russian usage.

Gogol, *Meditations on the Divine Liturgy* (London, 1926).

CHAPTER IV

CATHOLIC CHURCHES OF THE BYZANTINE RITE

1. THE ITALO-GREEKS

THE Italo-Greeks, more accurately called now Italo-Greek-Albanians, or even Italo-Albanians, are the only Orientals who have been in communion with Rome since before the Eastern schism; they therefore have an historical interest out of proportion to their numbers and present importance.

For several centuries before the birth of Christ Hellenic colonists had made Sicily and southern Italy predominantly Greek: the provinces of Calabria and Apulia are known historically as *Magna Graecia*. From at least the second century after Christ there were Christian communities in these parts, and the present inhabitants regard their churches as apostolic foundations (Acts 23:11–14).[1] The first seven hundred years of their ecclesiastical history are full of difficulties, but it seems certain that, after the superseding of Greek by Latin in the liturgy at Rome about the middle of the third century and the crystallizing of different liturgical rites, Roman and Byzantine usages existed side by side in southern Italy and Sicily; and there is no doubt that all bishops of these Christians were under the direct jurisdiction of the Bishop of Rome.[2]

---

[1] Pope St. Agatho (d. 681) was a Sicilian Greek, and Pope St. Zacharias (d. 752) a Calabrian Greek.

[2] Liturgical rite has essentially nothing to do with patriarchate. The notion that all subjects of the same patriarch should have his rite is partly a result of the aggressive "uniformizing" of Constantinople. The Pope was patriarch of Byzantines in Illyricum as well as metropolitan of those in *Magna Graecia*. The great archbishop of Canterbury, St. Theodore, was a Greek monk of Calabria; when Pope St. Vitalian appointed him in 664 to rule over us Latins he had to "change his rite" — and his style of hair-dressing (see Bede's *Ecclesiastical History*, IV, 1).

About the year 732 the Iconoclast emperor Leo III the Isaurian began forcibly to subject these Greek districts which Justinian had joined to the Eastern empire to the patriarch of Constantinople, and metropolitan sees were erected at Naples, Syracuse, and elsewhere. To avoid disputes the popes accepted the situation. But the conquest by the Normans of southern Italy, begun in 1017, and then of Sicily (at that time in Saracen hands), removed the possibility of these Greek churches following Constantinople into schism in 1054, and they came again under the immediate jurisdiction of the pope, as they have ever since remained.[3]

The influence of the Normans and the increasing Latin element was not favourable to the Greek Catholics; several of their eparchies (dioceses) were suppressed, whole parishes turned Latin, the numerous monasteries became decadent. By the beginning of the fifteenth century the Byzantines were on the verge of extinction. But there was an influx of refugees from Constantinople after 1453, and then for a hundred years there came colonists and mercenaries from Albania, following the alliance of Skanderbeg with Ferdinand I of Naples. Some of the immigrants were Latins, some Byzantines; these last saved their dying rite in Italy,[4] and account for the Italo-Greeks of today being mainly of Albanian descent. Nevertheless the decay continued, and the last Byzantine bishopric disappeared at the end of the sixteenth century; some of the monasteries hung on much longer. From before 1600 the Byzantines were subject to the local ordinaries, who encouraged and urged them (to put it mildly) to join the Latin rite; in consequence, the Byzantine rite was given up altogether in Apulia and Terra d'Otranto, and greatly decreased elsewhere. (To the average Western bishop of those days, Eastern subjects were a nuisance, and at least suspect of heresy all the time. That

---

[3] At a council held by Pope Urban II at Bari in Apulia in 1098 certain Italo-Greek bishops threw doubt on the procession of the Holy Ghost from the Son ("*Filioque*"). They were confuted by St. Anselm, archbishop of Canterbury.

[4] Pope Clement XI (1700–21) was a descendant of one of these Albanian families, which had settled in the Papal States.

Orientals have as much right to their "peculiarities" as Latins have to theirs did not occur to them: the popes, indeed, seem to have been the only ones who never lost sight of this).

Moreover, there was difficulty in recruiting and training their clergy, though the Greek College at Rome was open to them. An Oratorian priest, George Guzzetta, started an Albanian community at Piana in Sicily in 1716 and a seminary at Palermo in 1734; during the century or so of their existence these Byzantine Oratorians did much good work but were handicapped by their insistence on the Western principle of clerical celibacy; the seminary is still in being. There was a seminary for Calabria at Ullano from 1732 till 1860. Pope Clement XII authorized the consecration of a bishop, who should ordain priests but have no jurisdiction, for Byzantines in Calabria, and one for those of Sicily was appointed by Pius VI.

Meantime, in 1742, Pope Benedict XIV issued the constitution *"Etsi pastoralis,"* which was a sort of compendium of canon law for the Greeks and Albanians: their rites and customs are to be kept, their privileges are confirmed, no Latin ordinary is to interfere with their lawful usages or invite them to become Latins, and a Byzantine vicar general must be appointed; the Latin rite has no precedence as such over the Byzantine: "before God there is neither Greek nor Jew nor barbarian nor Scythian, for all are one in Christ." The effect of this was to restore self-respect to the Greco-Albanians and put a brake for the time being on their cultural and ecclesiastical decay; moreover, *"Etsi pastoralis"* paved the way for other and more far-reaching papal pronouncements on the true place of Orientals in the Church.

PRESENT STATE

Italy. In 1919 Pope Benedict XV constituted a separate eparchy for the Byzantines of Calabria, with its see at Lungro. It has twenty village parishes and one in the town of Lecce. Though it is not in this jurisdiction, mention must be made of the church built for the Greek colony at Leghorn in 1605; the hundred parishioners are mixed Melkites, Italo-Greeks, and Italo-Albanians.

Sicily. The Byzantines of Sicily have eight parishes, and these were made into a separate eparchy in 1937, with its see at Piana dei Greci. This town, near Palermo, has seven Byzantine places of worship.

Parochial clergy. These two dioceses (which are immediately subject to the Holy See) have a hundred churches and chapels, served by sixty priests, of whom over half are in Sicily. They make their studies in the junior seminary founded by Pope Benedict XV at the abbey of Grottaferrata, at the Palermo seminary founded by Father Guzzetta, and at the Greek College in Rome (see page 115). The Italo-Albanian priests retain their right to marriage before ordination and a few are married. The use of the traditional Greek clerical costume has been restored indoors and for formal occasions; most rectors of churches call themselves protopopes, i.e., archpriests.

Religious institutes. Both in the earlier and later Middle Ages the centres of Byzantinism in southern Italy were the numerous monasteries. To arrest their decline, Pope Gregory XIII in 1579 united them all into a congregation on the model of the Benedictine one of St. Justina of Padua; unfortunately it was also joined to the Spanish Basilian order, a purely Western institute (founded 1559; now extinct), and this hastened the decay in Italy by a prolonged process of voluntary latinization; the houses were Greek almost only in name. Rodotà, the first ordaining bishop for Calabria, could still speak in 1758 of forty-three struggling Oriental monasteries "where once there were about a thousand"; today there are none left at all, with the distinguished exception of Grottaferrata and its dependencies.

About the year 980 a Greek abbot, St. Neilos of Rossano, and his monks fled before the Saracen raids on Calabria and, having long enjoyed Benedictine hospitality at Monte Cassino, established a monastery at Grottaferrata in the Alban hills in 1004. It was within the domain of the turbulent lords of Tusculum, and frequently figures in the history of the Papal States, as when that disgraceful pope Benedict IX retired there to spend his last years in penitence. Pope Pius II made the Greek cardinal Bes-

sarion its abbot *in commendam*, and he did much for Grottaferrata. But his successor, Cardinal Julian della Rovere (afterwards Pope Julius II), rebuilt it as a fortress ("Uomo di spiriti
bellicosi," as the monastic chronicler justly observes), and later
commendatory abbots — and others — did much harm. These
gentlemen, whose sensitive classicism was such that it could not
bear the barbarous Latin of the office hymns, destroyed or hid
much beautiful Greek work of the Middle Ages, plastering it
("plaster" is the right word) with the riotous intemperances of
baroque. Not all the monks took this lying down, and their chronicler remarks drily that whereas Cardinal Guadagni is commemorated above the church door in *stone*, the angels venerating our
Lady's eikon within the church are only *stucco*.

The commendatory abbots did not end till 1824, and the life
and worship of the monastery continued to suffer. Further decay
was stopped by Pope Leo XIII in 1881, who ordered a rigorous
reform and restoration of its Byzantine integrity, which was carried through with gratifying results. And in 1937 the Holy See
made it an abbey *nullius* (*dioecesis*), that is, the people of the
surrounding district are ecclesiastically subject to the abbot as
their ordinary.

These monks have always had a reputation for learning, and
their library contains valuable manuscripts, including a famous
Typikon of the eleventh century, on which their editions of the
Greek liturgical books are based. The monastery has a school of
illumination and Greek palaeography, and a specialty is made
of the repair of old and decayed manuscripts. Greek frescoes and
mosaics, pushed out of sight by renaissance taste, have been
brought back to light, and in 1907 the Archimandrite Arsenios
Pellegrini established a museum of antiquities.

For nearly nine hundred years, then, there have been Greek
monks at the very gates of Rome, the capital not simply of the
Latin but of the Catholic world. Their byzantinism has not always
been above reproach; but that reproach has now been taken
away, and they are a living witness at her heart that the Catholic
Church is not solely a West-European institution. After visiting

Grottaferrata, Professor Karolidis, of the University of Athens, wrote in a Greek newspaper that "Here is an oasis of Hellenism right at the centre of Latin civilization." And this Byzantine monastic community goes back unbrokenly and organically through the ages to the time before the tragic separation of Eastern and Western Christians had taken place.

The community has a score of hieromonks and monks, mostly Italo-Albanians. In addition to a junior seminary for their rite, they conduct a printing establishment and an orphanage. In 1920 they took over the old monastery of Mezzoiuso in Sicily and made it a novitiate for the training of monks for apostolic work in Albania itself and later on in Greece,[5] while in 1932 a daughter-house was started near Lungro. In 1935 the missionary College of St. Basil in Rome was entrusted to them.

There are Byzantine sisters of several congregations engaged in teaching and other good works in Calabria and Sicily.

The Faithful. Of the twenty-five villages of Italo-Greek-Albanians in Italy and Sicily where the Greek observances are maintained the chief are Lungro, San Demetrio Corone, Piana dei Greci, and Palazzo Adriano. The people are all peasants, rather poverty-stricken in Italy, more prosperous in Sicily. There are 35,000 of them in the one country and about 16,000 in the other, of whom a fair proportion (here and there whole villages) speak a somewhat debased Albanian as their usual language. A Greek dialect is still spoken in certain villages of Terra d'Ontranto; there is evidence that it is derived primarily from the Greek of ancient times and not from later Byzantine colonies. It seems unavoidable that they should all in time become completely italianized and be absorbed into the Latin rite — but that time is still a long way off.

OTHER JURISDICTION

United States. There were large emigrations of Italo-Greeks at

---

[5] Some dissident Orthodox Greeks are rather proud of Grottaferrata and sympathetic toward its monks, because it was founded before the schism and has an unbroken Greek tradition.

the end of the nineteenth century, mostly to the states of New York and Pennsylvania. Many of them were lost to the Church for lack of priests of their rite. The first priest was sent from Palermo in 1904, and he opened two churches in New York. There are no statistics of their number in the United States today. Twenty years ago they were said to be 20,000, but there has been a tendency greatly to overestimate the number of Catholic Orientals of some rites in America. In any case the great majority of the Italo-Greeks frequent churches of the Latin rite.

PARTICULAR CUSTOMS

As their history would lead us to expect, the liturgy of the Byzantines underwent very serious modifications during the course of time in southern Italy, but in Sicily it was much better observed. These innovations have to a considerable extent been corrected and in most churches the Greek rite is now observed with a very fair degree of fidelity. They use the excellent books printed at Rome. But as the churches are nearly all too poor to afford *eikonostases,* and as statues, side-altars, etc., have been admitted into them, there is not much to distinguish them from the Latin churches. The Italo-Greeks adopted the Gregorian reckoning with the Catholic West in 1582, the first Easterns to do so. They have modified the Constantinopolitan kalendar by celebrating certain feasts (e.g., All Saints, All Souls, St. Joseph) on their Roman as well as their Byzantine dates and by the addition of more modern feasts, e.g., Corpus Christi, the Sacred Heart, St. Antony of Padua. Confirmation is separated from Baptism and conferred by a bishop, and absolution is given in the Roman form. Pope Benedict XV restored the privilege of confirming to priests in the eparchy of Lungro but the reform has not yet been effected; but in practice the bishop himself often baptizes, and then confirms immediately after.

Their church music is a traditional version of that of Constantinople, and in some churches Albanian hymns are still sung (unhappily, organs have been introduced into their churches in America). As is natural, Benediction of the Blessed Sacrament (in a form of their own) and all the other "popular devotions" of the West have long been known among them. A curious local observance in some churches is for men to receive Communion standing (according to their rite) but women kneeling.

BIBLIOGRAPHY

Fortescue, *The Uniate Eastern Churches* (Italo-Greeks and Melkites) (London, 1923).

Gaisser, *I canti ecclesiastici italo-greci* (Rome, 1905).

Rossini, *Canti tradizionali delle Colonie Italo-Greco-Albanesi* [the melodies made chromatic] (Birmingham, 1926).

Buccola, *Badia di Grottaferrata* (Grottaferrata, 1913).

2. THE RUTHENIANS OR UKRAINIANS

"Ruthenian" is the official ecclesiastical descriptive term for certain bodies of Catholics of the Byzantine rite found in Eastern Galicia, Podcarpathia, Hungary, and the Bukovina, with colonies in North America and elsewhere. They all belong in origin to one people. The land that lies between Vilna in the north and the Carpathian mountains in the south was part of Poland from about 1350 to 1793 and again from 1921 to 1939; in Russian history the territory is known as "The Western Lands," and it includes the provinces of Eastern Galicia, Volhynia, and Polesia. It has a very mixed population, consisting mostly, in order of numerousness, of Ruthenians (or Ukrainians), Poles, and White Russians. There are many more Ukrainians and White Russians to the east, but these are no concern of ours at the moment.

The Ruthenians are Slavs and, moreover, they may be justly regarded as the original Russians. After the fall of their great city of Kiev in 1240 to the Mongols the centre of state power gradually shifted to Moscow, and eventually the Muscovites, who were less purely Slav than the people of the southwest, reserved for themselves the name of Great Russians and called the others Little Russians.[6] Each of these three elements, Great Russian, White Russian, and Ruthenian, has its own language, descended from a common tongue that was spoken by them all before the twelfth century.

During the nineteenth century considerable cultural and political self-consciousness arose among the Ruthenians or Little Russians, which by the end of World War I developed into an

---

[6] In the West the Russians were first called Ruthenes and then Muscovites. The White Russians are sometimes called Byelorussians, to distinguish them from the other "White" Russians, so-called because they opposed the "Red" revolution.

acute nationalism. That is no concern of mine here, and I mention it for only one reason: a manifestation of this nationalism
was to refuse the name Ruthenian, because that is what their
foreign governors, Poles, Hungarians, etc., called them. They call
themselves Ukrainians.[7] However, so far as the Catholics are
concerned "Ruthenian" is still their official *ecclesiastical* designa-
tion, and so I employ it in this book, varying it by "Ukrainian"
when it seems convenient to do so: I use both terms without any
political significance whatever.

GENERAL ECCLESIASTICAL HISTORY

St. Vladimir, the apostle of Russia, was a Northman and his
capital Kiev, "the God-protected mother of Russian cities," was
the heart of what is known now as "The Ukraine." For two hundred and fifty years it was the political and ecclesiastical centre
of Russia, and the chief hierarchs continued to call themselves
metropolitans of Kiev for two hundred years after they had
resided at Moscow. Accordingly, for all the time from 988 until
the Metropolitan Isidore had to flee from Moscow in 1443 after
promulgating the Union of Florence, the religious history of the
Ruthenians was much the same as that of the Russians in general
(see pp. 124–125).

In 1458 Pope Pius II nominated a monk called Gregory to be
metropolitan of Kiev, and by arrangement with Casimir IV of
Poland he was allowed to exercise jurisdiction over the eight
eparchies of the Kiev ecclesiastical province that were then under
the control of Poland and Lithuania.[8] This lasted only till the
beginning of the sixteenth century, when they slipped back into
schism. During the second half of that century the Jesuits came
to Vilna, Yaroslav, Polotsk, and elsewhere and at once set themselves to work for the definitive reunion of the Ruthenian bishops
and their flocks, the leading spirits being Father Peter Skarga

---

[7] Historically, this is the less significant name of the two. *Ukraine* only
means "the borderland" or "marches."

[8] All White Russia and the Ukraine west of Kiev was under the suzerainty
of Poland and Lithuania from the middle of the fourteenth century till
1772–1795.

(d. 1612) and Father Antony Possevino (d. 1611). At length
in 1595 Michael Ragoza, metropolitan of Kiev, and the bishops
of Vladimir, Lutsk, Polotsk, Pinsk, and Kholm met at Brest-
Litovsk in Lithuania and petitioned the Holy See to admit them
to its communion, and on December 23 the reunion was solemnly proclaimed in the hall of Constantine at the Vatican. Only
the bishops of Lvov[9] and Peremysl stood out.

Just as the Eastern schism was brought about largely through
political, social, and cultural considerations, so these had their
part in the Union of Brest. Among them were the desire of the
Polish crown to unify the peoples of its dominions, the wish of
the Holy See to consolidate a Christian *bloc* against the Turks,
and the hope of some of the Orthodox leaders to raise the moral
and intellectual level of their clergy to that of the Western clergy.
The secular factors contributed much to the bitterness of the
struggle that followed. The enemies of the union, led by the
above two bishops and Prince Ostrozhsky, began a violent opposition; but Ragoza (d. 1600) was succeeded by two energetic and
capable prelates, the second of whom was an outstanding figure
in Ruthenian church history, Joseph Benjamin Rutsky, a convert
from Calvinism. While he occupied the see of Kiev (1614–1637),
the bishop of Polotsk, Josaphat Kuntsevich, was slain out of
hatred of the faith in November, 1623; fourteen years later his
chief opponent Melety Smotritsky himself became a Catholic.[10]

In 1620, encouraged by the dissident patriarchs of Constantinople and Jerusalem and aided by Protestant sectaries, a dissident
hierarchy was set up side by side with the Catholic one, and
eventually in 1632 the attacks of the Zaporozhsky Cossacks of the
Dnieper forced the Polish king, Ladislas VII, to recognize it; in
the following year the city of Kiev was lost to the union, the
famous Orthodox theologian, Peter Mogila, becoming its metropolitan. There followed a period of pressure and persecution from

---

[9] This Russian spelling is the easiest for English-speakers. *Lviv* is Ukrainian, *Lwow* Polish, *Lemberg* German, and *Leopolis* Latin.
[10] St. Josaphat was canonized in 1867 and his feast extended to the
Western church by Pope Leo XIII in 1882. We keep it on November 14.

schismatic Cossacks, Lutheran Swedes, and Mohammedan Tartars that ended only with the election of John Sobjeski to the throne of Poland in 1674. In 1692 the bishop of Peremysl brought his flock into the Church, in 1677 the bishop of Lvov had done the same, and in 1702 another dissident bishop; schism had now practically disappeared from Polish territory. The metropolitan continued to have the title of Kiev but lived at Radomysl, in the Ukraine.

At this time the Ruthenian Catholics must have numbered about twelve millions, but during the seventeenth and eighteenth centuries practically the whole of the nobility and the bigger landowners (boyary) became polonized and passed to the Latin rite, in spite of a decree of Pope Urban VIII in 1624 that forbade them to do so. This divided and greatly weakened the faithful, many of whom had been reduced to serfdom by the Poles, for the trials that were to come.

Some writers do not scruple to represent the Galician Ukrainians since 1595 as "groaning under the yoke of Rome," held in unwilling submission to the Holy See by the governments and subservient prelates of Poland and Austria. It may be freely admitted that at the time of the Union of Brest methods were sometimes used by both sides that would not be tolerated by enlightened Christians today. But that these Ruthenians as a whole were sincere in their Catholicity their subsequent history shows; the loving flock of Andrew Szepticky were not unwilling Catholics longing for separation: there was unrest among them — but the sources of it were not to be found in Rome.

From early in the eighteenth century Russia began more and more to interfere with the internal affairs of Poland, and in 1772 there began that process known as "the partition of Poland," the earlier part of which was concluded in 1795.[11] The fate of the Ukrainians varied according to the power into whose hands they

[11] To much of the territory acquired at this time (White Russia, Volhynia, part of the Ukraine) Russia made a claim for which a case could be made. What happened in 1815 was quite another matter. The Russian statesmen themselves distinguished sharply between the "Western Lands" and "Congress Poland," and at first treated them quite differently from each other.

fell. Russia eventually got back all the territory in which there were any Ukrainians, except Galicia, and it soon became apparent that the government's intention was to obtain control over and then suppress those Catholics who were not Latins. Catherine II and Alexander I reduced the Ruthenian episcopal sees to three, monasteries were closed, and churches handed over to the Orthodox. Many of the Byzantine Catholics quietly accepted the new state of affairs; they could hardly see the difference — the church services were practically the same, and that was the main thing for them. But many others resisted, and after the Polish insurrection of 1830 more repressive measures were taken. An unfaithful Catholic, one Joseph Siemashko, was nominated to the episcopate by Nicholas I and, on the death of the faithful Metropolitan Bulgak in 1838, this man induced the two remaining bishops to sign, and over 1300 clergy to assent to, an act of union with the state Church of Russia. The Czar had a medal struck to commemorate the occasion; it bore the inscription, "Separated by violence in 1596, reunited by love in 1839." This was hardly in accordance with the facts, for the remaining clergy and very many of the lay people refused to follow them, so the government resorted to open force. Catholic baptisms and weddings were forbidden and Orthodox priests intruded into the churches; all religious houses were shut and their goods confiscated; those who resisted were flogged or exiled to Siberia, and 160 priests were degraded and imprisoned in remote monasteries. The Ruthenian Catholic Church was dead in Russia. Only in the Kholm district, which was ceded by Austria in 1815 and was less severely dealt with, did it linger on till 1875 and even a few years longer, during which some Jesuits ministered at the peril of their lives.[12] When

---

[12] This grievous persecution was not primarily religious, but arose from the notion that every subject of the Russian state must be a member of the Russian church. The Latin Catholics of Poland also were persecuted, but their Catholicism was not regarded as so iniquitous because they were not Russians or regarded as "perverts from Orthodoxy." Nevertheless that Russia did not otherwise or in general oppress the Ukrainians is shown by the fact that, while Jews, Poles, Lithuanians, and Great Russian sectaries emigrated wholesale, Ukrainians did not: they were quite "at home." Ukrainian emigration was from Austria-Hungary, a foreign land.

Nicholas II granted religious toleration in 1905 over 300,000 of these former Catholics and their children returned to the Church, one third of whom were *Uporstvujushchie*, "Obstinates," old people who for thirty years and more had refused to attend the Orthodox churches; but as Catholic Byzantines were still illegal they had to become Latins. The new Catholics in Volhynia (see p. 127) are also descendants of the White Russians and Ukrainians who were forcibly "decatholicized" during the nineteenth century.

THE GALICIAN RUTHENIANS

The story of the Ukrainians of Galicia, who came under the sway of Austria, was a less unhappy but far from satisfactory one. There were (apart from Kholm, which was to go to Russia in 1815) two episcopal sees, Lvov and Peremysl (the last two sees to join the Union of Brest are the only ones that have survived), now under different civil rule from their metropolitan, which caused difficulties. The Holy See solved them in 1807 by making Lvov an archiepiscopate and uniting with it the old metropolitan see of Galich, which had been revived a few years before. Two of the occupants of this see have been elevated to the cardinalate, Michael Levitsky in 1856 and Sylvester Sembratovich in 1895.[13] It was not till 1885 that the huge eparchy of Lvov was reduced in area by forming a new one from it, Stanislavov.

Under the rule of the Austrian emperors the Ruthenians had full religious liberty; serfdom was abolished in 1848 and in 1860 Galicia was given a measure of civil autonomy and its own assembly. The Ruthenians, having lost their natural leaders by polonization, were all peasants, but from the middle of the nineteenth century a cultured and enterprising middle class began to develop and an *intelligentsia* made its appearance. For this they had to

---

[13] Very few Orientals have been made cardinals. The office is radically in relation to the local church at Rome: that is why they are called "Cardinals of the Holy Roman Church." They elect the bishop of Rome — who is as well supreme pontiff of the Universal Church, *ex officio* and *iure divino*. Father Leo Sembratovich, who was Ukrainian pastor at Detroit from 1929 to 1939, was a nephew and at one time secretary of Cardinal Sembratovich.

thank their married clergy, from whose children this new class was chiefly recruited. The Ruthenians were jealous of their former overlords the Poles, and the ill-feeling of the Poles was aggravated by the later policy of the Austrian government, which favoured the Ruthenians in order to counterbalance Polish influence and fostered the "Ukrainian movement" as a political move against Russia. On the other hand, the Ruthenians themselves were not of one mind politically: at the time of the outbreak of war in 1914 they were divided into five parties.

Their subsequent troubles did much to unite them. First they were suspected of pro-Russianism, and many were interned with considerable brutality, including 300 of the clergy. General Brusilov captured Lvov on September 3, 1914, and again many were interned or deported to Russia, this time on suspicion of being pro-Austrian and to conciliate the Poles. Among those deported was their archbishop, Andrew Szepticky. Full liberty was given to Orthodox clergy to cross the Podhorze and the Bug and do what they could with the Catholic Ruthenians. In circumstances in which there was so much, humanly speaking, in favour of schism, the solid Catholicity of the Ruthenians was well vindicated. Only twenty-nine priests turned Orthodox, and of these, twenty-seven were chased from their cures by their flocks; among the 1800 Ruthenian parishes of Galicia the state Church of Russia was able to establish only about one hundred temporarily in communion with itself.

At the end of 1917 a Ukrainian republic was proclaimed at Kiev and in October, 1918, a Western Ukrainian republic at Lvov, whereupon Poland assumed sovereign authority over the whole of Galicia. From November, 1918, the Ukrainians and the Poles were at war and the struggle was pursued with detestable bitterness and unscrupulosity on both sides. It is difficult to avoid the conclusion that a deliberate attempt was made by the Polish government to cut off the supply of Ukrainian clergy and cripple the resources of Ukrainian culture: but such misfortunes have overtaken both sides since then that it is better to be silent about the excesses of those days when these two peoples, both Slav and both Catholic, were at each other's throats. Ukrainian resistance was short-lived; and eventually, in 1923, in consideration of a promise (never fulfilled) by the Poles to give the Ukrainians an autonomous constitution, the Conference of Ambassadors confirmed Eastern Galicia as a province of Poland.

It is not difficult to imagine the results of these events — two deportations, two military invasions, and a civil war — on the Ukrainian people and the Ruthenian church; their marvelous recovery was due in the first place to the activity and ability of Metropolitan Szepticky, who laboured day and night under the most trying difficulties both of the situation in itself and of obstacles deliberately put in his way. As an example of the one, the sixty priests in the deaneries of Rogatin and Drogobich in 1913 had by execution, deportation, and natural decrease been reduced to five in 1920; of the other, from the beginning of the civil war the metropolitan was interned in his house by the Poles and not completely at liberty for over twelve months.

Andrew Szepticky was not only the greatest Eastern hierarch of his time, he was also one of the outstanding figures in the whole Church. He was only thirty-five when, in 1900, he was appointed to the see of Lvov and the primacy of the Galician Ukrainians. During the forty-four years of his episcopate his influence spread in a most remarkable way: he was recognized as the moral leader of Catholic Ukrainians abroad as well as at home, the Rusins of the Podkarpatska Rus looked up to him with love and reverence, many Orthodox Ukrainians and even Russians came under his spell — the spell of goodness, gentleness, sincerity, and fearlessness. People sought his spiritual counsel from so far away as France and Holland and England, and the Holy See sent him on a visitation of the Ukrainians of the United States and Canada.

One who knew the Metropolitan Andrew intimately tells us that he humbly aspired to martyrdom. And in a real sense the last thirty of his eighty years of life were one long martyrdom. Persecuted and oppressed first by the Russian and then by the Polish government from 1914 to 1923; the great works of the following constructive years — the monastic foundations, the seminary so carefully watched over, the tireless visitations, the great pastoral letters, the undertakings for the conservation and advancement of Ukrainian culture — all thrown down and trampled on when the Soviet army entered Lvov in 1939 and imprisoned him in his house; then the Nazis, and then the Russians again; the grinding sufferings of his children and neighbours, Ukrainians and Poles; and his own personal ill-health, which became almost complete physical paralysis and continual pain. But his great mind and noble spirit never failed.

Andrew Szepticky died on November 1, 1944. His death marks the end of an epoch in the religious history of the Galician Ukrainians, an epoch that began with the Union of Brest-Litovsk in 1595 and the martyrdom of St. Josaphat Kuntsevich in 1623: it closes with this other martyr — and yet others. There ends, too, the troubled era, with its sad history of Ukrainian-Polish disagreements and mutual excesses, that in Galicia followed the restoration of Poland in 1919. For within a few months of the passing of the "Father Metropolitan" (as he liked to be called) the great political powers recognized the annexation of certain territory — "The Western Lands" — by the U.S.S.R. And Galicia is a part of this territory.

When the Russians occupied Galicia in 1939 Metropolitan Szepticky, his brother Abbot Clement, the aged Bishop Gregory of Stanislavov, and others were confined to their residences; a large "contribution" in money was imposed on the primate and the archiepiscopal properties were confiscated. Other ecclesiastical buildings were either heavily taxed or seized outright. All three diocesan seminaries were forcibly closed and turned into barracks, as well as the Studite and many of the Basilian monasteries and numerous convents of nuns, whose schools were taken from them. Clergy and religious were forbidden to enter schools, hospitals, orphanages, barracks, etc., and many clergy were imprisoned. Printing-works, libraries, and archives of ecclesiastical bodies were seized, church holidays suppressed, and a campaign of vilification of the clergy began. These measures were not enforced with equal rigour everywhere, and in country districts depended on the temper of the local inhabitants. In general the staunchness of the faithful under these trials was superb, and indeed is said to have impressed the invaders. These were in due course driven out by the German counterinvasion; there were then more oppression, deportations, and shootings, which did not intimidate Metropolitan Szepticky from denouncing Nazi persecution of Jews. And then the Russian armies returned — this time to stay.

Andrew Szepticky's successor was Joseph Slipy, who had been the metropolitan's archdeacon and rector of the Lvov seminary. He had been, like Joseph Bocian years before, secretly ordained bishop during the Soviet occupation in 1939, and narrowly escaped execution by the Russians when they were driven out by the Germans in 1941. At first the Russian attitude to the new metropolitan was somewhat conciliatory; he was even told that he was at liberty to communicate with the Holy See. But this was at the time when, with the permitted election of a patriarch, the official relations between church and state authorities in the U.S.S.R. were beginning to approximate in some respects to those of tsarist days; and consequently there developed in the Western Lands a religious situation analagous to that after the partitions of 1772–1795. Particularly in this: Latin Catholics may perhaps be tolerated, but Ukrainian Catholics of Byzantine rite — no. It would be hopeless for the Russians to try and convert Poles to Russian Orthodoxy, but the Polish Ukrainians are another matter — they already share in the Slav-Byzantine culture. Obviously it is desirable from the Soviet point of view to detach as many people as possible from ultimate allegiance to a religious leader outside the U.S.S.R. — the pope — and from membership in a closely knit supranational church. They see this as clearly as did the imperial Catharine II, Alexander I, and Nicholas I.

And sure enough, within a few weeks of Metropolitan Szepticky's death, the Orthodox Metropolitan Nickolay was sent by the Soviet Government to Lvov to organize an attempt to bring the Galician Ukrainians into the Russian Orthodox Church. The

degree of his success was little, and a few months later there
was a development that showed how little: the Soviet police
arrested the Metropolitan Slipy of Lvov and his auxiliary,
Bishop Niketas Budka (formerly exarch of the Ruthenians in
Canada), Bishop Gregory Chomyshyn of Stanislavov and his
auxiliary, Bishop Ivan Latyshevsky, Bishop Nicholas Czarnecky,
and a large number of priests and deported them into the interior of Russia. Thus at one stroke the Catholic Ukrainians were
deprived of their bishops. And shortly afterwards it became
known that Metropolitan Slipy was probably dead, and that
Bishop Chomyshyn and Bishop Latyshevsky had died. The third
diocesan bishop, Josaphat Kochylevsky of Peremysl, despite the
fact that he was still domiciled in Poland, was arrested also,
together with his auxiliary, Bishop Gregory Lakota. Later he
was released, and then, it is said, again arrested.[14] Of the
Galician bishops, only the other auxiliary of Lvov, Mgr. John
Buchko, is at liberty, because he was in Italy; and he
can do nothing for his brethren across the Russian border,
where the Catholic Ukrainians are given the alternative of reject-
ing Catholicity or being deported from their homes into the
depths of the U.S.S.R. The Soviet authorities found some tools
for their work among the Catholics themselves: an "initiative
group for the reunion of the Greek Catholics with the Russian
Orthodox Church" was formed in 1945, and in it were certain
priests representing each of the three Catholic dioceses, the
chief being the archpriest Gabriel Kostelnyk. If we may judge
from a manifesto signed by these men, it is Ukrainian nationalist
passions that have led them astray.

In March, 1946, this group, calling itself "the Synod of the
Uniate Church in the Western Ukraine," reported to Marshal
Stalin that the Union of Brest was revoked and that the Byzantine
Catholics of the Western Ukraine had returned to the Russian
Orthodox Church. Only a handful of the clergy followed
Dr. Kostelnyk and his bogus "synod," and of the remainder

---

[14] Reports have been very conflicting, and certainty about any individual
is rare.

many have had to go into hiding; the laity remained faithful to
Catholicity in overwhelming numbers. At the time of writing, the
conditions of the penal times in Great Britain have come to
Galicia.

In every respect this is a more brutal and unscrupulous repeti-
tion of the events of 1800–1875 (see above, p. 71). No doubt it
will be a long and difficult process to detach the Galician Ukrainians from their allegiance to Catholic unity; but, deprived of
their religious leaders and guides and of normal religious institutions and means of teaching, and cut off from the centre of
unity at Rome, resistance cannot but weaken as the present generations pass away — unless some unpredictable change comes
about in the situation. The pages that follow must therefore be
regarded as past history, a record of the situation in September,
1939; and as a memory of the biggest and most important of the
contemporary Catholic Eastern churches and of the greatest and
best-beloved of its shepherds, the God-pleasing bishop Andrew
Szepticky, and of his fellow bishops, of their clergy and of their
flocks who were faithful, many of them at the price of life.

STATE IN 1939

Organization. The Ruthenians or Ukrainians of Galicia form a
single ecclesiastical province containing, in spite of their numbers, only three eparchies, viz., Lvov, Peremysl (with the added
titles of Sanok and Sambor), and Stanislavov. The archbishop's
full style is "Archbishop of Lvov, Metropolitan of Galich, and
Bishop of Kamenez, Primate of Lodomeria." Each Ruthenian see
has a chapter of canons, as in the West. (Such chapters are
unknown to Eastern canon law.)

Parochial clergy. The great seminary of Lvov was founded in
1783 and has had a very fruitful career; it entered on a new
phase which seemed of much promise and importance in 1931,
when it was erected into an academy of theology in fulfilment
of the university aspirations that it has always had. In 1939 there
were in the seminary about 220 theological students and 120
juniors. The other two eparchies also have seminaries, both estab-

lished at the end of the eighteenth century. The Ruthenian College at Rome was erected by Pope Leo XIII in 1897, the Emperor
Francis Joseph of Austria providing a generous subsidy. It was
first confided to the direction of the Ruthenian Basilian monks
in 1904. It houses about 50 students. Others went to Innsbruck
University and to the *Augustineum* at Vienna. Of the 2150 secular priests in 1939, 77 per cent were married, but the celibate
ideal was beginning slowly to gain ground; this has an important
economic aspect, for while, as has been said, a married clergy
has in the past been a source of strength to Ukrainian religion
and culture, nevertheless the burden of a family is often very
grievous to pastors in the poor rural parishes that predominate.
Of the 1267 parishes of Lvov, 482 did not have a resident pastor
in 1932.

Each bishop has an *archdeacon* (who, contrary to Eastern custom, is a priest) among his officials, and there are numerous *deans*
in charge of districts (the Byzantine name for such, archpriest
or protopope, has been dropped). The diaconate, as among most
Catholic Byzantines, is invariably a step to the priesthood and
not a permanent office even in the monasteries. Roman titles of
honour are conferred on the Ruthenian clergy, resulting in some
very surprising prelatical costumes. Ordinary clerical dress is a
black cassock and a round cap rather lower than the Russian
brimless *kalemaukion;* the *rason* has been given up, and secular
priests are often indistinguishable from Latins; most of them are
clean-shaven, at any rate in the towns and in America.

Religious institutes. The most interesting monastic body not
only in Galicia but among all the Catholic Eastern churches is the
Studites, of whom a brief account will be found on pages 223–225.
They are, however, less in the public eye than the more numerous
and old-established "Basilians," to whom the Ruthenians owe so
much. At the time of the Union of Brest there was a number of
monasteries among the Ruthenians, and within the next twenty
years St. Josaphat Kuntsevich and Joseph Benjamin Rutsky had
inaugurated a reform at the monastery of the Holy Trinity at
Vilna. In 1617 this was organized as a congregation, with a supe-

rior general and a form of organization based on that of the
Society of Jesus — already the monastic idea was being superseded. Before the suppression by the Emperor Nicholas I in 1832
there were 96 Basilian monasteries in Lithuania, Russian Poland,
and the Ukraine, and by 1882 what little remained of the Order
of St. Basil in Galicia was in dire need of reform, after having
been for long the backbone of the Ukrainian clergy. In that year
Pope Leo XIII entrusted the work to the fathers of the Society
of Jesus, who carried it out with efficiency and thoroughness,
beginning at the monastery of Dobromil whence it spread to the
other houses. But the Ukrainian Basilians became in the process
exactly like a Western religious congregation and, beginning as
monks, have now become, in fact if not in name, clerks regular,
though they are bound to choir-office. They take vows, temporary
or solemn, and each religious is either a priest or a lay-brother;
the last named must know some useful trade. In this capacity the
Basilians have done a very great pastoral and educative work
among the Catholic Ukrainians, especially in the country districts,
and have carried their activity overseas to the Americas.

They had 25 monasteries, 161 priests, 203 clerics, and 205 lay-
brothers in 1938, and are now known officially as the *Basilians of
St. Josaphat*. Their abbot general (*archimandrite*) lives at Rome
and there is an abbot provincial (*protohegumenos*) for the Galician province, for Podcarpathia, for North America, and for
Brazil; the local superior is an abbot (*hegumenos*). They have
abandoned the traditional monastic dress of the East and wear
a black tunic with hood, belt, and cloak (*mandyas*), and their
choir-office is recited, not sung.

In 1913 Mgr. Szepticky introduced some *Redemptorists* from
Belgium into his eparchy, from whom have sprung a Byzantine
vice-province of that congregation.

There are about a thousand Ukrainian nuns in Galicia, all engaged in active works of charity (except a few Studites). Three
hundred of them are Basilians, and the rest belong to local
congregations.

The Faithful number about 3½ million in Galicia. At least 90

EASTERN AND WESTERN CLERGY IN PROCESSION IN RUMANIA
A Byzantine Bishcp is carrying the Blessed Sacrament, covered, in a Ciborium

Courtesy, Dom Benedict Morrison

MAR ANTONY ARIDA
Maronite Patriarch

CHURCH OF THE RUSSIAN COLLEGE, ROME

RUSSIAN CLERGY ASSEMBLED IN ROME
In center, Bishop Peter Bucys

CLERGY OF THE COPTIC RITE
In center, the Bishop of Thebes, Anba Mark Khuzam

COPTIC BISHOP, PRIESTS, AND DEACON

SYRIAN PATRIARCHAL CHURCH, BAIRUT

MAR IGNATIUS GABRIEL TAPPUNI
Syrian Patriarch of Antioch and Cardinal of the Holy Roman Church

THE SYRIAN LITURGY
The Celebrant Blesses the People With the Holy Things

per cent of them are peasants, and they are people of outstanding intelligence, cultural activity, and farming ability among the huge block of peasant peoples that stretches from the Pindus Mountains to Danzig and from the Black Sea to Tirol. They have remained faithful to communion with Rome throughout the generations of subjection to Polish and polonized Ukrainian landlords under the Polish and Austrian kingdoms, and during the difficult years under the Polish republic after World War I. What will be their future, God alone knows. There are hundreds of thousands of them among the displaced persons in Germany, Austria, France, Italy, and elsewhere; and at the time of writing these hapless people are threatened with forcible "repatriation" over the soviet border.

OTHER JURISDICTIONS

The Bukovina. There are some 70,000 Catholic Ukrainians in the Bukovina, all of which territory was part of the Rumanian kingdom after 1918. In 1930 they were organized separately under an episcopal exarch of their own, who was a vicar general of the Rumanian bishop of the Maramures. In 1940 the U.S.S.R. annexed the northern part of the Bukovina, where most of these Catholics (and many more Orthodox) Ukrainians live. Their dependence on Maramures has therefore no doubt come to an end.

United States. From 1879 there have been emigrations of Ukrainians to the United States, both from Galicia and Podcarpathia (see pp. 72 ff.; 88). The first priest to be sent was Father Ivan Valansky, who in 1886 opened the first Catholic church of the Byzantine rite in America, at Shenandoah, Pennsylvania. The number of immigrants increased rapidly and in 1907 Pope Pius X appointed a bishop of their rite for them, not, however, as ordinary at first but as an auxiliary to the local Latin bishop; he was Soter Ortynsky, the first Oriental Catholic bishop in America.

The arrival of numerous Byzantine Catholics in the country was naturally fraught with difficulties. Not only did they bring with them all their own political and national rivalries (e.g., between Galicians and Podcarpathians) — this was perhaps to be expected; but they also had a bad reception, or none at all, from their Latin brethren in the United States. It is difficult to write of this matter in measured terms, so I quote the words of the late Andrew Shipman, of New York: "These Ruthenians have continued to practise their ancient Greek-Slavonic rites and usages . . . strange to the Catholic accustomed only to the Roman rite, and [they] have made [the Ruthenians] objects of distrust and even active dislike." Those words were written over thirty years ago, and there has been a considerable change since then. A greater knowledge of our Eastern brethren, fostered by numerous publications, by the work of St. Michael's Guild, and by such things as the annual conference on Oriental rites sponsored by Fordham University, has led to better understanding and therefore to better relations. The old bad attitude, however, is still not entirely a things of the past — may it soon be so.[15]

The question of a celibate secular clergy has for long been one of the chief difficulties. The bishops of the United States found the presence of married priests embarrassing, and the apostolic letter "Ea semper" of 1907 decreed that only celibate Ruthenian priests should be admitted or ordained in North America. This, and other innovations in their customs, was strongly resented, the Orthodox made the most of them, and 10,000 Ruthenians joined the dissidents. Eventually the Holy See did not enforce the prohibition of married priests in the United States (though no married men may be ordained there) and otherwise modified "Ea semper," but further legislation by the decree "Cum data" in 1929 again caused trouble.

In 1924 the Ruthenians were put under the direct jurisdiction of two exarchs, bishops of their rite, one for the Podcarpathians and the other for the Galicians. The last-named number 300,000 with about 140 priests and 158 churches or chapels, and their bishop, Mgr. Constantine Bohachevsky, resides at Philadelphia, which is a principal Ukrainian district. In 1942 he was

---

[15] An excellent article on this subject was written by Father Desmond A Schmal, S.J., in the *Ecclesiastical Review* (Washington, D. C.) for November, 1937. For Shipman and his fine work, see Pallen's *Memorial of Andrew J. Shipman* (New York, 1920).

given an auxiliary, Mgr. Ambrose Senyshyn, Basilian monk, the first Oriental Catholic bishop to be consecrated in the New World. They have a dozen churches in New York and its vicinity, St. George's on East Twentieth Street being the first; St. Michael's and St. Nicholas's at Yonkers and SS. Peter and Paul's in Jersey City are fine examples of Slav-Byzantine church buildings. There is a junior seminary in Connecticut and a senior seminary at Washington, D. C., with houses of Basilian and other nuns. The fine church of St. Nicholas at Chicago is served by Basilian monks.

Canada. Ruthenian emigration to Canada began in the nineties of the past century, chiefly from Galicia. The first church, SS. Vladimir and Olga's, was opened at Winnipeg in 1900, with a Slovak pastor, Father Damascene Polivka, but the dearth of clergy was so chronic that for a time (and still in a measure) the emigrants were a prey to proselytizers. The first priests to come to the rescue, at the instance of Mgr. Langevin of St. Boniface, were French-Canadians and Belgian Redemptorists (Father Achille Delaere was their moving spirit), who soon were allowed to adopt the Byzantine rite. In 1913, at the instance of Mgr. Szepticky, the Holy See appointed a bishop as exarch with personal jurisdiction over the Ukrainians of Canada, but the shortage of clergy has continued to be so great that the religious state of the people is still far from satisfactory. The rule against married priests means, practically, that only widowers and monks can be sent from Europe and the supply of American-born priests is insufficient, while in general the attitude of the Canadian Latins has been as unhelpful as in the United States.

There are about 300,000 Ukrainians in Canada, mostly farming in Alberta, Saskatchewan, and Manitoba, though there are numbers in Montreal and other cities, with only 120 priests to look after them. Of these, 39 are Basilian monks, whose monastery is at Mundare in Alberta, and 20 Redemptorists, who have establishments at Yorkton and Ituna in Saskatchewan. There are 380 churches and chapels, of which only 36 have resident priests: the holy Liturgy is celebrated in most of them only about monthly.

The bishop, Mgr. Basil Ladyka, lives at Winnipeg; he has established a junior seminary, and some 50 students are preparing
for the priesthood in various Latin seminaries and in religious
houses. He has an auxiliary bishop. Much good work is being
done by nuns of various congregations, who number about 120.

Both in Canada and the United States, there is considerable
literary activity among the Ukrainians; newspapers are published
in their language, and those who have been able to avail themselves of "higher education" have done so well as strongly to
confirm the high opinion of Ukrainian abilities that is current in
Europe. Except for the small bodies mentioned below, the
Ukrainians and Rusins of North America are practically the only
Catholic Ruthenians left leading a normal free life in a free
country, and with their ecclesiastical organization unimpaired.
Theirs is a great responsibility, to uphold before the world and
in the Church the great traditions of Slav-Byzantine Catholicity.

Brazil and Argentine. There are 52,000 Ruthenians, mostly in
the state of Parana in Brazil, with a dozen priests, of whom several are Basilian monks. The 15,000 of the Argentine have only
one or two priests. They are all under the jurisdiction of the local
bishops, subject to special regulations of the Sacred Eastern
Congregation.

Elsewhere. The few thousand Ukrainians scattered in other
parts of the world before 1939 were unprovided with churches,
except at Brussels and Vienna, where there is the fine baroque
church of St. Barbara, taken from the suppressed Jesuits in 1775
and made the chapel of an ecclesiastical college for Ruthenians
and Rumanians by the Empress Maria Teresa. It became a parish-
church for Byzantines in 1784 and has had a very eventful history.
A seminary was attached thereto from 1852 till 1892, and this
Barbareum gave 400 priests to the several Catholic Byzantine
bodies of the Austro-Hungarian Empire.

PARTICULAR CUSTOMS

A number of small modifications have been introduced into the
Byzantine liturgy (which in ordinary speech they refer to as

"The Divine Worship") by the Ruthenians in the past two hundred years. While none of these innovations were necessary, and some of them definitely undesirable, it is to be noted that some points of divergence from standard Russian usage so far from being innovations are precisely those observances which were swept away by the patriarch of Moscow, Nikon, in the seventeenth century, whereby the great schism of the Starovery was caused.[16]

Apart from certain differences in the text, the following are among the changes made (particularly by the Synod of Zamosc in 1720); but they are not universal or uniform in all Ukrainian churches: the amice and alb are worn in place of the *stikharion;* a large paten and purificator are used instead of the *diskos* and sponge, and *ripidia* have disappeared; after the *proskomide* the holy doors of the *eikonostasis* are opened and so remain throughout the Liturgy; the order of some of the chants is altered; the words *i ot Syna* (*Filioque*) are added to the creed and reverences are made at "his only Son" and "was made man"; at the consecration and elsewhere a bell is rung; hot water is not put into the chalice before Communion, nor blessed bread distributed; the people receive the Blessed Sacrament in both kinds from a spoon, but usually kneeling; washings of the fingers have been introduced; the vessels are left on the altar till the end of the Liturgy; and there is a sequence of liturgical colours for vestments, elsewhere unknown in the East. A deacon is rarely seen assisting at the Liturgy except in cathedral and monastic churches, and then he is often a priest. Concelebration takes place only on certain pontifical occasions, with the result of the appearance of side-altars in large churches.

In the bull "*Apostolatus officium*" by which Pope Benedict XIII confirmed the acts of the Synod of Zamosc there was a note of warning against spoiling the integrity of the Byzantine liturgy, and in approving the *typikon* (constitutions) of the Studite

---

[16] Mgr. Szepticky reconciled a number of these "Old Believers" to the Catholic Church, and gave them a large chapel at Lvov, where all their traditional ritual customs are (or were) observed.

monks in 1923 the Sacred Eastern Congregation declared: "It is
the wish of this Congregation that the monks observe the Byzantine rite in all its purity, getting rid of all the alterations whatso-
ever in use among the Ruthenian people and sanctioned by the
Synod of Zamosc." It is one of the objects of those monks to encourage the restoration of liturgical purity among the people,
but many of the clergy are attached to the old ways as "our tradition." It is a pity, for more reasons than one; Ruthenian "hybridization" is continually used as an argument to prove that
"Rome does not really respect the Eastern rites" and to dissuade
dissident Orientals from returning to unity. In fact, the new edition of the service books in preparation in Rome provides for the
abandonment of these peculiarities where the people wish it.

For the administration of the sacraments (especially Penance)
and other rites, the Byzantine offices have been here and there
interpolated with prayers translated into Church-Slavonic from
the Roman books, without a shadow of necessity, and the propagation of Western "popular devotions" leads sometimes to fantastic results. The one Eastern usage above all that the Ruthenians ought to have got rid of they have preserved: the Julian
kalendar. Their objection to going to a Latin church even when
no other is available (noticeable in America) is unhappily largely
due to their historical relations with the Poles, which have tended
to make them suspicious and hostile toward all Latin Catholics.
Such an attitude, whether among Easterners or Westerners, shows
an insufficient understanding of what Catholic Christianity really
means.

A number of less ancient Western feasts have been introduced
into Galicia, sometimes with altered date: e.g., Corpus Christi,
the Holy Trinity, the Sacred Heart, Christ the King. Among the
holydays are St. Josaphat, "the Martyr of Unity," St. Vladimir,
and his two sons, SS. Romanus and David (Boris and Gleb). The
Russian habits of fasting have been modified, but the Eastern
identification of fasting and abstinence is retained. Ukrainian
racial feeling has happily ensured the preservation of their most
lovely church music; and in Galicia their distinctive church build-

ings, many of them in wood, are of great interest and beauty. Like most Catholic Orientals the Ruthenians now make use of the Western form of rosary, but their version of the Hail Mary is different and includes a mention of the mystery pertinent to each decade.

BIBLIOGRAPHY

Likovsky, *Union de l'Eglise romaine conclue à Brest en 1596* (Paris, c. 1898).

Guépin, *Saint Josaphat et l'Eglise gréco-slave,* 2 vols. (Paris, Poitiers, 1897–1898).

Korolevsky, *Le Metropolite André Szeptyckyj* (Grottaferrata, 1920).

Tiltman, *Peasant Europe* (London, 1934).

Delaere, *Mémoire sur les tentatives de schisme . . . des Ruthènes de l'Ouest canadien* (Quebec, 1908).

Scott, *The Ukrainians: our most pressing problem* (Toronto, c. 1930).

Felinsky, *The Ukrainians in Poland* (London, 1931).

Konovalov, *Russo-Polish Relations* (London, 1945).

Pelesz, *Geschichte der Union der Ruthenischen mit Rom* (Vienna, 1880).

Korczok, *Die griechisch-katholische Kirche in Galizien* (Leipzig, 1921).

Dmytrievsky, *L'Union des Eglises et les Persécutions Polonaises en Ukraine* (Brussels, 1939).

Eastern Churches Quarterly, Vol. VI, No. 6 (Ramsgate, 1946), the full text in English of Pope Pius XII's encyclical letter *"Orientales omnes,"* on the 350th anniversary of the Union of Brest and the current persecution, a most striking document; Vol. VI, No. 8 (Ramsgate, 1946), the Ukrainians in North America.

3. THE PODCARPATHIAN RUTHENIANS
or RUSINS

Probably since the year 1339, certainly since the middle of the fifteenth century, there has been a settlement of Ruthenians and Byelorussians on the southern side of the Carpathians, at the western end of Slovakia. This district is now commonly called Ruthenia, but Podkarpatska Rus is the more accurate name, and Rusins is a convenient appellation for the people who live there. They early came under Hungarian rule, but until they got a bishop of their own in 1491 they were ecclesiastically under the bishop of Peremysl in Galicia.

In 1646 their bishop, Basil Tarasevich, and some of his flock returned to Catholic communion, and six years later the rest followed (Union of Ungvar). A monk named Peter Rostoshynsky, who had received episcopal ordination while still a dissident, was appointed to be their bishop. Very troublesome conflicts of jurisdiction arose between the successors of Rostoshynsky, the Latin primate, and the Ruthenian metropolitan north of the Carpathians. These were resolved in 1771 when Pope Clement XIV, at the request of Queen Maria Teresa, established the Ruthenian eparchy of Mukachevo (Munkacs), suffragan to the primate of Hungary. Another see was set up in 1818, at Preshov.

During the nineteenth century the magyarizing and latinizing policy of the Hungarian government caused much discontent among the Rusins, and, especially after a Russian missioner, Father Alexis Kabaluk, arrived among them in 1910, some of them left the Church. The Hungarians tried to stop this movement by force; in 1913, for example, thirty-two Rusin peasants were sent to prison on the occasion of their professing dissident Orthodoxy.

In the course of World War I the Hungarian government was even more oppressive to the Rusins, on the ground that they were pro-Russian; consequently, when after the war Hungarian authority was removed and the Podkarpatska Rus became part of Czechoslovakia, all was set for schism. It broke out seriously in 1920, and was fomented for political ends by elements in the Czech government. The leading Orthodox missioner was a Russian monk of Pochaev in Poland, Father Vitaly, who had founded a monastery and book-publishing house in Slovakia. Within three years seventy villages, involving 100,000 people, had turned Orthodox. The cause was, as so often, fundamentally racial and cultural. The Rusins were very conscious of their affinities with the northern Slavs, and their experience was that the policy of the local Catholic authorities, civil and ecclesiastical, was to make them Magyar or Slovak; moreover their clergy, often trained in Hungarian seminaries, had got culturally and socially out of touch with their peasant flocks.

Very few of these clergy took part in the separatist movement, and after a time the schism was to a considerable extent mended. But it left a deep wound. It is an excellent example of an unresolved "social conflict" being at the bottom of religious separatism (cf. Vol. II, Cap. 1).

There is no need to go into details — even were they clearly known — of the political maneuvers as the result of which the U.S.S.R. annexed the Podcarpatska Rus during World War II. It is sufficient to say that the religious position of the Catholic Rusins there is the same as that of their brethren in Galicia (see pp. 76–78): all schools, monasteries, convents, and the like have been closed, 150 churches have been seized, other property has been confiscated, and the faithful are subjected to the strongest pressure to enter into communion with the Russian Orthodox Church. Soon after the Ukrainian bishops were arrested and deported to the U.S.S.R. in 1945, the same fate overtook the bishop of Mukachevo, Theodore Romza, and his auxiliary.

PRESENT STATE

Organization. Here, as above, we can only speak of things as they were before the Soviet annexation. There were two eparchies

of Ruthenians, Mukachevo (with residence at Uzhorod) and
Preshov, of which the latter had been in administration since before 1928. Both cathedrals have chapters of canons. Before 1939
it had been projected to make the Rusins a complete ecclesiastical province, under a metropolitan with one or more suffragans.
Apart from the Rusins now under Soviet rule, there are some
100,000 Rusins and Ukrainians, many of them refugees, now in
Czechoslovakia, in the jurisdiction of the bishop of Preshov.

Parochial clergy. These are trained in the college of their rite
at Uzhorod (Ungvar) or in Latin seminaries. They are mostly
married, and a French observer who knows them well characterizes them as "well-instructed, affable, of a real Christian spirit . . .
worthy of all respect, of simple habits free from pretensions and
'bossiness' "; but the priesthood tends as it were to pass from
father to son and to form a sacerdotal caste.

Religious institutes. There were three small monasteries of
Basilians of St. Josaphat (see p. 79), and two small houses of
Byzantine *Redemptorists,* of which the first three at least are
doubtless now dispersed. But it would seem that events elsewhere may lead to a monastic revival in the "free" jurisdiction of
Preshov above referred to. In Galicia, the Basilians have been
rigorously suppressed; for example at the well-known monastery
of Zovkva, not far from Lvov, thirty-six out of thirty-eight monks
were shot, and its printing-press and library partly destroyed
and partly carried off to Kiev. But there are monks among the
Ruthenian refugees in Czechoslovakia, who are now found as far
west as the former Sudetenland; and the Byzantine Redemptorists have in fact begun the formation of a vice-province for
Slovakia, with headquarters at the monastery of Veliky Mikhalo-
vice; a third house is in course of establishment near Preshov.

The Faithful are nearly all peasants, very self-sufficient and
particularist, but sincerely religious. They have been called the
"poorest peasants in Europe," but under the Czechoslovak
government they fared considerably better than many minorities
in other countries and their state was improving. Unfortunately
there was something of a gap, social and cultural, between

them and their better educated clergy. They numbered over half a million in 1939.

OTHER JURISDICTIONS

Hungary. Those Rusins still domiciled in Hungary form an administration apostolic under an episcopal exarch at Miszkolcs. They number about 20,000.

Poland. There are some few Rusins north of the Carpathians in territory that is still Polish. They were organized separately in 1934, under an episcopal exarch whose headquarters was at Rymanov.

United States. In Europe the Ukrainians of Galicia out-numbered the Rusins by six or seven to one, but in the United States the last-named are the more numerous, being over 300,000. This is in part due to the fact that Slav-Byzantine Catholics originating in the plain of Hungary and in Croatia are included with them. It is commonly said that Rusins are more tenacious of their own usages and customs than are Ukrainians; this is in a measure borne out in America, where they played a pre-dominant part in the troubles referred to on page 82. But these troubles were of an extremely complex nature, involving not only questions of rite and discipline but also political, social, economic, psychological, and personal considerations.

A big step in pacifying the Rusins in the United States was made in 1924, when the Holy See gave them a bishop of their own, subject to the delegate apostolic at Washington, whose cathedral is at Homestead, Pennsylvania. He has over 150 priests, who serve 186 churches. The present bishop is Msgr. Basil Takach, who in 1946 was given a coadjutor, with the right of succession as ordinary, in the person of Bishop Daniel Ivancho.

Canada. The Podcarpathian Ruthenians of Canada and else-where are organized with their Galician brethren (p. 83).

PARTICULAR CUSTOMS

The particulars already given of the modification of the Slav-Byzantine rite in Galicia apply also to the Podcarpathians. This was precisely one of the elements in the schism of 1920, and steps were taken to remedy these just grievances by a restoration of their own usages. It is hoped that the movement will spread to the United States, where there is so much to encourage Orientals to imitate Western practices, regardless of their suitability to Eastern religious tradition. The Podcarpathians sedulously maintain general congregational participation in the liturgical singing, their traditional music being a particularly lovely variation of that of the Galician Ruthenians. The wooden churches of the Podkarpatska Rus, especially those built in the Boiko and Hucul styles, are extremely attractive: certain features are, curiously enough, reminiscent of Far-Eastern architecture; others, less curiously, remind one of the timber churches of Scandinavia.

BIBLIOGRAPHY

Vassily, "The Podcarpathian Schism" in *Pax,* Nos. 147 and 150 (Prinknash Abbey, 1934).

Grigassy, *Prayer Book for . . . Rusins in America* (Braddock, Pa. n.d.).

Hanulya, *The Eastern Ritual* (Cleveland, Ohio, 1942). Rusin usage.

Heisler and Mellon, *Carpatho-Ukraine* (London, 1946).

Eastern Churches Quarterly, Vol. VI, No. 8 (Ramsgate, 1946). The Rusins in North America.

4. THE HUNGARIAN RUTHENIANS

The so-called Hungarians of the Byzantine rite are in fact
Ruthenians from the Carpathians and some Rumanians who,
living in the great Hungarian plain, have lost their own languages
and become almost completely magyarized. For long they were
divided between five Ruthenian and Rumanian eparchies, till
in 1912 Pope Pius X, to the satisfaction both of the faithful
concerned and of the Hungarian civil authorities who feared
the influence of foreign bishops, united them all into the new
eparchy of Hajdudorog. After the war of 1914–1918 over half of
the parishes concerned were returned to the jurisdiction of
Rumanian bishops on the formation of the kingdom of Greater
Rumania.

Present State

Organization. The Bishop of Hajdudorog is a suffragan of the
Latin archbishop at Esztergom. His catheral is at Hajdudorog,
but he lives at Nyiregyhaza where he has another episcopal
church, with a chapter of canons. Aspirants for the priesthood
are trained in the general Ruthenian seminaries. There is a
Basilian monastery at Mariapocs.

The Faithful. Even since the dismemberment of the eparchy
in 1919 its subjects are still numerous, 142,000, mostly peasants.
The rest of the Catholics of Hungary, two-thirds of the total
population, are Latins; there are said to be 150,000 dissident
Orthodox. The groups of Rusins round Miszkolcs are organized
separately (see p. 90). In the United States Hungarian Ruthenians are included with the Rusins.

Particular Customs

The Byzantine rite is used according to the version of the
Ruthenian liturgical books. But having lost their own language,

the people of Hajdudorog found difficulty in maintaining their congregational singing in Slavonic, and a movement arose in the middle of the nineteenth century to substitute Magyar (Hungarian) as their liturgical language. Translations of hymns, etc., and then of the liturgies were made, and these were adopted without authorization in a number of churches. In 1912 Greek was authoritatively imposed for all liturgical services and three years were given for the change to be effected. For several good reasons this has not taken place (e.g., Greek — and Byzantine chant — is even more difficult for the people to learn than Slavonic); accordingly, Magyar is now used in all churches, with the approval of the bishop. For those services not yet translated, the singers continue to do as best they can with Slavonic. In the 1920 edition of the Liturgies the Greek text of the *anaphoras* is printed parallel with the Magyar.

5. THE YUGOSLAVS

The small body of Catholic Yugoslavs of the Byzantine rite is made up of a nucleus of croatized Serbs to which other elements have been added. When Matthias Corvinus, King of Hungary, recaptured Bosnia from the Turks he established on the border military colonies of refugee Serbs (Uscochi, "refugees") of the Orthodox Church. They nominally came into communion with Rome but it was not made real until 1611, when their bishop, Simeon Vretanjic, was recognized by Pope Paul V as Byzantine vicar of the bishop of Zagreb. Simeon's profession of faith was received by St. Robert Bellarmine, and he lived at the monastery of Marca, a great centre for Serbian reunion, of which there was some talk at this time, many Serbs having fled into Hungary from the Turks (nine individual bishops were reconciled between 1596 and 1704). Other episcopal vicars followed, but the period was troubled and in 1739 Marca was burnt down by brigands at the instigation of an Orthodox bishop. The Catholic Serbs of Croatia were then given a diocesan bishop by Pope Pius VI in 1777; his see was at Krizevci, under the primate of Hungary.

During the eighteenth century there was a migration of Podcarpathian Ruthenians to the southwest, and another of Galicians to Bosnia and Slavonia at the end of the nineteenth; there are also some Rumanians and Bulgarians from Macedonia in this heterogeneous collection, held together by the Catholic faith and their common Eastern rite.

PRESENT STATE

Organization. The Bishop of Krizevci, who is now a suffragan of the Latin archbishop of Zagreb, has jurisdiction over all Catholics of Byzantine rite in Yugoslavia. These Catholics share in the persecution to which Christians in that country are now subjected, and in 1945 Bishop Janko Simrak was committed to prison by the partisans of Marshal Tito; in consequence of hardships then suffered he died in 1946.

Parochial clergy are formed in the seminary of Zagreb (founded 1685), which is directed by Basilian monks. The parishes are arranged in archpresbyterates or deaneries. Most of the clergy are married. There is a cathedral chapter of four canons.

Religous institutes. There are *Friars Minor* of the Byzantine rite working in this eparchy. They wear the *rason* over the brown Franciscan tunic and cord, with *kalemaukion* instead of the hood. The *Basilian nuns* are represented by four convents.[17]

The Faithful total 55,000 souls, among whom Ruthenians are most numerous and the Serbs next. The last-named call themselves Croats and speak Serbo-Croat; the other elements all conserve the language of their respective countries of origin. The people are nearly all peasants. Their principal centres are in upper Croatia the Backa, Slavonia, and Bosnia. A few have emigrated to North America, notably Cleveland and Chicago, where they are included with the Rusins. In Yugoslavia most Croats are Catholics of the Latin rite and the Serbs are Orthodox.

The common liturgical language of these people is Church Slavonic. They observe the Byzantine rite and usages in, on the whole, a high degree of purity.

Mention can be appropriately made here of a most remarkable man who, in the seventeenth century, devoted his life to the cause of the political union of all the Slavonic peoples under the leadership of Russia and their religious union under the leadership of Rome. This was Iuri Krizanic (1618–1683); he was a Croatian Catholic priest, of the diocese of Zagreb, whose attitude to the problem of the reconciliation of East and West anticipated much that is often regarded today as contemporary development. His eventful life and learned writings were for-

---

[17] In 1945 a community of Franciscans of the Slav-Byzantine rite was started in the United States by Father Josaphat Ananevich and others. Their house is near Hazleton, Pa.

gotten till the nineteenth century, when they were rediscovered by the Russian "slavophils"; William Palmer wrote of him in *The Patriarch and the Tsar* (1871–1876). A sympathetic account of this man and his prophetic ideas by an Orthodox writer can be read in the *Eastern Churches Quarterly*, Nos. 7–8 of Vol. IV.

BIBLIOGRAPHY

Picot, *Les Serbes de Hongrie* (Prague, 1873).
Simrak, *Graeco-Catholica Ecclesia in Yugoslavia* (Zagreb, 1931).

6. THE RUMANIANS

The Rumanians are in part descendants of the "veterans of Trajan," colonies of Romans chiefly from Illyria and Italy planted by him in the province of Dacia at the beginning of the second century of the Christian era; fusing with the Thracian natives, overrun by Visigoths, Gepides, Slavs and others, they gave rise to a new people, predominantly Latin in language and characteristics but modified by Greek, Slav, and other influences.[18]

The first Dacian Christians were of the Latin rite (according to some, St. Niketas of Remesiana was one of their evangelizers), and so remained until they were conquered by the Bulgars. Then in the ninth century they were subjected to Byzantine bishops, who imposed their own rite, and in due course the Rumanians were drawn into the schism of Constantinople. For long the Rumanians were dependent on the prelates of the Bulgarian and other churches; it was not till the fourteenth century (when Rumanian principalities independent of Turks, Hungarians, and Poles began to be formed) that three separate metropolitans were given to Valachia and Moldavia. Latin missionaries were active from the thirteenth century, attracted particularly by the pagan Kumans in the Danubian plain, and dioceses were erected; but the majority of these Catholics turned Orthodox or Calvinist at the time of the Reformation. Damian, the Moldavian metropolitan, signed the act of union at the Council of Florence, but it was not acceptable to most of his church and he and his successor had to seek refuge in Rome.

In accordance with a decree of the Fourth Lateran Council, the Rumanians of Transylvania (The Ardeal), which had been conquered by the Hungarians in the eleventh century, should have been given vicars of Eastern rite by the Latin bishops of the conquerors; this was not done, however, and they gradually

---

[18] Rumanian is almost an Italian dialect, with a large Slavonic vocabulary.

fell away. After the Council of Florence St. John of Capistrano rallied 30,000 of them to the union, but it lasted only about 25 years. The Protestant Reformation wrought havoc in Transylvania both among Latins and Orthodox, who became "Calvinist by creed, Eastern by certain externals." There was even a Calvinist "superintendent" for the Orthodox, and resisters were persecuted by their Hungarian and German masters. But in 1687 the Emperor Leopold I of Austria drove the Turkish overlords from this province, and the Jesuit chaplains of his army set themselves to deal with the religious situation.

THE CATHOLIC RUMANIANS

In 1697 the Orthodox metropolitan of Alba Julia, Theophilus Szeremy, moved by the reasoning of Father Ladislas Baranyi, S.J., called a synod which signed an act of union with Rome. Within a few weeks Theophilus was dead, not without suspicion of having been poisoned by Calvinists. In the following year Athanasius Anghel Popa was consecrated bishop for Transylvania at Bucarest, where he was solemnly warned by the Orthodox patriarch of Jerusalem, Dositheos (who was visiting Rumania), of the dangers of Protestantism. Athanasius took the advice to heart — but not in a way Dositheos intended. On arrival at Alba Julia he got in touch with Father Baranyi, and in a few weeks had signed, together with thirty-eight protopopes (deans), a profession of faith and a declaration of desire to become "members of the holy Catholic Church of Rome."[19]

The bishop and archpriests had stipulated that their "discipline, church ritual, liturgy, fasts, and customs remain unchanged; if not, neither do our seals bind us." Assurance was

---

[19] It must be noted that this reunion was not entirely inspired by disinterested conviction of the truth of "Roman claims" and abhorrence of schism: not entirely, and perhaps not even primarily. Fear of Protestantism and need of protection therefrom were apparently the principal motives of both Theophilus and Athanasius. Such unsatisfactory features have been at the root of many "reunions," and must be faced and taken into consideration. Sometimes the reunion is spoiled thereby *ab initio;* at other times, as in the case of the Rumanians, the reunion nevertheless works out well and becomes permanent.

given of this,[20] and in 1701 the union was finally confirmed at Vienna and Athanasius solemnly enthroned. Thus many priests and 200,000 other Rumanians were brought into communion with the Holy See.

The Calvinists were furious and the Orthodox no less; there was an outbreak of violence. For a time the union was in danger, but the Jesuits came to the rescue and the neo-Catholics were eventually stabilized. It was not till 1735–1751 that foreigners, Serbs mostly, stirred up the schism which reduced the Catholics by half, from which are descended the dissident Orthodox in Transylvania today. Some of the effects of this were modified and the Catholics greatly strengthened and encouraged by the activities of their fourth bishop, the holy Peter Paul Aron (1752–1764).

In 1721 the Latin bishop of the Ardeal invoked canon 9 of the Fourth Lateran Council against the successor of Athanasius, John Pataky, claiming that Pataky was simply his "ritual vicar." Pope Innocent XIII replied by a declaration that Pataky was the bishop-in-ordinary of the Catholics of his rite, but that he should reside at Fagaras instead of Alba Julia; future bishops would be appointed on the presentation of the Austrian emperor. Empress Maria-Teresa obtained the erection of a second episcopal see in 1777, and two more followed in 1853, when Fagaras became an archbishopric.

A curious abuse, shared with the Orthodox, persisted among the Catholic Rumanians until the middle of the last century; namely, the granting of decrees of complete dissolution of marriage in cases of adultery.

On the establishment of the kingdom of Great Rumania in 1919 the Catholics found themselves for the first time under a sovereign of their own nationality.

PRESENT STATE

Organization. The Catholic Rumanians of the Byzantine rite

---

[20] Otherwise, the reunion was to be only conditional. Theologically, its basis was the acceptance of the "four points" of Florence (see p. 13).

form an ecclesiastical province, consisting of the metropolitan see of Fagaras and Alba Julia (resident at Blaj), with the four suffragan sees of Gherla and Cluj, Oradea Mare, Lugoj, and Maramures (residence at Baia Mare). The archbishop of Fagaras has jurisdiction over the small minority of Catholics of his rite who live in the "Old Kingdom," including the Bukovina. All five bishops are *ex officio* senators of the realm; by the concordat of 1929 they are nominated by the Holy See, the civil government approving the nominees. Representatives of all the clergy have an advisory voice in the selection of the metropolitan who has almost patriarchal powers. The cathedrals have chapters of canons.

Parochial clergy. These number over 1500, of whom 90 per cent are married. There are seminaries for their training at Blaj, Oradea Mare, and Cluj, and a Pontifical Rumanian College was erected at Rome in 1930. A faculty of Catholic theology was granted in the national University of Bucarest in 1932. The parishes are arranged in 116 deaneries, of which the deans, called "protopopes," have considerable powers; they constitute an ecclesiastical court of first instance. The clergy wear a plain cassock and (like their Orthodox brethren) put on the *kalemau-kion* only in church; the *rason* has been almost entirely given up, except by bishops and they wear it only on certain formal occasions. Clean-shaven clergy are now often seen in towns, even among the dissidents.

Religious institutes. A few years ago there were no monks or nuns left among the Catholic Rumanians.[21] There is now a small monastery of the *Basilians of St. Josaphat* (see p. 79) at Bicsad, which has started a daughter-house at Moiseu. The *Conventual friars minor* have opened a college at Oradea Mare for Byzantine candidates for their order; some of the friars have passed to the rite. Since 1923 the *Assumptionists* have a vice-province of the Byzantine rite in Rumania, and in 1938 they transferred

---

[21] Thanks to the Emperor Joseph II. He would allow only Hungarian monasteries in Transylvania, so Rumanian aspirants had either to turn Latin or Orthodox.

their Institute of Byzantine Studies from the shores of the Bos-
porus to Bucarest. They have opened a special house for the
spiritual formation of the clergy at Blaj (the *Casa Domnului,*
"Lord's House"), and been entrusted with the direction of the
old-established *Pavelian* school at Beius, and other works.[22] The
Jesuits provide for Byzantine candidates in their provisional
novitiate at Satu Mare, and there are *Brothers of the Christian
Schools* at Oradea.

The Assumptionists have opened two Eastern convents of their
Oblate sisters, and a teaching and nursing congregation, the
Sisters of the Most Holy Mother of God, founded by the late
Metropolitan Suciu, in 1921, has several houses.

The concordat between Rumania and the Holy See stipulates
that all members of religious orders shall be Rumanian subjects.

The Faithful form the second largest body of Catholic Orientals, nearly 1½ million (the Latin Catholics are about 1¼
million),[23] whose prestige and influence is out of all proportion to
their numbers, especially in Transylvania where the Orthodox
have only a bare majority. The rural Rumanians are a pious
people; and in spite of the secular submission to foreign powers,
the Rumanian professional classes in Transylvania are the elite
of the country. The Catholic clergy laid the foundations of
Rumanian literary and academic culture in the past century.
Relations between Catholics and Orthodox are on the whole
good. It is often difficult to see what divides them, and the
Catholic bishop of Oradea Mare, Mgr. Valeriu Frentiu, believes
that their reunion is an administrative and personal problem
rather than a doctrinal and "ideological" one; strong opinions
in favour of reunion are expressed by Orthodox clergy from
time to time.

---

[22] Things have changed a lot since the days (1875–1888) when a seminary
had to be taken from the charge of a certain Western congregation because
all the best subjects were being enticed to become Latins and join it. But
similar things still happen in some parts of the world.

[23] Since the eleventh century these have been looked on by the Rumanians
at large as "foreigners" and "oppressors," as to a large extent they were,
being mostly Hungarians and Germans. By the concordat the Latins have
rather to "take a back seat"; e.g., only one of their five bishops is a
senator, while all the Byzantine Catholic bishops are.

OTHER JURISDICTIONS

United States. Many Catholic Rumanians have been lost to the Church through insufficiency of clergy; there are now some 8000, subject to the Latin bishops, half of them around Cleveland, Trenton, and Rockford. Their first church was built at Cleveland in 1906, St. Helen's, due to the labours of Father Epaminondas Lucaciu, who had been sent to the United States two years before. There is a good Rumanian church at Aurora, Illinois, and a dozen others, but insufficient clergy of the rite.

PARTICULAR CUSTOMS

The Rumanians keep their Byzantine rite in a high degree of purity, some of the few small modifications being shared by the Orthodox. The Gregorian kalendar was adopted by both in 1924 for the celebration of fixed feasts only; Easter is therefore still observed according to the Julian reckoning. The liturgical language is Rumanian, which began to take the place of Staroslav in the seventeenth century — the first example since the early centuries of a Catholic liturgy being authorized for celebration in a vernacular. In Transylvania there is a traditional church music, derived from the chant of Byzantium, but the national architecture has been almost ousted by the neo-classic in that province; *eikonostases* reach nearly to the roof. At the Catholic Rumanian church of San Salvatore alla Coppelle in Rome the congregation at the Easter ceremonies is made up almost entirely of Rumanian dissidents.

Certain extra-liturgical practices from the West have been introduced among the faithful.

BIBLIOGRAPHY

Jorga, *Histoire des Roumains* (Bucarest, 1922).
Kormos, *Rumania* (Cambridge, 1944).
Netzhammer, *Aus Rumänien*, 2 Vols. (Einsiedeln, 1913).

7. THE MELKITES

After the Council of Chalcedon the Monophysites in the patriarchates of Alexandria, Antioch, and Jerusalem dubbed the orthodox Catholics "Melkites," from Syrian *malko,* "king," because they professed the orthodoxy of the emperor. The name stuck and is often used without qualification to designate the Catholic Byzantines of Syria and Egypt, though the dissident Orthodox are equally Melkites.[24] After the Arab invasion in the seventh century the Melkites of all three patriarchates came for a time more and more under the ecclesiastical domination of Constantinople, and by the end of the thirteenth century they had abandoned their own liturgies to the Monophysites and adopted that of imperial Byzantium.

There was another important change after Chalcedon, in the *personnel* that made up these patriarchates. Alexandria was originally Greco-Egyptian, Antioch and Jerusalem Greco-Syrian. Today, the Orthodox of Alexandria are predominantly Greek (though the Syrian element has been recently enlarged by emigration), those of Jerusalem are Syrian ("Palestinian") under a Greek ecclesiastical caucus, those of Antioch are almost entirely Syro-Arab. The Catholic Melkites, both of Egypt and Syria, are fundamentally Syro-Arabs, racially more or less one with the Catholic (West) Syrians and Maronites, but with more Greek blood.

Though numerically insignificant the patriarchate of Antioch is still of great historical interest and ecclesiastical importance because of the large number of its patriarchs and bishops who were

---

[24] In the popular speech of the Levant the word "Catholic" primarily means "Catholic Melkite." A Syrian divides the principal Christians into "*Rûm* (Roman = Orthodox) *wa Kathulik wa Lateen wa Maroniyeh.*" This shows a nice historical sense, for of the half-dozen Catholic rites represented in Syria, Palestine, and Egypt, the Melkites are hierarchically the "authentic local Catholics": the present Syrian and Maronite bodies are due to heresies in the past, the Armenians are largely refugees, and the Latin rite also is a foreign importation.

in communion with Rome between the Byzantine schism of 1054[25] and the definite emergence of two hierarchies, Catholic and dissident Orthodox, in 1724: so much so that it has been claimed that throughout that period the Antiochene patriarchs (even while resident at Constantinople) considered themselves subject to the pope as supreme pontiff.[26] But this is certainly an exaggeration.

When the Crusaders captured Antioch in 1098 they acknowledged the Catholicity and jurisdiction of its patriarch, John IV; but after the death of the papal legate Adhemar du Puy, their attitude altered and they treated John so badly that he fled to Constantinople.[27] It is not believable that his successors there were not in schism. But Theodosius V signed the act of union at Lyons in 1274 and resigned his see rather than repudiate it; others must have followed his example, for Saracen writers of the fourteenth and fifteenth centuries make a clear distinction between the Melkites who submit to the pope of Rome and the other Christians (Jacobites, etc.) who do not. It was John IV's flight to Constantinople that started the series of absentee Melkite patriarchs in the imperial city, which greatly helped to strengthen the spirit of schism; for Constantinople was always the spearhead of opposition to Rome.

The patriarch of Antioch, Dorotheos I, accepted the union of Florence, and there is reason to think that the three Melkite patriarchs did not relapse into schism again until the Turks cut off Syria from the West in 1516 and the Greeks seized the patriarchal throne of Jerusalem from the Syrians in 1543. But again in 1560

[25] The contemporary patriarch, Peter III, implored Cerularius not to separate himself and his church from Rome and the West.
[26] There have been some Catholic patriarchs of Alexandria, too, since the eleventh century, and two are reported at Jerusalem in the seventeenth.
[27] Thereupon the Crusaders instituted that anomaly, a Latin patriarch of Antioch. It was this playing fast and loose with Eastern sees and their holders (to say nothing of such things as their sacking of Constantinople in 1204) that made the name of crusader — and consequently of Catholic — stink in the nostrils of pious Orientals. There are still Latin patriarchs of Constantinople, Alexandria, and Antioch, titular prelates of the papal court, and one in residence at Jerusalem; he is, of course, really only an archbishop, for the pope is the only real Latin patriarch.

Joachim V was apparently a Catholic, and in 1585 the retired patriarch, Michael VII, and with the seventeenth century there began a strong movement toward definitive reunion. The patriarchs Athanasius II, Ignatius III, Euthymios II (who welcomed the Jesuits into his territory), Eutychios, Makarios III, and Cyril V, and the bishops Euthymios Saifi of Tyre, Gregory of Aleppo, Gerasimos of Saidnaia, Parthenios of Diarbekr, and others, all made formal profession of allegiance to the Holy See between 1600 and 1720; the Jesuit missionaries, indeed, seem to have recognized all Melkite bishops in Syria as the legitimate ordinaries of their rite.

When the patriarch Athanasius III, a schismatic, died in 1724, a nephew of Euthymios of Tyre who had been educated in Rome, Seraphim Tanas, was elected in his place; he took the name of Cyril VI. Thereupon those who were not in favour of communion with Rome (and some who were) selected a candidate, Silvester, and sent him off to Constantinople, where he was consecrated and put forward as the true patriarch of Antioch.[28] Silvester had the support of only five bishops out of fifteen, but he obtained the favour of the Turkish government first and Cyril had to take refuge in a remote Maronite monastery in the Lebanon.

THE CATHOLIC MELKITES

For a time there was a violent persecution of the Catholics, and even when it died down the reign of Cyril continued to be troubled; he fell foul both of the Jesuits and the Maronites, and Pope Benedict XIV had to send a severe instruction that the Maronites were not to induce Melkites to join their rite and that Melkites were not to call Maronites heretics. Cyril VI Tanas resigned in 1759, but the state of the Catholic Melkites continued to be disturbed. For example, a synod at Karkafah in 1806 pub-

---

[28] From this time on there are two lines of patriarchs, one for Catholics, one for dissidents. The Catholic patriarch is the historical as well as the spiritual successor of St. Evodius, St. Ignatius the God-bearer, and the Flavians. The Orthodox have contested the validity of the election of Cyril VI, but the synod of Constantinople itself admitted it by claiming to depose him.

lished a number of "acts" which later had to be condemned by the Holy See for their "conciliarism," there were quarrels between the patriarch Agapios III and the Metropolitan of Bairut, and from 1817 till 1832 there was a bloody persecution at the hands of the Turks — nine Melkites were murdered out of hatred of the faith at Aleppo on April 16, 1818.[29]

The rule of the great Maximos III Mazlum (1833–1855) was a period of reform and progress, culminating in his obtaining from the Turkish government complete civil autonomy for his people under their patriarch. In the time of his successor, Clement Bahath, there was for three years a small but very noisy schism caused by the imposition of the Gregorian kalendar in place of the Julian. Gregory II Yusuf (1864–1897) was another energetic and far-seeing patriarch. He suggested the formation of the seminary of St. Anne at Jerusalem, and at the epoch-making international eucharistic congress held in that city in 1893 Gregory was the outstanding figure. He had assisted at the Vatican Council and was well known to the West.

There has been a remarkable extension of his church in the regions of Tripoli, Galilee, and Transjordania; between 1931 and 1936 alone there were 10,000 reconciliations of dissidents.

PRESENT STATE

Patriarch. The supreme head under the sovereign pontiff of the Catholic Melkites is the "Patriarch of Antioch and of All the East"; since the days of Maximos III each holder has had the personal privilege of adding the titles of Alexandria and Jerusalem.[30] His jurisdiction extends to all the faithful of his church in what was in 1894 the Turkish empire and Egypt. He is elected by the bishops, residential and titular, of the jurisdiction united

[29] Earlier martyrs were David the Greek (1660) and Ibrahim al-Dallal (1742).

[30] On solemn occasions he is "The most blessed, holy, and venerable chief and head, Patriarch of the great cities of God, Antioch, Alexandria, and Jerusalem, of Cilicia, Syria, and Iberia, of Arabia, Mesopotamia, and the Pentapolis, of Ethiopia, Egypt, and all the East, the lord N., Father of Fathers, Shepherd of shepherds, High priest of high priests, and Thirteenth Apostle." "The East" is the Roman prefecture *Oriens.*

in synod. The Holy See confirms the election upon receiving noti-
fication and a profession of faith (although the elect is enthroned
at once after the synod) and sends the *pallium*.[31] Until this confirmation is received, the patriarch may not exercise his functions,
but this rule is often disregarded. Among the patriarchal rights
are the nomination of three persons from whom a bishop is
chosen for a vacant see, the appointment of titular bishops
(*synkelloi*) at will, the ordination of all bishops and their canonical deposition, the consecration of Chrism for his whole church,
the convening of a plenary synod, as well as certain civil rights
in respect of his flock. He confers the *omophorion* on his bishops
as the pope does the *pallium* on Western archbishops. His chief
residence is at Damascus,[32] with others at Alexandria and Cairo.
Altogether, the Melkite patriarch's position, *vis-á-vis* both his own
people and the Holy See, approximates more closely to that of a
pre-schism patriarch than does that of most other Catholic Eastern pontiffs; it is therefore the more remarkable that he has no
patriarchal *curia* beyond two councillors who are titular bishops:
every bishop is the sole judge of causes in his own eparchy.

Bishops. The sees are Damascus (the patriarchal eparchy),
Tyre, Aleppo, Bosra and the Hauran, Bairut, Homs, St. John of
Akka (Ptolemais), Sidon, Paneas, Tripoli, Baalbek, Zahleh, and
Transjordania (Amman). The first six of these are metropolitan
according to old lists, but all the bishops are called archbishop
and are subject directly to the patriarch. The authority of the
patriarch of Antioch was extended to the Melkites in the patriarchates of Alexandria and Jerusalem in 1772; for those of Egypt
he has vicars patriarchal (with the title of archimandrite) at
Alexandria, Cairo, and Khartum, and at Jerusalem a vicar with a
title of exarch.

---

[31] He sometimes wears it to be buried in. The *pallium* has no historical
significance in the East; it is the pope's recognition of communion with
the new patriarch.
[32] None of the five governing patriarchs (Catholic Melkite, Syrian, Maronite, Orthodox Melkite, and Jacobite) who have the title of Antioch live
there. "Antakiyeh" is now a Mohammedan town with about 30,000
inhabitants.

The Holy See has neither voice nor part in the appointment of Melkite bishops. When a see is vacant, the patriarch in consultation with the bishops puts forward two or three names and choice is made therefrom by the clergy of the eparchy and, in practice, the leading laymen.[33]

The patriarch and bishops still act to a large extent as judges in civil causes. They live as simply as do their parish clergy and most of the members of their flocks.

Parochial clergy. Before the days of Maximos III practically all the parishes were served by monks, who still have charge of many of them. A seminary was founded in 1811 at Ain Traz in the Lebanon, a great Melkite centre where three plenary synods have been held; its career was chequered and not very successful, and it was finally closed in 1899. After the Crimean War the Turkish government presented to France, as a *baksheesh* for her part in the campaign, the crusaders' church of St. Anne in Jerusalem. Here in 1882 Cardinal Lavigerie, at the suggestion of the patriarch Gregory II, opened a Byzantine seminary under the direction of the White Fathers.[34] By the end of its first fifty years this institution had produced eight bishops, 126 priests, and three permanent deacons, of whom Mgr. Lagier says, "Their modesty, unworldliness, cultured wide-spiritedness, and dignity of soul make up a priestly *ensemble* that is surpassed nowhere in the Catholic Church" (but they are very French). All the St. Anne's priests have voluntarily accepted celibacy, but there is also a number of married priests among the Melkite clergy, who are hard-working and highly respected men. A few aspirants are sent to the Greek College at Rome, and there are several diocesan junior seminaries

The names of *exarch* and *archimandrite*[35] are conferred as titles of honour, the holders of which affect certain distinctions of dress.

---

[33] By a special privilege, approved by Pope Pius VII, the metropolitan of Aleppo is elected by the clergy and twelve laymen (who, however, have only an advisory part), without reference to the patriarch.

[34] The Society of Missionaries of Africa, founded at Algiers by the cardinal in 1868. Lavigerie played an important part in the abolition of the slave trade, and his society worthily carries on the tradition of his genius.

The clergy wear the traditional Byzantine *rason* and *kalemaukion* and some retain the custom of long hair.

Religious institutes. For two hundred years the monks were the mainstay of the Catholic Melkite church. In 1708 Euthymios Saifi of Tyre built a monastery at Masmuseh, near Sidon. He put its members under the "rule of St. Basil," but his object was to form a congregation more on the lines of the clerks regular of the West; nevertheless they are canonically reckoned as monks. His foundation prospered and grew, receiving the name of *Salvatorian* Basilians from its mother-house "of the Saviour," Dair al-Mukhallis; this house still flourishes and here Melkite monastic life can be seen at its best. The *Shuwairite* Basilian monks were founded about the same time at Shuwair by two hieromonks from the Orthodox monastery of Balamand ("Belmont"), near Tripoli. Their organization was more strictly monastic than that of the Salvatorians, but they also were soon engaged in parochial and mission work. Almost from the beginning there was friction between the Shuwairite monasteries in the Lebanon mountains and those of Aleppo, which was ended in 1832 by the formation of a separate congregation of *Aleppine* Basilians (the others are sometimes called Baladites, i.e., rustics).

These three congregations all developed under direct Western influence, principally of the Jesuits and Capuchins, and their earlier constitutions were modeled on those of the Maronite Antonians, which were to a considerable degree "made in Italy." Nevertheless, the members of these organizations are an indigenous product, and cannot be mistaken for anything other than they are — Eastern religious who have developed in certain conditions and in response to a particular demand. On account of the shortage of secular priests the Melkite Basilians have throughout their history been principally engaged in serving parishes, and the value of the service they have done to the Catholics of their rite is incalculable. To a monk of Shuwair, Abdullah Zahir, was

---

[35] Any bishop may confer this title on any priest he pleases. The White Father Père Abel Couturier, that "ghost from the *lauras* of Pharan," was named archimandrite by the patriarch and by the bishops of Ptolemais and Sidon as well.

due the establishment of the first Arabic printing press in the Ottoman Empire, early in the eighteenth century.

The Salvatorians have seven monasteries and seven "cells" (*metokhia*) with 190 monks, nearly all priests; the Shuwairites, five monasteries and five cells, with 110 monks, and the Aleppines, three monasteries, six cells, 50 hieromonks and 25 monks. Of the total of 330 hieromonks nearly two thirds live in and serve parishes. They wear the traditional Byzantine dress.

An apostolic visitation of the Melkite Basilians resulted in 1934 in a complete reorganization. The visitors were the late Dom Benedict Gariador, abbot general of the Cassinese Benedictines of the Primitive Observance, Dom de Lajudie, monk of the same congregation, and Dom Menez, monk of Solesmes, under the presidency of the patriarch, Mgr. Mogabgab. The new constitutions, while organizing each congregation on the lines of the later Western orders, with an effective superior general (protoarchimandrite) at the head of each, provide for a greater degree of monastic regularity in the monasteries. But local superiors are appointed by the superior general, who can also transfer monks from one house to another at will.

After he retired from the see of Baalbek in 1894 Germanos Muakkad[36] founded the society of *Missionaries of St. Paul*, at Harissa in the Lebanon. Its numbers are still small, but they do a great work in giving missions and retreats and running a polyglot printing establishment.

All three Basilian congregations have convents of nuns affiliated, totaling over 150 members, whose life till recently was strictly contemplative and the most traditionally Eastern of any nuns in the Catholic Church, being entirely free from foreign influence. It is still mainly so, but since 1941 the nuns of the Salvatorian branch have been a missionary congregation. There are two small societies of sisters who teach, care for the sick, etc., and there is a number of Melkites among the Maryamat, an inter-ritual congregation of teaching sisters.

---

[36] Dr. Adrian Fortescue said of him, "I have rarely met any man who gave the impression of being a saint as did Germanos Muakkad."

The Faithful. There are nominally 150,000, but certainly more, Catholic Melkites in the patriarchal territory, 25,000 of whom are in Egypt and many in Galilee and Transjordan (the dissident Orthodox Melkites of the three patriarchates total some 400,000). In Syria many and in Egypt all of them live in the towns, and form prosperous communities whose social and religious prestige is high; in the rural districts of Syria and Transjordania increasing numbers of peasants become Melkite Catholics. By blood these claim to be pure Arabs of the Hauran, especially of the Banu Ghassan, originally from the Yemen in southern Arabia, and descended from Solomon and the Queen of Sheba — a common Oriental boast. In some of the more remote parts religious education is insufficient, and in the towns the influence of Freemasonry (imported by returned immigrants) has been most harmful.

In extensive districts of Syria the Melkites are recognized as the principal authentic local and indigenous expression of Catholicism (see footnote on p. 104), but in Palestine their position is not so satisfactory. Here the course of history has brought about a predominance of Latin influence, and lately the formation of a native clergy and laity of the Roman rite, in spite of canon 98 and other legislation. But in Galilee and Transjordania there is a movement of Palestinian Catholics and Orthodox back to their proper Melkite Catholic church. The resulting atmosphere of rivalry between Latins and Byzantines is very regrettable, and indeed there is not always among the Catholic bodies of Syria in general that accord, good feeling, and mixing with one another that one would wish to find. Their rivalries are of old standing, and are kept alive particularly by some of the laity and lower clergy. The Latin minority is often ignorant about Orientals, patronizing, and superior; the Melkites, as heirs of Constantinople, Alexandria, Antioch, and Jerusalem, have a touch of Byzantine aggressiveness about them — they have not forgotten that the Latin church is not native to Palestine, Syria, and Egypt; the Maronites have more than a touch of that self-satisfiedness which sometimes characterizes a body of people who have for centuries

Courtesy, *Universe*

BISHOPS OF THE SYRO-MALANKARA AND (Center) SYRO-MALABARESE RITES

Mar Augustine of Ernakulam

Mar Theophilos of Tiruvella

Mar Ivanios of Trivandrum

MALABARESE CHURCH, IRAPOLY

GREGORY PETER XV AGAGANIAN
Patriarch of Cilicia and Katholikos of the Catholic
Armenians, Cardinal of the Holy Roman Church

Bishop

Vartapet

Protodeacon

Subdeacon

CLERGY OF THE ARMENIAN RITE

maintained their orthodoxy under oppression in the face of those whose orthodoxy is a more recent acquisition; the little group of the "pure" Syrian rite is less involved in these unhappy squabbles.

Other Jurisdictions

United States. There has been emigration of Melkites to America for fifty years, with the loss of many to religion. There are now 20,000 in the United States, with a score of priests, subject to the American ordinaries. Their chief churches are around New York, New England, and Detroit. Here they call themselves Syrian Greek Catholics. The first Melkite priest in America was a Basilian monk, Father Abraham Bashawatah, and the first church was at Brooklyn. The Melkite church on Washington Street, New York City, is a melancholy example of what havoc can be worked in an Eastern church building by Western "hybridization."

Elsewhere. There are two or three thousand Melkites in other parts of the world. They have churches at Constantinople, Marseilles (founded 1821), Paris (St. Julien-le-Pauvre), Montreal, Sydney, and Brisbane.

Particular Customs

The Melkites are more jealous for the good observance of their rite than many Eastern Catholics in the Levant. The Byzantine liturgy and other rites are celebrated normally entirely in Arabic, and have been modified only in small points, chiefly of externals. Their chant is in substance that of Constantinople. "And from the Son" is sung in the creed, and Baptism is administered by seating the child in the font and pouring water over it. The segregation of women during divine service is insisted on with all the rigour of the ancient canons. A number of the smaller churches are too poor to have an *eikonostasis*.

The use of the traditional spoon for giving Holy Communion is being more and more superseded by the practice of dipping the holy Body in the sacred Blood and administering them by hand; this reform led to a notable increase in communions even before the decree of Pope Pius X in 1905. The Melkites accorded a degree of external *cultus* to the Blessed Sacrament before any other Catholics of Eastern rite. So early as the end of the seventeenth century an old Arabic *Pentekostarion* was found at Damascus containing an office for Corpus Christi, and since the plague was stayed at Aleppo in 1732 the feast has been observed with increased solemnity. Benediction of the Blessed Sacrament, with a completely different ceremonial from that of the West, has been introduced into some eparchies, as has the entirely unnecessary innovation of giving absolution by the Western indicative formula (in Arabic, of course).

One or two Western devotions are practised among the Melkites, e.g., the rosary, but there are no statues in the churches, only pictures. Their kalendar is, except for the Gregorian reckoning and Corpus Christi, that of Constantinople. In addition to Sundays there are now 32 holydays, but hardly regarded as of obligation. The ancient customs of fasting and abstinence have been modified (see p. 56).

BIBLIOGRAPHY

Charon, *Histoire des Patriarcats melkites,* 2 vols. (Paris, 1911).

Fortescue, *The Uniate Eastern Churches* (Italo-Greeks and Melkites) (London, 1923).

Gorra, *Sainte Anne de Jérusalem* (Jerusalem, 1932).

Couturier, *Cours de Liturgie Grecque-Melkite,* 3 vols. (Paris, 1912).

Couturier, *Syllitourgikon* (the music in Eastern and Western notation) (Paris, 1926).

8. THE GREEKS

Before the rise of Constantinople to civil and ecclesiastical power the country now called the Kingdom of the Hellenes was, as part of the Roman prefecture of Illyricum, within the patriarchal jurisdiction of the Roman pontiff. But eastern Illyricum was part of the Eastern Empire, and from the fifth century the patriarch of Constantinople claimed to have jurisdiction over it. The question was a source of never ending dispute between Old Rome and New Rome until the mediaeval schism, when what is now Greece was definitely involved on the side of Constantinople and became part of its separated patriarchate, sharing its political and religious history until the establishment of the modern Greek state in the early part of the nineteenth century. Then, in 1833, the Greek assembly declared the national church autocephalous and it was so recognized by Constantinople seventeen years later.

After the Greek-speaking lands fell into the hands of the Turks, Pope Gregory XIII, in 1576, founded the Greek College at Rome, primarily for refugees from Greece who wanted to study for the priesthood; but, although there were many individual Greek bishops, priests, and others who returned to unity during the seventeenth and eighteenth centuries,[37] it was not found possible to form a Catholic community of Byzantine rite among the Greek people, so the college was utilized for others of that rite, especially Ruthenians.

For this and for other reasons, less easy to understand, the long history of the college has been very chequered and at times

---

[37] Cyril Kontaris, oecumenical patriarch of Constantinople, saved his church from Protestantism and in 1638 entered into communion with the supreme pontiff. He was dethroned, imprisoned at Tunis, and there murdered by the Turks in 1640. The cause of his beatification as a martyr was introduced at Rome, but has never been finished.

troubled. Despite this it has produced a remarkable number of great men. There may be mentioned Leo Allatius (d. 1669), a Greek of Khios, whom Fortescue refers to as "perhaps the most learned Greek since Photios," a man as distinguished in profane as in sacred learning; Josaphat Azales (d. 1621), who tried to reconcile the monks of Athos with Rome; Demetrios Kyriakos, a famous hellenist in the seventeenth century; Peter Arcudius (d. 1633), a most learned theologian; and Peter Rodotà, the eighteenth-century historian of the Italo-Greeks, whose work can never be superseded as a source.

Upon the foundation of a special college at Rome for the Ruthenians in 1897, the Greek College was reorganized and confided to the care of Benedictine monks; it is now a charge of those of the Belgian congregation. Since then many of the anomalies and drawbacks of the college in the old days have disappeared. While employed there the monks adopt the Byzantine rite (some belong to it permanently), and the college chapel of St. Athanasius is now one of the best Byzantine churches in Rome.

The students are now principally Greeks and Italo-Greek-Albanians, with a few Melkites and occasionally other elements.

THE CATHOLIC GREEKS

In 1829 the sultan Mohammed II emancipated his non-Latin Catholic subjects from the civil authority of the dissident patriarchs, and a body of Greek Catholics of the Byzantine rite came into existence. The leading spirit in its formation was a Latin priest from Sira, Father John Hyacinth Marango, who in 1856 started work at Constantinople with the object of persuading the Orthodox to return to unity. The results were hardly commensurate with his enthusiasm and energy,[38] but by 1861 he had a small nucleus at Pera, in whose direction he was succeeded in 1878 by Father Polycarp Anastasiadis, a former student of the Orthodox seminary at Halki. In 1895 Pope Leo XIII invited the French

---

[38] Nevertheless, it was due to him that two contemporary Orthodox bishops, Meletios of Drama and Benjamin of Neapolis, died Catholics.

Assumptionists to go to Constantinople, where they organized a seminary and two parishes of the Greek rite, and began those learned studies of Oriental religious matters whose fruits are so valuable to scholars.

Pope Pius X gave these Greeks a titular bishop as ordinary (exarch) in 1911, in the distinguished person of Isaias Papadopoulos, who had led a Catholic movement in the Thracian village of Malgara and suffered much for the faith. He was called to Rome in 1917 and his place was taken three years later by Mgr. George Kalavassy, who in the face of great hardship and difficulties established himself and part of his flock at Athens. In 1932 those at Constantinople were made a separate ordinariate, with Mgr. Dionisios Varoukhas as bishop. The Catholics of Malgara and Dandeli emigrated to near Salonika.

PRESENT STATE

Organization. The two ordinariates of Greece and Turkey are subject to the Sacred Eastern Congregation at Rome, which appoints the bishops.

Parochial clergy. These are fifteen in number, all voluntarily celibate, with one permanent deacon. There is a clerical school at Athens, preparatory for the Greek College at Rome; the Assumptionist Oriental seminary at Kadi-Keuy (Chalcedon) has been closed since 1915. The clergy conduct a boys' orphanage and a printing press.

Religious institutes. The secular priests are united in a society ("of the Most Holy Trinity"), but it is not a religious congregation. Several of the Assumptionist priests are of the Greek rite, but their Institute of Byzantine Studies is directed by Latins. The *Sisters of the Theotokos Pammakaristos,* founded by Mgr. Kalavassy, conduct a school at Athens.

The Faithful. They number less than 2500. Those who emigrated to Athens in 1923 have had to suffer a good deal of harsh treatment at the hands of their dissident brethren, for Catholics of Eastern rite were not known in Greece (there are 43,000 Latins, mostly of foreign origin but now completely hellenized) and they were accordingly accused of dishonest propaganda. A law of 1938, rigorously curbing the activities of non-Orthodox religious bodies, was probably aimed particularly at the Byzantine Catholics and at a certain Protestant sect: it is likely to have gravely increased the difficulties of both of them.

These Catholics, whether Latins or Byzantines, are the only people who can properly be called "Greek Catholics."[39] There is now a Byzantine church on the island of Sira.

In 1929 some of the Greek community in *Lyons,* dissatisfied with the ministration of their bishop for Western Europe, asked to be received into the communion of the Catholic Church. A priest was sent to them from Athens by Mgr. Kalavassy.

OTHER JURISDICTIONS

There are three tiny groups of Greek Catholics separate from the above, which should be mentioned here rather than with the Italo-Greeks as is usually done.

Corsica. When the Turks conquered Greece seven hundred people fled from Boitylos in the Morea in 1675 and the Genoese Republic gave them a home in Corsica. They accepted the jurisdiction of the Holy See, and settled down first at Paomia and then at Ajaccio. In 1770 the first French governor, the Count de Marboeuf, built for them the township of Cargèse, which their descendants now occupy. They number 500 souls and, though they have nearly lost their Greek language, they still keep their Greek rites, only a little modified by Western practices, e.g., Confirmation is separated from Baptism and administered according to the Roman rite by the bishop of Ajaccio. They have one church.

Algeria. A colony from Cargèse went to Algeria in 1875 and founded the village of Sidi-Maruan. They number some 250, with one church.

Malta. When the Knights of St. John of Jerusalem occupied

---

[39] The name is nevertheless often used in popular speech of and by the Catholic Melkites, Ruthenians, and others, especially in North America. The Hellenes are sometimes distinguished as "Pure Greeks."

Malta upon being driven from Rhodes by the Turks in 1522, a church was built at Valletta for those Greeks of Byzantine rite who accompanied them. That community exists to this day, though now numbering hardly a score of souls, and till 1942 used the same church, which was handsomely furnished. In that year it was utterly destroyed during an air raid. The church was dedicated in honour of our Lady of Damascus, named for an eikon brought from Rhodes; this eikon was saved, and will in due course be set up again in the new church which is to be built.

The Catholic Greeks of Greece and Turkey use the Byzantine rite and customs, in ecclesiastical Greek, according to pure Constantinopolitan usages, without any admixture or addition of specifically Western observances.

BIBLIOGRAPHY

Fortescue, *The Orthodox Eastern Church* (London, 1911).

Attwater, "A Greek Parish in Corsica" in *Eastern Churches Quarterly*, July, 1943.

Armstrong, "The Greek Catholic Church of . . . Malta" in *Eastern Churches Quarterly*, January, 1943.

9. THE BULGARS

The Bulgars are in origin a Finno-Turkish people (completely slavonized long ago) who established an independent kingdom in their present country and its borders during the seventh century. About the year 865 their Czar Boris, largely for political motives, accepted Christianity from Constantinople and imposed it on his people. But Boris wanted his church to be independent, and turned to Pope St. Nicholas I, asking him to give Bulgaria a patriarch. Nicholas sent an archbishop. This precipitated a long contest for jurisdiction over the Bulgars, both Rome and Constantinople claiming that they were in their patriarchate. The Slavs, too, had a hand in the conversion of the Bulgars. When the Germans made things impossible for the followers of St. Methodius in Moravia and Pannonia, a number of them fled into Bulgaria about the year 885 and evangelized the heathen there. Their leader St. Clement and four of his clergy, together with SS. Cyril and Methodius, are venerated as the Seven Apostles of the Bulgars.

The Emperor Basil II ("the Bulgar-slayer") conquered Bulgaria in 1018, and the ecclesiastical province of Okhrida was eventually involved in the Byzantine schism. But it continued to be an autonomous church till 1767, when it was reduced to complete dependence on the Greek patriarch of Constantinople. Eastern Bulgaria recovered independence in 1185, and from 1204 to 1234 was in unambiguous communion with Rome, its primatial see being at Tirnovo. Then the politics of the Czar John Assen II dragged the church of Tirnovo into schism and, when Bulgaria was conquered by the Ottoman Turks in 1393, its territory was united to that of Okhrida; but it managed to maintain a semi-independence till 1767.

When in that year all the Bulgarian eparchies were brought

under the direct control of Constantinople they were subjected
to a ruthless process of hellenizing: Greek became the com-
pulsory liturgical language and only Greeks were appointed to
episcopal sees. National consciousness awoke in Bulgaria and
when, in 1856, the Turkish government decreed the freedom
and equality of its Christian subjects, Bulgarian representatives
demanded for their church a number of far-reaching reforms.
(Political freedom was their ultimate object; it was gained in
1878.) The patriarch of Constantinople made certain concessions,
including the appointment of some bishops of Bulgarian nationality. But it was too late; Bulgaria was now demanding an autonomous national church, and in 1870 it was granted by an
imperial *firman* from the Ottoman *Porte:* the Bulgarian Church
was to be autocephalous under an exarch (primate) and synod.
Whereupon in 1872, a council of the Church of Constantinople
declared the Bulgars excommunicated, which sentence was not
lifted till 1945.

THE CATHOLIC BULGARS

At the beginning of their struggle with Constantinople there
was an influential minority of Bulgars who sought ecclesiastical
independence of the Greeks by means of reunion with Rome.
Assured by the Catholic Armenian archbishop of Constantinople,
Mgr. Hassun, that their rites and customs would be respected,
they sent a deputation to Rome in 1861, where Pope Pius IX
himself consecrated their leader, the archimandrite Joseph Sokolsky, as prelate of the Catholic Bulgars of the Byzantine rite.

But the movement was spoiled in an unforeseen way. The
growth of Catholicism in the Balkans was obnoxious to the
political aims of Russia and, diplomacy having failed, a month
after his return to Constantinople Sokolsky was kidnapped, taken
to Odessa, and interned for the remaining eighteen years of his
life in the monastery of the Caves at Kiev.[40] Then the Russian
diplomats set themselves to encourage the Turks to favour an

---

[40] That Sokolsky connived at his removal and reverted to Orthodoxy has
been asserted, but not proved.

independent Orthodox Bulgarian church, whose establishment killed the Romeward movement.

At this time there were over 60,000 Bulgars reunited with Rome.[41] They were given another prelate, and Augustinians of the Assumption and other Western congregations were sent to help them. But by 1872 three quarters of them had returned to Orthodoxy, and most of the remainder lived, not in Bulgaria, but in Macedonia and Thrace. Accordingly, in 1883 Pope Leo XIII appointed them a vicar apostolic in each of these districts. After the Balkan war of 1912–1913 the Orthodox Bulgars of Macedonia again contemplated reunion with Rome, and again were frustrated by political forces. This war brought ruin to both vicariates; parish after parish was destroyed, many of the faithful massacred, others forced into the Orthodox Church, at the hands of the Greeks and, to a lesser degree, the Serbs. After the European war of 1914–1918 what remained of the Catholic Bulgars sought refuge in their own country.

PRESENT STATE

Organization. The Catholic Bulgars now form an exarchate. The exarch (Bishop Ivan Garuvalov in 1947) resides at Sofia and depends on the Sacred Eastern Congregation through the delegate apostolic to Bulgaria.

Parochial clergy. These number 41, about half of whom are married. The Assumptionists (who have a few priests of the Byzantine rite serving parishes) conduct junior seminaries at Yambol and Plovdiv (Phillippopolis), studies being completed at Oriental seminaries elsewhere; the fine seminary at Karagatch, near Adrianople, was destroyed during World War I.

Religious institutes. The *Resurrectionists,* a congregation of Polish origin having both Latin and Eastern members, have a few priests of Byzantine rite in Bulgaria. There is a convent of

---

[41] One of the most remarkable among them was the aged monk Pante-leimon, who tried to introduce frequent Communion among the monks of Mount Athos. He became a Catholic in 1863 and founded two monasteries, one for men and one for women. They failed after his death in 1868. He was ordained only in 1865, at the expressed wish of Pius IX.

Eucharistines, engaged in charitable works at Sofia, and an enclosed Carmel (the first of Byzantine rite) was founded at Sofia in 1935.

The Faithful now number only 5500 all told, mostly engaged in agriculture but with good communities at Sofia and Varna. The Augustinians of the Assumption do admirable educational work among them. There is a number of Catholics of the Latin rite, but the overwhelming majority of the Bulgars are dissident Orthodox.

The Bulgarian liturgy is the Byzantine according to Slavonic usages, and innovations are avoided; even the Julian kalendar is in use. Church music is either an adaptation of the Greek chant or Russian polyphony. The Bulgars are not in origin Slavs, but the use of Church Slavonic as a "national custom" seems to have begun soon after their conversion, when the followers of St. Methodius from Moravia introduced the practice at the court of the Czar Boris, who adopted it as a sign of independence of Constantinople.

BIBLIOGRAPHY

Songeon, *Histoire de la Bulgarie* (Paris, 1913).
Canisius, *Aux Avant-Postes du Monde Slave* (Louvain, 1931).
Kristov, *Pantéléimon* (Paris, n. d.).

10. THE RUSSIANS

The Russians date their conversion to Christ from about the year 988, when St. Vladimir, grand-prince of Kiev, gave the new religion to his people. Russia received the faith from both Northmen and Greeks, but the second influence was soon preponderant: her rites of worship, her canon law, her earlier metropolitans came from Constantinople. And since this was the period of Cerularius, she was given anti-Western ideas as well. In the circumstances of the times it is impossible that the fact and significance of communion with the Holy See of Rome can have had much importance in their religious consciousness. Greek influence was predominant in their church and, in the words of Father Pierling, S.J., "One looks in vain for an exact date or outstanding event that can be registered as the point of departure for the separation between Russia and Rome. It came about by implication, without shock or apparent reason, simply because of Russia's hierarchical submission to the patriarch of Constantinople."

There were, however, contacts and normal relations between Russia and the West until the middle of the thirteenth century, when the Mongol invasion isolated her for a hundred and fifty years. When full liberation from that yoke at length came, the Russian Church had become a self-sufficient national institution, and the idea of Catholicity was associated with enemies and rivals on her western borders. At the Council of Florence Russia was represented by a Greek, Isidore, metropolitan of Kiev (Moscow), who was in favour of reunion. Pope Eugenius IV created him cardinal (and the great Bessarion of Nicaea as well) and sent him home as legate to confirm the union, but the grand-prince of Muscovy, Basil II, and his other bishops would have none of it and Isidore had to escape to Rome.

In 1589 the patriarch of Constantinople, Jeremias II, acknowledged Russia as a separate patriarchate of the Orthodox Church,

with its patriarchal see at Moscow ("The Third Rome"). Six years
later took place the union with Rome of the metropolitan of
Kiev and other bishops in southwest Russia, under the rule of
Poland, whose people included those whom we now call Ruthenians or Ukrainians (see p. 67 ff.). Peter the Great abolished the
patriarchal office in 1700, and set up a "Holy Governing Synod"
to rule the Russian Church in concert with the civil power
(1721). This lasted till the revolution of 1917, when a patriarch
of Moscow was again elected. At that time the number of
dissident Russian Orthodox Christians was about 110 millions
(including sects).

THE RUSSIAN CATHOLICS

During the centuries after the Council of Florence there
were very few Catholics indeed under Russian rule until the
partition of Poland in 1772–1795.[42] Toward the end of the nineteenth century, largely under the influence of the great philosopher and theologian Vladimir Solovyev, began a movement in
favour of Russians who became Catholics keeping their own rite.
Such a thing was legally impossible — a Byzantine *had* to be
Orthodox — even after 1905, when Nicholas II issued an edict
of religious toleration.[43] But from that time groups of Russian
Catholics of Byzantine rite were formed here and there (a few
converts from the sect of *Starovery*, "Old Believers"). In 1917
the Ruthenian archbishop of Lvov, Andrew Szepticky, in whom
Pope Pius X had recognized plenary powers over the Catholic
Byzantines in Russia, appointed Leonid Feodorov to be their

---

[42] Before the revolution there were some two million Latin Catholics
in Russia (excluding Poland and Lithuania), three-quarters of them White
Russian and hardly any of them Great Russian. It is curious to note that,
despite her anti-papal activities, the Empress Catherine II invited the
Jesuits to White Russia and refused to allow the promulgation of Clement
XIV's brief of suppression in 1773. She was thus the means of maintaining
the unbroken continuity of the order.

[43] There were in fact Catholics of Eastern rite before 1905. Solovyev
himself made his profession of faith before Father Nicholas Tolstoy, a
Byzantine priest, in 1896 at Moscow; and there was Father Alexis Zer-
chaninov, who was exiled to a monastery — the Bolshevists sent him to
Tobolsk.

exarch. The provisional government of that year gave official recognition to them, with Father Leonid at their head, but after the outbreak of the Bolshevist revolution he was imprisoned at Solovky and his small flock scattered. Father Leonid died after great sufferings at Vjatka on March 7, 1935. He had spent fourteen of his twenty-two years of priestly life in jail: first under the Czars as a Byzantine Catholic; then under the Bolsheviks as a Christian. It is hoped that the cause of the canonization of this very remarkable man will be introduced at Rome.

Among his flock were the twenty-five nuns who had been founded by the heroic Mother Anna Abrikosova, the wife of a priest. They followed the rule of the Third Order of St. Dominic, adapted to their rite, and did much good work in Moscow, deeply impressing their Orthodox neighbours; most of them were sentenced to varying periods of detention in Solovky, Siberia, and elsewhere, a religious congregation being looked on as a "counter-revolutionary activity." It is gratifying to note that three of these young nuns were Poles, who had given up their own rite to work for reunion and therefore were specially obnoxious to the Soviet authorities.

Mother Anna died in the Butyrky prison at Moscow, and the chaplain of the nuns, Father Nicholas Alexandrov, met his death as a confessor of the faith in the fearful penal camp at Solovky. Mention must also be made here of Father Potapy Emelyanov, a monk of Pochaev and parish priest of Bogdanovka, near Kharkov. Led by him, his parishioners asked to be received into Catholic communion in 1918, and as a consequence they were bitterly ill-treated, first as "Bolsheviks" by Ukrainian separatists and then as "renegade Russians" by the Bolsheviks. Father Potapy was arrested and flogged for the sixteenth time in 1920, and taken to Solovky in 1927, where he died ten years later. At the time of his act of union Father Potapy had never either met a Catholic or read a specifically Catholic book.

PRESENT STATE

Western Europe. In 1939 the Catholics among the Russian

emigrés in Paris, Lyons, Lille, Berlin, etc., numbered about 1500. They were in charge of a bishop of their rite,[44] who resided at Kaunas in Lithuania, where there were a thousand more. There is a Russian ordaining bishop of Byzantine rite in Rome.

A centre for Russian studies, with a junior seminary attached, was established by Dominican friars of the Slav-Byzantine rite at Lille. This in 1937 was transferred to Paris, where the friars serve the Catholic Russian church. The Byzantine Jesuits also had an important Russian establishment, including a boarding-school for boys, at Namur. This, too, was transferred to Paris, in 1941, where it flourished during the war years and very favourable relations with the Orthodox were maintained. There is another junior seminary at Munich.

Eastern Europe. After 1919 reunion work was undertaken among the Orthodox of eastern Poland, most of whom were descendants of the Oriental Catholics "reconverted" to Orthodoxy by the Russian government in the nineteenth century (see p. 71). A few of them (some 20,000 in fifty parishes) returned to unity, and it was the desire of Pope Pius XI to unite them under a diocesan bishop immediately depending on the Holy See. The chauvinistic policy of the government of Poland made this impossible, so a resident episcopal visitor apostolic was given them in 1931.

Work for reunion among these people obviously belonged to their Ruthenian neighbours in Galicia, but again political considerations were in the way, so it was especially entrusted to certain Western congregations who have members qualified and willing to adopt the Eastern rite. The *Jesuits*[45] had their

---

[44] This bishop, Msgr. Peter Bucys, had been superior general of the congregation called "Marians," founded in 1673 by Father Stanislaus Papczilski near Warsaw. It has both Byzantine and Latin members, who work in Poland, Lithuania, the Far East, and elsewhere.

[45] Father Vladimir Ledochowski, the provost general, began to prepare an Oriental branch of the Society of Jesus in 1920, at the wish of Pope Benedict XV. There are now over fifty priests of the society who are Byzantines, and chapels of the rite have been provided in Rome at the *Casa generalizia* (St. Vladimir's) and at the *Gregorianum* (Our Lady of Kазан's)

headquarters at Albertyn, near Vilna, on which depended fifteen or more priests, all of Slav-Byzantine rite. It was a completely Oriental establishment, and over forty scholastics were being trained there for work among all or any of the Slavonic peoples. A similar work was being carried on by the *Redemptorists*, who have had a Slav-Byzantine branch since 1905, originating among the Ukrainians in Canada. Their principal house in eastern Poland, outside Galicia, was at Kovel. *Capuchin* friars of Eastern rite also worked there successfully. The *Missionary Sisters of the Sacred Heart* were founded at Warsaw specifically for reunion work among the White Russians, in 1927.

These particulars are all stated in the past tense, for the provinces concerned, Volhynia, etc., are now once again part of Russia. The institutions referred to, and others, were ruined by war after 1939, and under the Soviet regime there is no hope of building them up again for so long ahead as human eye can see. The apostolic visitor referred to above, Bishop Nicholas Czarnecky, was deported to the U.S.S.R. with the other Catholic Byzantine bishops in 1945. Another victim was Father Niemunsevich, of Albertyn, who was shot by the Nazis.

United States. There are a few hundred Catholic Russians in the United States, with two small churches, in New York and Los Angeles. They have no special organization. The training of monks of the Slav-Byzantine rite has been begun at the Benedictine abbey of St. Procopius at Lisle, Illinois.

The Far East. A centre for a number of Catholic Russians in China and Manchuria is at Harbin, where their ordinary has his headquarters. They have a junior seminary, an orphanage, and two schools, the one for girls conducted by Ursuline nuns (under an English superioress) who have adopted the Eastern rite. The other chief centre, now the more important, is at Shanghai where, built up in the first place by the Archimandrite Nicholas, there are a church, school, and college, and several priests for the five hundred or more faithful.

Many of the clergy serving these scattered groups are former dissident Orthodox priests. The clergy of the future are being formed at the *Russicum* college in Rome, founded for that purpose in 1929. This college is in the Via Carlo Cattaneo, and is directed by members of the Society of Jesus; the adjoining church of St. Antony the Abbot is, as well as the college chapel, the public church for Russian Catholics in the City.

In 1935 all Russians of Eastern rite were withdrawn from the jurisdiction of the pontifical commission for Russian affairs and came under the Sacred Eastern Congregation.

These Russian Catholics have the Byzantine liturgy, in Church Slavonic, in strict accordance with the Russian so-called synodal books, and their religious customs and outlook are completely Oriental. Russians attach considerable importance to liturgical purity and "hybridization" is carefully avoided. Married men are, of course, entitled to be ordained deacon and priest, but voluntary celibacy is encouraged.

BIBLIOGRAPHY

Pierling, *Rome et Moscou* (Paris, 1883).
d'Herbigny, *Vladimir Solovyev* (London, 1918).
Bennigsen, *et al., Religion in Russia* (London, 1940).
Volkonsky, "Aperçu sur l'origine de l'Eglise catholique byzantine-slave en Russie" in *L'Unité de l'Eglise*, No. 42 (Paris, 1930).
Attwater, "Leonid Feodorov" in St. Michael's Guild pamphlet *The Eastern Churches* (New York, 1939).
Berg, *Die römisch-katholische Kirche und die orthodoxen Russen* (Berlin, 1926).
Iswolsky, *Light Before Dusk* (New York, 1942).

11. OTHER BYZANTINE ELEMENTS

Albania. Two thirds of the Albanians are Mohammedan; the rest are dissident Orthodox and Latin Catholics in the proportion of about two to one.[46] From 1628 there was a body of Catholics of the Byzantine rite in the coastal region of Chimarra, served for a time by Basilian monks from Sicily, but the mission collapsed in 1765. They had a vicar apostolic from 1692 till 1737.

Since 1922, when the Orthodox Albanians began to agitate for independence from the patriarch of Constantinople, there has been some talk of reunion with Rome. About 1920 this step was taken by the archimandrite Germanos at Elbassan, and he ministers to the small group of people who followed him.

Georgia, or Iberia, lies between Armenia and Russia, south of the Caucasus, and was evangelized during the fourth century, probably from Armenia and Syria.[47] Later, it came under the influence of Constantinople and drifted into schism in the earlier years of the thirteenth century. From then on Western missionaries worked in Georgia, and at least one king and one katholikos were formally Catholic. In 1801 the Emperor Alexander I annexed Georgia to his dominions, and its Orthodox church became an exarchate of the Church of Russia; it was released from this at the revolution, only to fall into the hands of a Soviet socialist republic.

In 1917 there were 2½ million Orthodox Georgians and about 40,000 Catholics, of whom 32,000 were of the Latin rite and the rest of the Armenian (Byzantine Catholics were not allowed in

---

[46] The mountainous district of the north is pretty solidly Catholic. There our priests are most picturesque people, with huge moustaches but no beard.

[47] The national apostle is a rather mysterious female saint, Nino. She is commemorated in the Roman Martyrology on December 15, under the style of *Sancta Christiana, ancilla.*

imperial Russia). Today there are a few hundred of the Byzantine rite, whose liturgical language is Georgian. They are ministered to by priests of a congregation founded at Constantinople by Father Peter Karischiaranti in 1861 to minister to his countrymen of whatever rite. He also founded an auxiliary sisterhood. There is (or was) an administrator apostolic at Tiflis for all the Georgians in U.S.S.R.

It is planned for a Georgian Byzantine priest to be in residence at Paris, where a small number of Catholic Georgian residents frequent the "foreigners' church," rue de Sèvres.

Estonia. Estonia is predominantly a Lutheran country, but there are 200,000 Orthodox (a third of them Russians) and a few Latin Catholics. For some years Catholic priests of the Byzantine rite (Capuchins and Jesuits) ministered in two centres, Narva and Esna. Progress was slow but promising; but the Soviet annexation of Estonia has put an end to the work indefinitely.

Finland. Finland is a Protestant country with a small Orthodox minority, including some Russians. The beginning of a Byzantine Catholic centre was made at Terrioki in 1938, but it was broken up by the Russo-Finnish war in the following year. It is hoped to begin the work again at Helsinki or elsewhere.

Latvia. There were the beginnings of a Catholic Byzantine group in this country, thanks to a Russian priest, Father Vasilyev, and Professor Valpitro of Riga University. Soviet domination has no doubt brought this work to an end.

BIBLIOGRAPHY

Peacock, *Albania* (London, 1914).
Tamarati, *L'Eglise Géorgienne* (Rome, 1910).
Karst, *Litterature Géorgienne chrétienne* (Paris, 1934).

CHAPTER V

THE ALEXANDRIAN RITE

1. THE COPTS

FROM its beginnings the heresy of Monophysism (see p. 4) had its stronghold in Egypt, where the patriarch of Alexandria, Dioscoros, was its spokesman and leader. After six years of controversy and violence he was deposed and his teaching condemned by the Council of Chalcedon in 451. Practically all the clergy and people of Egypt (and many in Syria) refused to accept the decisions of the council, not altogether on account of religious enthusiasm but because political passions also were involved: it was bad enough to be subject to a foreign emperor without having "Byzantine theology" as well. The century that followed was an outrageous period of ecclesiastical quarreling, minor schisms, persecution, political chicanery, and physical violence. The see of Alexandria was bandied between hierarchs who were sometimes orthodox but more often monophysite, till in 567 two lines of patriarchs were definitely established: one for the mostly foreign minority of orthodox Catholics, the other for the solid mass of Egyptian Monophysites, today called the Coptic Church.[1] With the modification that the orthodox line is now in schism from Rome, that is still the position.

The monophysite Egyptians continued to be troubled by domestic quarrels, by the Catholics, and in 616–628, by Persian invaders who bitterly persecuted them. Eleven years later the Arab conquest was begun, and the anti-imperialist Copts are

---

[1] A Copt is simply an Egyptian (Arabic *Kibti*=Gk. [Aἰ] *gúpt* [ιos]), in actual use a Christian Egyptian.

132

said to have given aid to the Khalifah against the Byzantines. They had their reward, and for century after century were oppressed by Arabs, Mameluks, and Turks; massacres were frequent and apostasies so numerous that today 90 per cent of the Egyptians are Mohammedan. But there were also many martyrs. The Copts did not get on well with the Crusaders, and though two legates of the Coptic patriarch John II signed an act of union at the Council of Florence it never became effective. An attempt at reunion by the patriarch Gabriel VIII in 1594 was no more successful.

Early in the seventeenth century Capuchin missions were established in the Levant by Father Joseph of Paris (Joseph Leclerc du Tremblay, "Grey Eminence"), and a foundation was made at Cairo in 1630. For a time it prospered, under the direction of Father Agathangelo of Vendôme. The patriarch opened all his churches to the friars, and Father Agathangelo gave spiritual conferences in the schismatical monasteries of the Lower Thebaid.[2] Unhappily, and not for the only time in history, the great obstacle to reunion was the European Catholics resident in the country. Father Agathangelo referred to the household of the French consul as a "synagogue of Satan," and the general behaviour of the Europeans was such than when the Coptic patriarch complained bitterly that "the Roman Church in this country is a brothel" Father Agathangelo could not deny his reasons for saying so. He appealed to the cardinal prefect of Propaganda to have the worst offenders excommunicated. But nothing was done, and Father Agathangelo went off in despair to Ethiopia and to martyrdom.

THE CATHOLIC COPTS

In 1675 the Friars Minor of the Observance were given charge of a prefecture apostolic in Upper Egypt and the Jesuits came to Cairo, but the Coptic mission languished until 1741,

---

[2] One of the two books he used for this purpose was *On the Holy Will of God*, by Father Benedict of Canfield (William Fitch), the first Capuchin missionary in England in penal times. Father Agathangelo and his companion, Father Cassian, were beatified in 1905.

when the dissident bishop living at Jerusalem, Anba Athanasius, became a Catholic and was put in charge of those of his rite. At this time the learned Raphael Tukhi was editing and publishing the Coptic liturgical books in Rome and was made ordaining bishop for Coptic seminarists in the city. The first two successors of Anba Athanasius as vicars apostolic, John Faragi (1781) and Matthew Righet (1788), could not receive episcopal consecration, apparently because there was no Catholic bishop in Egypt and a voyage to Europe was too difficult. The third, Maximos Joed, was nominated in 1824 and consecrated by a Byzantine, Ignatius V Kattan, Melkite patriarch of Antioch. Meanwhile, the Catholic Copts had no churches of their rite and had to use those of the Franciscans; this and the overlapping of jurisdictions caused numerous difficulties. It was believed that the khedive Mohammed Ali wished the Catholics to have a patriarchate of their own, and accordingly it was erected by Pope Leo XII in 1824. But it was not made operative, and there was a further succession of three vicars apostolic, of whom the learned Aghapios Bishai represented his church at the Vatican Council.

In 1893 the Franciscans made over ten churches to the sole use of the Copts, and two years later Pope Leo XIII divided them into three dioceses and appointed Cyril Makarios as administrator; in 1899 he was advanced to the rank of patriarch. From this time onward the Catholics of the Coptic rite have continued to increase in numbers and effectiveness. Anba Makarios held a synod of his church at Cairo in 1898, and continued to govern it for ten years, when certain difficulties made it necessary for him to resign. He went into schism for a time. The patriarchal throne has since remained vacant, being administered now by Anba Mark Khuzam, the bishop of Thebes.

PRESENT STATE

Patriarch. His title is "Patriarch of Alexandria of the Copts." His powers are stated in the decree of erection of the see to be the same as those of the other patriarchs, but these vary. The civil power recognizes him (and during a vacancy the administrator) as the competent judge in the matrimonial and testamentary causes of his people.

Bishops. The Coptic sees are Alexandria (comprising the whole of Lower Egypt, with residence at Cairo), Hermopolis Major (residence at Minieh), and Thebes (residence at Tahta). The bishops are at present appointed by the Holy See.

Parochial clergy. The senior seminary founded by Pope Leo XIII at Tahta in 1899 was reorganized in 1920, and the junior seminary, conducted by the Jesuits at Cairo from 1879 till 1907, was reopened in 1927. Both are now directed by the Coptic secular clergy, the junior seminarians studying under Jesuit professors at a neighbouring college. Other aspirants go to the Oriental seminary at Bairut. The clergy have been bound to celibacy since the synod of 1898, but dispensations are sometimes accorded, especially in the case of married priests converted from Monophysism. About four fifths of the eighty Coptic priests are celibate.

Religious institutes. The *African Missionaries of Lyons* administer three districts in Lower Egypt, under the jurisdiction of the vicar apostolic of the Latins in the Nile delta. Two of their priests have adopted the Coptic rite. The *Friars Minor* have recently opened the College of St. Cyril at Ghiza to train aspirants of this rite for their order. The *Coptic Sisters of the Sacred Heart* have convents and schools in Cairo, Tahta, and Sohag.

The Faithful. In 1894 there were 5000 Catholics of the Coptic rite; in 1946 there were 63,000.[3] With a few individual exceptions they are of the poorest class of Egyptian *fellahin*. The Jesuits have done much educational and spiritual work for them since 1879, and the Friars Minor minister to many in their Egyptian vicariate.

---

[3] There are still 900,000 dissidents. The better among the laity and lower clergy tend to be dissatisfied with their own church and to turn toward Catholicism. But as we lack means to build churches and schools and train priests, Protestant missions reap much of this harvest. For some years abjurations of heresy have averaged over 1100 a year.

LITURGY AND CUSTOMS

Church buildings. A church of the Coptic rite has a distinctive arrangement. It is divided for the whole of its width into sanctuary, choir, and nave, and further subdivided for men and women, by screens of carved and inlaid wood, often open lattice work, and as the central door is not closed the altar is never entirely hidden. Within the triple-domed sanctuary (*haikal*) are three altars in a line, each in an apse, standing clear of the wall; they are of brick or stone with a wooden top, without gradines, wholly covered by linen or silk cloths; on each are a crucifix and two candles and a sort of box (*al-kursi*) in which the chalice stands during the Liturgy. On the *haikal*-screen are a few pictures and others, with mosaics and wall-paintings, around the church. Actually many Catholic Coptic churches át the present day are tiny tumble-down buildings with no screens and having a "Western" altar with gradines and flowerpots, but preserving the wooden *mensa* (tablet); the Blessed Sacrament is reserved in a tabernacle. Such innovations as seats and statues are sometimes seen. The cathedral of the bishop of Thebes at Tahta is planned in the traditional way; the same applies to Minieh, but it has been long unfinished for lack of funds.[4]

Vestments. These correspond to those of the Byzantine rite. The chasuble (*burnus*) is open all down the front, rather like a cope. Bishops wear the Latin mitre, but for crozier have the Eastern twined serpents; they also wear the *omophorion* but not the *sakkos*. Servers are seen in surprising costumes — cottas, albs, stoles, and lace collars. Out of church the clerical hat (the dissidents wear a turban) is a black cylinder about six inches high, growing wider to the top — a thoroughly Egyptian-looking headdress (bishops cover it with a veil). All wear the wide-sleeved *rason* over the cassock.

---

[4] The average superficial area of the three Catholic Coptic pro-cathedrals was about 16 square yards. There is a curious bit of folklore to account for the lavish use of ostrich-eggs as an ornament in Coptic and other Levantine churches. They may have really been used originally to prevent mice climbing down the cords and getting at the oil in the many hanging lamps.

Liturgical books. These were arranged and printed in Rome by Raphael Tukhi between 1736 and 1764. Mgr. Makarios published the missal, ritual, and office-book at Cairo (1898–1906), and some of them have been reprinted there since, the Divine Office in 1930, revised by Mgr. Khuzam.

Altar-vessels and bread. The vessels are very similar to those of the Latin rite, with three small and two large veils to cover the offerings, but the paten is larger and deeper. The bread (*korban*) is leavened, round, and thick, marked with twelve crosses. *Ripidia* are carried in processions, and a hand-cross is used to give some blessings.

Music. The Coptic lay people have a remarkable knowledge of the text of their liturgy and they take an active part in a solemn celebration, singing the traditional chant by heart, with copious variations. Some of this music was first written down by the Jesuit fathers Blin and Badet at the end of the past century. Cymbals, triangles, and occasionally the flute (*mizmar*) are the only instruments.

Liturgical language. This is Coptic (i.e., the last stage of Egyptian, a tongue otherwise dead for centuries),[5] with many Greek words and some phrases. Arabic is the vernacular of Egypt and more and more tends unofficially to displace Coptic in the Liturgy: it is used officially for the Divine Office and certain occasional rites. The Bohaïric dialect of Lower Egypt is used throughout the country.

THE EUCHARISTIC LITURGY

The Coptic Liturgy is a form of the original Greek Liturgy of Alexandria with three alternative *anaphoras:* an adaptation of the Byzantine "St. Basil" for use on ordinary days and Sundays; "of St. Mark," or "St. Cyril," used on his and St. Cyril's feasts and when a bishop is consecrated; and "of St. Gregory Nazianzen," for great feasts (this last is addressed throughout to our Lord). The Catholics have a form of "Low Mass," which

---

[5] Father Wansleben, O.P., claimed to know an Egyptian at Cairo in the seventeenth century who spoke Coptic naturally.

is celebrated in a low voice. The Coptic Liturgy (*Korban*) may be concelebrated with any number of celebrants on specific occasions; there is no Liturgy of the Presanctified. An English version of this Liturgy can be found in the present writer's *Eastern Catholic Worship*.

THE DIVINE OFFICE

There are seven "hours," collectively called *al-Agbieh*, namely Prayer of Sunset (*al-Ghurub*), of Repose (*an-Naum*), of Midnight (*Nusf al-Lail*), of the Dawn (*al-Bakar*), and of the Third, Sixth, and Ninth Hours; bishops and religious have an extra evening office, "of the Veil" (*as-Satar*). The night-office has three nocturns of twelve psalms and a Gospel each, with *troparia*, and prayers, and the Creed after each nocturn; the other hours each consists of twelve psalms (some "at choice"), a Gospel and *troparia* (*al-Bakar* has nineteen psalms); all the hours have several short prayers, the *Trisagion*, Our Father, and *Kyrie eleison* (41 times). Nearly all the Office is in Arabic since 1906.

THE SACRAMENTS

Baptism is a long ceremony. After prayers and blessing of the oil of catechumens the priest anoints the forehead, breast, hands, and back of the child. Then there are exorcisms, renunciations, and profession of faith by the godparent, and the anointings of the breast and hands are repeated. The water is blessed at great length: there are three lessons and a Gospel, prayers for the sick, dead, and others not immediately concerned, a little oil of catechumens is poured into the water three times and it is breathed upon crosswise thrice; there is a marvellous panegyrical exorcism and benediction of the water, modeled on the prayer of the eucharistic *anaphora*, and a little chrism is added. Then the deacon brings the child "from the west to the east over against Jordan" (the font), and the priest immerses it three times saying, "N., I baptize thee in the name of the Father...," etc. Baptism is administered by pouring water in cases of necessity, of adults, and of conditional baptism.[6] The rite ends with a characteristic "prayer at the pouring away of the water."

Confirmation follows immediately. The child is anointed with chrism on the forehead, mouth, hands, breast, back, and soles of the feet, in such a way as to make 21 anointings, with varying formulas; then the priest imposes his right hand and breathes on the child, saying, "Receive the Holy Ghost and be a cleansed vessel. . . . ." The child is dressed in a white robe, with a girdle and fillet ("crown") and final prayers are said, followed by a procession and Liturgy.

Penance. Absolution is given in a long deprecatory formula: " . . . Do thou, O God, grant him forgiveness of his sins, and may he be absolved by the all-holy Trinity, Father, Son, and Holy Ghost, through my unworthy mouth. . . . "

Eucharist. Communion in both kinds has never been abolished among the Catholic Copts, but in practice it is at present unusual. Ordinarily the communicant receives in one kind, kneeling, the words of administration being, "This is in truth the body of Emmanuel our God." The receiver answers, "Amen."

Anointing. Again a very long rite, in which seven priests one by one light seven lamps or candles, with an epistle, psalm, Gospel, and prayer at each lighting. Finally the Gospel-book is laid on his head and the sick man is anointed once on the forehead and wrists, with a prayer that he may be healed in body and soul, and further prayers (including "Glory to God in the highest") said. In practice one priest only is present and he lights all seven lamps, with the prayers appropriate thereto; an abridged version of this rite was published for Catholic use in 1933.

Orders. Singers are ordained by a prayer and a blessing, readers and subdeacons by imposition of hands on the temples; deacons and priests receive two impositions of the right hand

---

[6] This is often necessary for converts from the dissidents, owing to the careless and fanciful ways in which some of their priests administer the sacrament.

on the head, and are invested with the girdle and stole respectively. The formula for ordaining a bishop names the powers which he is to exercise, and all bishops present lay their hands twice on his shoulders and forearms and breathe on his face. The formula for a priest is: "Fill him with the Holy Spirit and the grace and wisdom . . . ," etc. "We call you N., to be a priest for the ministry of the altar which was first given to right-believers, in the name of the Father. . . . Amen."

Marriage. The wedding service consists of two parts, the betrothal (epistle and Gospel, three long prayers, the Creed, a thanksgiving, and a blessing of the wedding garments) and the crowning. After an epistle (Ephes. 5:22–6:3), Gospel (Matt. 19:1–6), litany, and prayers, the priest blesses oil and anoints both parties on the head and wrists; then he crowns them while "Worthy the bridegroom and his bride" is sung thrice. The rite is concluded by exhortations, broken up by antiphons sung by the choir.

Kalendar. The Copts date their years according to the "era of the Martyrs," i.e., beginning from August 29 or September 13, 284, the date of the accession of Diocletian. Their year has twelve months of thirty days each, and a "little month," ordinarily of five days (these lines are written on Pharemuthi 7, 1650, i.e., April 2, 1934, according to them), but the Catholics of Lower Egypt fix Easter by the Gregorian computation and those of Upper Egypt by the computation of the patriarch Demetrios (d. 231).

Feasts are divided into three classes, and there are numerous saints' days, most of them Egyptian. A number of festivals are common to the Coptic and Roman kalendars, but most of them fall on different dates; they commemorate the Primacy of St. Peter the Apostle on Mesore 7 (July 31), together with the High-Priesthood of Aaron. Peculiar festivals are those of the Four Incorporeal Living Creatures (Ezech. 1:5–14), referring them to the four evangelists, and of the Four and Twenty Elders (Apoc. 4:4). These are also commemorated in the eucharistic liturgy. Of more recent Western feasts, Corpus Christi and the

Sacred Heart are the principal ones adopted. Sundays and nine other days are holydays of obligation.

Penitential seasons. During Lent (47 days) fasting from food, drink, and tobacco lasts till noon and abstinence is observed even on Sundays. Abstinence is further observed on every Wednesday and Friday (except in paschal-time), for sixteen days before Christmas, three before SS. Peter and Paul, and fifteen before the Assumption. A fortnight before Lent begins there are three days of penitence called the "fast of Nineveh." This observance is known in all Eastern churches except the Byzantine: it commemorates the penance of the Ninevites at the preaching of Jonas.

General observations. Copts make the sign of the cross from left to right, and the Catholic lay people show respect by genuflecting instead of the customary prostration on both knees, which in confined to the Liturgy. Water is solemnly blessed at the Epiphany (a common Eastern custom, referring to our Lord's baptism), at the Supper of the New Covenant, i.e., Maundy Thursday, and on SS. Peter and Paul's day; on the last two days there is a washing of feet in every church. The usual Western devotions, Benediction of the Blessed Sacrament, rosary, stations of the cross, etc., are practised, but the effects of Western influence are far less noticeable in Upper than in Lower Egypt, as might be expected.

BIBLIOGRAPHY

Khuzam, *The Catholic Coptic Mission* (Cairo, 1929).
Bute, *The Coptic Morning Service* (London, 1908).
Woolley, *Coptic Offices* (London, 1930).
Blin, *Chants liturgiques des Coptes* (Cairo, 1889).
Macaire, *Historie de l'Eglise d'Alexandrie* (Cairo, 1894).
O'Leary, *The Saints of Egypt* (London, 1938).

2. THE ETHIOPIANS

The Ethiopians[7] proper are partly of Semitic stock, and their ancestors before the Christian era probably emigrated to Africa from southern Arabia. They now occupy the mountainous country between the Sudan, Kenya, and the sea. They are homogeneous neither in race nor religion, but the nucleus is Ethiopic and Christian.

The first authentic evangelization of the Ethiopians of which there is record was toward the middle of the fourth century, when two youths from Tyre, Frumentius and Aedesius, spared from a massacre of their fellow voyagers, attained influence at the Ethiopian court at Aksum and preached the Gospel there. St. Frumentius was eventually consecrated bishop for his converts by the then archbishop of Alexandria, the great St. Athanasius himself. A more extensive evangelization was carried on some hundred and fifty years later by the "Nine Saints," who were monks and probably Monophysites from Syria. In the time of Justinian there was lively competition between the Catholics and Monophysites of Egypt for control of the Ethiopic mission; the last-named won, and the Ethiopian church has ever since remained hierarchically dependent on the Coptic patriarch of Alexandria, and accordingly monophysite. Until the sixteenth century little is known of the history of Christianity in Ethiopia: especially after the Arab conquest of Egypt communication even with the oppressed mother-church was difficult and often interrupted. There was a religious and intellectual revival in the

---

[7] "Ethiopia" and "Ethiopians" are to be preferred because those are their own names for their country and themselves, and there is nothing against them. The more usual "Abyssinia" and "Abyssinians" originated as an offensive nickname, "the mongrels."

thirteenth century, followed by the arrival of Dominican missionaries, who for a time had some success. A bishop of Syrian nationality was sent from Jerusalem, but persecution began and the mission was broken up. The relics of the martyrs are still venerated, even by the dissidents, around Neebi. A further Dominican effort in the fifteenth century led to the sending of an embassy to the Council of Florence and another to Rome, of which the only result was the establishment by Pope Sixtus IV of a church, monastery, and hospice for Ethiopian pilgrims behind St. Peter's, San Stefano dei Mori, "of the Moors."[8] At the end of the century there was an abortive mission by the Friars Minor.

At the beginning of the sixteenth century Ethiopia was engaged in a struggle with Mohammedan invaders, and the negus Labna Danghel (1508–1540), who had come into contact with Catholicity through the Portugese military expeditions in the Red Sea, asked the king of Portugal to get the pope to send a prelate who would take the place of their primate from Egypt, hoping thereby to get Portuguese military aid as well. After a curious incident in which a Portugese adventurer, a physician named Bermudez, became abuna[9] for a short time, St. Ignatius Loyola organized a mission, and in 1555 Pope Julius III appointed a Portuguese Jesuit, Nuñez Barreto, as "patriarch of Ethiopia," with two other bishops and ten priests. Barreto never reached his destination and, though his fellow bishop Andrew Oviedo was able to, the mission had not much success: Labna Danghel's successors were not favourable to Catholicity, the danger of

---

[8] A monk who lived here, Tasfa Sion, published in 1548–1549 a translation of the New Testament into Ge'ez, which included the "common parts" and one *anaphora* of the Ethiopian Liturgy with a Latin version — the first published text of it. The monastery was unoccupied by 1700 and came for a time into the hands of the Copts, when it sheltered their great liturgical scholar, Raphael Tukhi (d. 1787). It is now the Pontifical Ethiopian College. A manuscript (Brit. Mus. Harl. MS. 5512) written here for the Ethiopian bishop Sahyun in 1549 contains a reference to "the cardinal of England," i.e., Reginald Pole.

[9] *Abuna,* "our father," is the title of the metropolitan of Ethiopia since the days of St. Frumentius himself, who was called *Abuna* or *Abba Salama,* "father of peace."

invasion was less pressing and, moreover, the Portugese had asked for one third of the kingdom, as well as the religious submission of the people, as the price of their assistance.

The mission had practically died out when a new development took place with the arrival, in 1603, of Father Peter Paez, a Jesuit of outstanding ability, of whom "the learned men of Gondar, even the most anti-Roman of them, still speak with admiration" (incidentally, he rediscovered the sources of the Blue Nile). He gained great influence over the negus Susneyos (Malak Sagad III, 1607–1632), who undertook a number of religious reforms and after some years was reconciled with the Holy See. At once abuna Simeon excommunicated him, stirred up the people, and civil war broke out; it lasted for five years. Susneyos was victorious and proclaimed union with Rome for his whole kingdom.

About this time Paez died (he was buried close by Lake Tsana), and Pope Gregory XV sent Father Alfonso Mendez to take his place. Many of the Ethiopians were again in revolt: they had been badly upset by decrees against concubinage, divorce, and so forth, and now the mistaken zeal of Mendez began to alter their rites and ceremonies to conform with Roman usages, and to impose celibacy on a pastoral clergy of whom practically every one was legitimately married. On the other hand, many of them welcomed the union; and all might have been well had not Susneyos and his officials sought to impose the reforms, necessary and unnecessary alike, by methods of the grossest cruelty and persecution: documents published by St. Bonaventura's College at Florence in 1928 disclose a state of affairs that is almost unbelievable. The upshot was that when Fasilidas succeeded his father as negus in 1632 he let loose a counterpersecution and banished all Catholic priests from his country; in this work he was helped by a German Lutheran physician named Peter Heyling. The successor of Mendez, Appolinario de Almeida, who for eight years faced every suffering and danger, was put to death with two companions, as were the Capuchin friars Agathangelo of Vendôme and Cassian of Nantes, who were beatified as martyrs by Pope Pius X in 1905.

MAR EMMANUEL THOMAS (d. 1947)
Patriarch Katholikos of Babylon of the Chaldeans

THE CHALDEAN LITURGY
The Celebrant Sings the Gospel

ARMENIAN CATHEDRAL AT BZOMMAR

CHALDEAN CHURCH AT MOSUL

RUSSIAN PRIEST

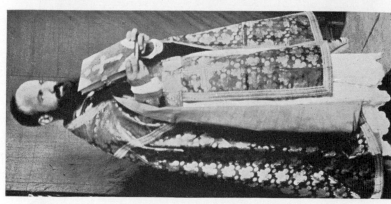

SYRIAN PRIEST

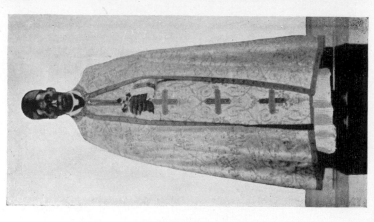

ETHIOPIAN PRIEST

Pope Urban VIII had entrusted a new Ethiopian mission to the Franciscans, but it was fruitless, except in persecution for the missioners: the cause of unity had been ruined in Ethiopia for many generations to come.

This is one of the two outstanding examples of large bodies of Christians being lost to Catholic unity primarily through European arrogance and insufficiency; both were in the seventeenth century, and in both the Portugese were the Europeans at fault: the other one was Malabar (see p. 212 ff.). Cardinal Hinsley, writing about Ethiopia in the *Dublin Review* of October, 1935, said justly: "The coercive measures against the schismatics, enforced by Susneyos and more or less countenanced by the Jesuits, even though in accord with Abyssinian mentality and the customs of the age, were inexcusable in the eyes of the Church and before the court of Christian civilization. But indiscreet zeal soon brought its own punishment, and the zealots were the pitiable victims."

THE CATHOLIC ETHIOPIANS

Ethiopia was closed to Catholic priests for two hundred years: a native bishop, George Egziabahar, sent there from Rome at the end of the eighteenth century was simply murdered, and several Capuchins had suffered before him. An attempt to establish relations, in accordance with tradition, between the Ethiopians and the Catholic Copts through Theodore abu-Karim, vicar apostolic in Egypt, came to nothing. The ordinary fate of any Catholic priest in Ethiopia was violent death. But in 1839 the famous Irish-French traveller Arnauld d'Abbadie d'Arrast used his influence to get a prefecture apostolic established at Adua; it was confided to the Lazarists, with Blessed Justin de Jacobis at their head, who did a wonderful work until he was banished in 1855. In 1846 the Capuchins established a vicariate in the Galla country under Mgr. (afterwards Cardinal) Massaia, and another vicariate was organized from Alitiena by the Lazarists.

Mgr. de Jacobis opened a seminary which he put in charge of a distinguished ex-monophysite monk, Gabra Michael, who eventually reconciled the reigning negus with Rome. But in 1854 this ruler was deposed by the vigorous soldier Kassa (Theodore II), and abandoned his faith in the face of persecution. The dissident primate, Salama, was recalled, and he seized and tortured Abba Michael in a vain attempt to make him apostatize. Having been reprieved from death upon the intervention of the British consul Walter Chichele Plowden (who had supported Theodore's usurpation), he was sentenced to perpetual imprisonment and died from hardship and exposure three months later. Gabra Michael was beatified as a martyr in 1926. In such ways did the Catholic Church in Ethiopia begin slowly to recover the souls who were thrown away by European aggressiveness in the seventeenth century. The accession of Menelik II in 1889 brought peace to the missionaries and their flocks.

PRESENT STATE

Organization. The Catholics of the Galla and Kaffa districts, converts from heathenism, are all of the Latin rite and therefore are no concern of ours here; so are some of those of the Lazarist vicariate in the northern part of the country: it was some time before there were any facilities for enabling Catholic Ethiopians to continue in the usages to which they were accustomed. But this was remedied in the north by the time the Capuchins were given a separate prefecture in Eritrea in 1894, and in 1930 an ordinariate of Eastern rite was formed in that Italian colony, Abba Khidaneh-Mariam Kassa being appointed its first bishop, with the title of the old African see of Thibaris. His residence is at Asmara, which is a great educational centre. There is a technical college at Sanganeiti, and schools and orphanages elsewhere.

Parochial clergy. In 1919 Pope Benedict XV restored the church behind St. Peter's, the old St. Stephen's of the Abyssinians ("Moors"), to serve as the chapel for a college of their rite which he founded close by. This seminary is under the charge of the Capuchins, with an Ethiopian priest as spiritual director. There is an Oriental seminary for them in Eritrea, and the Lazarist seminaries in the neighbouring vicariate are available for aspirants of the Eastern rite. These are bound to celibacy, but married priests returned from schism are given a dispensation.

Religious institutes. Monasticism (often of a very loose kind) has always been widespread in Ethiopia, and there are today hundreds of monks among the dissidents. To provide for Catholics, twenty-three young Ethiopians and two priests were in 1931 accepted at the Cistercian abbey of Casamiri, in Italy, to be trained to form a nucleus of Catholic monks in their own country. Sixteen of these young men were "professed" in 1933, and a monastery has now been opened near Asmara. There are nuns, too, of a kind now surviving nowhere else in the Church: they take a private vow of perfect chastity, but are not bound to the common life; there are about a hundred of these sisters, living in their homes and engaged in works of mercy.

The Faithful number about 28,000 in Eritrea, and 2500 under the care of the Lazarist vicar apostolic elsewhere, having ninety priests (there are rather less Latin Ethiopians and probably some four million dissidents, with as many Mohammedans and heathens). They are an intelligent people, devoted to their religion, but for the most part ignorant and poor. There is a tiny colony of Catholic Ethiopians at Jerusalem.

In 1935 the Italian dictator Mussolini invaded Ethiopia and on May 8, 1936, announced the annexation of the whole country to the Italian crown. In the years that followed there was some outside criticism of the Holy See for its alleged alacrity and thoroughness in trying to use for ecclesiastical ends the political situation, brought about by barefaced aggression. But, quite apart from the fact that Rome did little more than reorganize already existing mission territory in view of new conditions, the Italian civil authorities actually favoured the Mohammedans at the expense of Christians. Even in Eritrea, Ethiopian Catholics (especially those who had some education) strongly opposed the invaders (not always for strictly patriotic reasons); and on the whole it would seem that the Italian invasion did less harm to the cause of reunion than might have been expected. In any case the Ethiopians had shown themselves little disposed to give up their religious isolation and errors. Eritrea was an Italian province for over fifty years, but in 1939 there were still only about 28,000 Ethiopian Catholics there in a population of over 600,000: this does not suggest the likelihood of any great change in the country at large.

Certain laws in restraint of foreign clergy have been revived, but their scope is not altogether clear. The future of the Church in Ethiopia is evidently with the national rite and the indigenous clergy.

LITURGY AND CUSTOMS

The Ethiopic liturgical rite is substantially that of the Copts, translated into Ge'ez, but owing to need of revision of the books the Catholics for some time used the Roman rite in that tongue, as they still do for some purposes. Pope Pius XI ordered that this revision should be carried out in strict accordance with the best Ethiopic liturgical tradition and this has been done so far as the text is concerned, but European influence has led to some regrettable modifications in accessories: a glaring example is the church of the Ethiopian College itself at Rome, which is completely Western, even to the Latin text upon the altar cloth.[10]

Church buildings. The normal plan of an Ethiopian church is now circular, divided into three concentric circles with the altar in the middle, but there are many old churches of basilican shape in Ethiopia and those of the Catholics are rectangular. The dissidents treat with great reverence the *tabot*, a box on the altar that contains the wooden altar-board (there are national legends about the Queen of Sheba and the Ark of the Covenant concerning this piece of furniture); Catholics replace it by a tabernacle containing the Blessed Sacrament, and the altar top is of stone.

Vestments. These are of the usual Eastern type, with a very

---

[10] This is the sort of thing that provokes non-Catholic Orientals to maintain that, whatever the Holy See may say, the Roman policy is to "hybridize" Eastern Christians with the ultimate object, or result, of making them Latins.

full chasuble having a sort of embroidered shoulder-cape attached, from which depend four short "orphreys"; bishops and other dignitaries wear a "crown" of a very exotic pattern. But Catholics often wear almost purely Byzantine vestments, and the bishop has the Roman mitre and crozier. Clerical dress consists of a round black cap (or else a *kalemaukion*) with a wide-sleeved gown over a cassock.

Liturgical books. The book of the Liturgy was published at Asmara in 1890 and 1913, but in an unsatisfactory form; an entirely new edition was undertaken at Rome, and it appeared, excellently printed by the Vatican Press, in 1945. Some years earlier the Ethiopic rite of ordination was printed for the first time. An edition of the Divine Office is expected before long; at present only the Psalter is available. The Ge'ez version of the Roman *Rituale* was last printed, at Asmara, in 1924; the proper Ethiopic rites will become available in due course.

Altar-vessels and bread. The altar-vessels are as in the Latin rite. The bread is an extraordinary example of hybridization: in Eritrea, unleavened is practically universally used by Catholics; elsewhere, unleavened at a "Low Mass" but leavened at a solemn celebration. Blessings are given with a hand-cross.

Music. The Ethiopian chant, enharmonic, of course, has received little study. To Western ears it is wailing and barbaric, and is accompanied *ad libitum* by drums, cymbals, and rattles or bells. Some of the chants bear a strong resemblance to those of the Jewish synagogue, and other influences can be detected.

Liturgical language. This is Ge'ez,[11] the classical Ethiopian tongue, a semitic language closely allied to Arabic, dead since before the thirteenth century. The present vernacular dialects, principally Amharic and Tigre, are probably descended from a sister language of Ge'ez.

THE EUCHARISTIC LITURGY

As has been said above, the Liturgy (*Keddase*) is "according to the order of our fathers the Egyptians," translated into Ge'ez

---

[11] Meaning "free," i.e., the language of the ruling people.

and modified by time. There are seventeen *anaphoras,* that "of
the Apostles" being most commonly used, and this one is, in
fact, independent of the Coptic rite, though derived from Egypt
through the ancient *Ethiopic Church Order.* The "common"
parts of the Liturgy are a form of the Alexandrian "St. Mark."
There is no concelebration or Liturgy of the Presanctified; the
Catholics have a form of "low" celebration for ordinary days.
There is an English version of the Liturgy in the present writer's
Eastern Catholic Worship.

THE DIVINE OFFICE

The Ethiopic office consists almost entirely of psalms, with
lessons from the prophets and short poetical compositions
interspersed.

THE SACRAMENTS

With the exception of the Eucharist and pontifical offices, these
are all administered according to the Roman forms, in Ge'ez,
pending the revision of the Ethiopian books. Until recently the
priest administered *Confirmation* after Baptism, but now it is
deferred and given by the bishop or his delegate.

Eucharist. Among Catholics there is diversity and a good
deal of freedom in the manner of receiving Communion. At a
solemn Liturgy it is always in both kinds, standing; at a "Low
Mass" generally in one only, but sometimes in both. At the
Ethiopian College in Rome communion in one kind is altogether
forbidden. The Body and Blood are administered separately (the
Blood in a spoon); the words used are, respectively, "The bread
of life which came down from heaven, the body of Christ,"
and "The cup of life which came down from heaven, the
precious blood of Christ." The recipient replies "Amen" to the
first, and "Amen, Amen" to the second.

Kalendar. According to Ethiopian chronology we are now
(1946) in the year A.D. 1938, but their annual kalendar is
similar to that of the Copts. Their new year's day is August 29
according to the Julian reckoning, September 11 according to

the Gregorian which the Catholics follow (at the cost of much complication).

Feasts. The kalendar of feasts is that of the Copts, with local saints added or substituted, *e.g.,* Takla Haymanot, on December 24. It has had to undergo a good deal of modification for Catholic use, for the dissidents celebrate, e.g., Pontius Pilate — because he said he was innocent! But no later Western feasts have yet been adopted.

Penitential seasons. There are forty fasting days in Lent, which includes Sundays (a unique observance); fifteen days before the Assumption; three days "of Niniveh" before Lent; the eves of Christmas and the Epiphany; and in a modified form every Wednesday and Friday. Strict fasting includes abstinence from eggs and milk as well as meat, but there is no fasting at all during the fifty days of paschal-time.

BIBLIOGRAPHY

Colbeaux, *Histoire politique et religieuse de l'Abyssinie* (Paris, n. d.), 2 vols.

Jones and Monroe, *Abyssinia* (Oxford, 1935).

Somigli, *Etiopia Francescana nei documenti dei secoli XVII e XVIII* (Quarrachi, 1928), 2 vols.

Selam, *De Indumentis sacris ritus Aethiopici* (Rome, 1930).

La Santa Messa in Rito Etiopico (Rome, 1938).

CHAPTER VI

THE ANTIOCHENE RITE

1. THE SYRIANS

THE position in the patriarchate of Antioch after the Council of Chalcedon was much the same as in that of Alexandria, except that even western Syria was never solidly monophysite like Egypt. Those that refused to accept the Council's decrees were to a considerable extent moved by political, anti-imperial passions, and were egged on by dissident Egyptian monks. The patriarchal throne of Antioch, like that of Egypt, was bandied between orthodox Catholic and monophysite occupants until the Emperor Justinian I imprisoned all bishops professing or suspect of Monophysism. The sect would then probably have died out in Syria had it not been for the action of the Empress Theodora, who favoured the heretics. At the request of the chief of the Ghassanid Arabs, Harath ibn-Jaballah, she procured the clandestine consecration of two monks in the year 543, one of whom, Jacob al-Baradai, spent the rest of his life secretly organizing the Monophysites in Syria. He gave them a patriarch (called "of Antioch" but residing in eastern Syria) and is said to have ordained twenty-seven bishops and over two thousand priests. From this time on there are two churches in Syria, that of the orthodox Catholics (Melkites) and that of the Mono-physites, commonly called the Jacobite Church, after its tireless organizer.

The Jacobites welcomed the Arab invasion in 636, and were alternately patronized and persecuted by their conquerors; large numbers of them turned Mohammedan. They had fairly amiable relations with the Crusaders, and in the twelfth and thirteenth centuries, as in the West and in Ethiopia, there was a revival of religious and intellectual life. Its great ornament was Barhebraeus (Gregory Abdul-Faraj), who was as good as he was learned. At the instance of Dominican and Franciscan missionaries there were several movements for union with Rome, notably in 1237 and 1247, but this promising phase was followed by a long period of internal disorder. After the Council of Florence there was a further prospect of union, but it came to nothing.

In consequence of the encouraging attitude of the then Jacobite patriarch, Naamat-Allah, Pope Gregory XIII sent a legate to Aleppo in 1583, who paved the way for the establishment of the Capuchins and Jesuits there in 1626. Jacobites at once began to come into communion with the Holy See and in such numbers that by 1656 they were strong enough to elect a Catholic, Andrew Akijian, to the vacant Jacobite see of Aleppo. He was consecrated by the Maronite patriarch, and five years later became Syrian patriarch. The dissident Jacobites resorted to violence, and the persecution went on for a hundred years. Andrew's successor was Peter, ex-Jacobite bishop of Jerusalem, to whom the Jacobites opposed a patriarch of their own. In spite of a guarantee of protection obtained by the German emperor from the Turks at the instance of the pope, Peter was thrown into prison at Adana in 1701, together with an archbishop and ten priests. The two prelates died in chains, leaving the Catholic Syrians without a leader, and during the succeeding eighty years they were all but destroyed by the severity of the repressive measures taken against them.

In 1691 their bishop at Mardin, Athanasius Safar, went to South America to collect funds for the establishment of a seminary — surely one of the first to cross the Atlantic on such an errand, and probably the first Syrian to set foot in the New World. Like so many who have followed him, Safar found the Americans to be generous people, and in 1696 he was able to buy a property in Rome. But the enterprise did not prosper, and in 1753 the college was closed and the buildings sold.

In Syria, as elsewhere in the Levant, the activities of the civil representatives of France were often most pernicious at this time. Their consul at Aleppo obtained Turkish support for Andrew Akijian by bribery; and in 1704 the ambassador at Constantinople (Ferréol; cf. p. 183) wrote, "It will be easy for me to make [Isaac bin-Jobair] patriarch of the Syrian at Aleppo." But it was not. Isaac refused the office and retired to Rome, where he translated *The Imitation of Christ* into Syriac.

THE CATHOLIC SYRIANS[1]

Before he died in 1783 the then Jacobite patriarch of Antioch nominated as his successor the archbishop of Aleppo, Mar[2] Michael Jarweh. He had recently become a Catholic and, hastening to take possession of the patriarchal residence at Mardin, he gained the support of four bishops and sent to Rome for confirmation of what he had done. The anti-Catholic party meantime elected another patriarch, who succeeded in getting a *berat* of recognition from the Turkish government before Jarweh, whom he put in prison. Jarweh escaped, first to Bagdad and then to the Lebanon, that secular refuge of persecuted Catholics. He established himself in a Maronite monastery, then a school, at Sharfeh, and governed his followers from there till his death in 1801. Michael Jarweh is accounted the first patriarch of Antioch of the Catholic Syrians.

In 1830 the patriarchal residence was moved to Aleppo and the Turks recognized the Catholics as a separate body from the Jacobites, their patriarch becoming civil head of the "nation" (*milleh*) in 1843. Between 1820 and 1850 five Jacobite bishops submitted to Rome,[3] and in the latter year the patriarch Gregory

---

[1] Sometimes called, with their dissident counterpart the Jacobites, *West Syrians*, or *Pure Syrians*, to distinguish them clearly from the Chaldeans and Nestorians, though a good half of them in fact live in Irak and the eastern parts of Syria.

[2] *Mar* (Syriac, "lord"; fem., *mart*) is used in all Syriac rites as a title for saints and bishops.

[3] For an account of one of them, see Attwater, *Eastern Saints*, s.v., A Syrian Saul.

Jarweh moved his residence to the centre of Jacobite influence, Mardin, persecution both by dissidents and Mohammedans having made Aleppo untenable. This led to more submissions, again including several bishops,[4] but the progress of the Catholic Syrians was abruptly checked by World War I.[5] In 1915 Mar Flavian Michael Malkeh, bishop of Gazirah, was murdered in prison by the Turks, with four of his clergy. The patriarch Ephrem II Rahmani (1898–1929), left Mardin and went to live at Bairut, where the patriarchal residence is now fixed. Rahmani worthily maintained the reputation of the Syrian Church for learning, and his reputation as a scholar extended to the West.[6]

PRESENT STATE

Patriarch. The Syrian Patriarch of Antioch is elected by the bishops of his church, and the choice has to be confirmed by the Holy See, which sends him the *pallium,* but enthronization takes place the Sunday after election.[7] He always takes the name of Ignatius (in memory of the great bishop of his see martyred at Rome *c.* 107) in addition to another name. He has jurisdiction over the faithful of his rite in the old Turkish empire and Egypt; he receives appeals from lower courts, appoints titular bishops at will, summons plenary synods, and consecrates the bishops and chrism for his whole church. He lives at Bairut and deals directly with the Sacred Eastern Congregation. The present

---

[4] And an ex-patriarch, Mar Abdal-Massih, in 1913, but he returned to schism soon after. The only other noteworthy case of schism in recent years was that of Mar Gregory Sattuf, Bishop of Homs, who went back to the Jacobitism in 1905 and later became patriarch. Their original abjurations of Jacobitism were chiefly due to quarrels and grievances — that is so often the case in these "submissions"; the reconciliation of Mar Ivanios in India is a most happy example of better things.

[5] The patriarch Philip Ankus assisted at the Vatican Council.

[6] He published the first full text, with Latin translation and introduction, of the Syriac *Testamentum Domini Nostri* (Mainz, 1899).

[7] What is the significance of this conferring of the *pallium?* Undoubtedly it was originally a token of recognition and communion, but latterly Rome has considered it as conferring jurisdiction. Nevertheless, the Melkite, Syrian, and Maronite patriarchs certainly exercise jurisdiction *de facto* before they receive papal confirmation.

patriarch, Mar Ignatius Gabriel Tappuni, was made a cardinal in 1936. (He was condemned to death by the Turks, but ransomed during World War I.)[8]

Bishops. The Syrian sees are that of Mardin and Amida, the patriarchal diocese, administered by a titular archbishop as vicar; Bagdad, Mosul, Aleppo, Damascus, which are archiepiscopal; Homs and Bairut, which are episcopal; but all the bishops are subject directly to the patriarch. The Jezira, Palestine, and Egypt are patriarchal vicariates. A vacant see is filled by the synod of bishops, who choose one from a number of candidates recommended by the clergy and people of the diocese.

Parochial clergy. Since the second synod of Sharfeh in 1888 priests have been bound to celibacy, but dispensations are accorded to converts from the Jacobites. There is a considerable prejudice against celibate pastoral clergy among some of the people. In 1930 the patriarchal seminary at Sharfeh (erected 1801) was put under the direction of the Subiaco Benedictines of the French province, who since 1901 had conducted a seminary of the Syrian rite at Jerusalem; this is still maintained by them but now as a junior seminary. The education and formation given by the Benedictines is entirely conditioned by the Syrian liturgy, and they bid fair to turn out priests as worthy as those of St. Anne's for the Melkites. Other aspirants to the priesthood go to the Dominicans' Syro-Chaldean college at Mosul, the Jesuits' interritual seminary at Bairut, and elsewhere.

The vicar general of each diocese is called *chorepiskopos,* and this title is sometimes accorded to priests occupying responsible posts outside the dioceses. It is conferred by the bishop with an imposition of hands; its insignia are a violet cassock and small hood (*masnaphto*), and sometimes the pectoral cross. Bishops-elect always receive the chorepiscopal blessing eight days before their consecration, if they have not already received it. The *periodeut* ("visitor") is a diocesan prelate who has charge of

---

[8] See footnote on page 72. Among his companions in captivity at Aleppo was Father Pascal Maljian, who was afterwards head of the Catholic Armenians in the United States.

the discipline of the clergy. There is no permanent office of archdeacon among the Catholic Syrians.

Religious institutes. The few monks and nuns of this rite were dispersed during World War I. There had been at Sharfeh from 1785 a congregation of "clerks regular" whose existence was very precarious; an attempt was made to revive them at Mardin in 1882 as the *Missionaries of St. Ephrem,* but they still number only a few priests. There is a wealthy and ancient monastery at Mar Behnam, near Mosul, with a few student brethren in charge of a secular priest.

These things being so, the assembly of Syrian bishops asked the Benedictines at Sharfeh to undertake the formation of a monastic foundation, under the Rule of St. Benedict but adapted in all respects to Syrian requirements. The object of the foundation is to combine monastic with active life — conduct of seminaries and schools, publishing, etc., but excluding the care of parishes. The first Syrian monk of this enterprise was simply professed in 1935, but its progress has been retarded by the war which so soon followed.

The Faithful of the Syrian rite number some 60,000 in the patriarchal territory, chiefly in Syria and Irak. Many of them were refugees from the Turks. The Jacobites, who have suffered from the same massacres and deportations, are only about 90,000 and show a tendency toward the Catholic Church. Mgr. Rahmani reported 800 reconciliations at Aleppo, 1000 at Homs, and 1500 among the refugees at Bairut in one year; more recently an episcopal vicar patriarchal had to be appointed for the converts in the Gazirah district of Irak. The Syrians are all very poor and simple, and have insufficient good schools of their own, though over a score have been opened for refugees since 1918; they are helped so far as possible by Western congregations working in Syria, particularly the Jesuits, and by the Maryamat sisters.

OTHER JURISDICTIONS

United States. There are 6800 Catholic Syrians (not to be confused with the Catholic Melkites or the Maronites, also

Syrians) in the United States, chiefly in New York state, Boston, and Cleveland. Even now they have no priests of their rite, and those of the faithful who still practise their religion mostly frequent the churches of their fellow Syrians, the Melkites or Maronites. A bishop was sent from Syria to visit these people some years ago, but the outbreak of World War II seems to have prevented anything new being done to improve their religious condition.

Elsewhere. There are another 7700 in various other parts of the world, almost entirely without clergy. There are two priests in the Argentine, and one each in Chili and Paris,[9] for the colonies in those places. Brisbane apparently has a church for its 700 faithful, but no priest. This defect is due to lack of clergy, and is a matter of great anxiety to the patriarch and bishops. Lacking one of their own, Syrians are encouraged to attend Catholic Melkite churches, which are more familiar to them than Latin ones.

LITURGY AND CUSTOMS

Church buildings. In a Syrian Catholic church there are generally three altars in a row, the middle one, under a *ciborium*, having a tabernacle, crucifix, and an indeterminate number of candles. The two side altars are sometimes only used as credence-tables. The altar top (*tablitho*) is of wood or stone, and always portable, covered by a "corporal" with a silk or linen cloth beneath. There is sometimes an open screen with three doors, but without pictures or lights hung on it. It should have a large curtain, with a smaller one for the altar alone, to be drawn across at certain times. *Ripidia* stand behind the altar for use in processions. In front of the sanctuary and separated from it by wooden railings is the choir, raised one step above the nave. Normally there are no seats, and men are accommodated in front, women behind. Round statues now take the place of pictures in some town churches, and confessional boxes have been adopted.

---

[9] Their church of St. Ephrem in the rue des Carmes was formerly the chapel of the Irish College.

The Catholics have some ancient churches around Mosul and the cathedral of Aleppo; others look like bad Latin churches.

Vestments. The eucharistic dress consists of a white alb (*kuthino*), stole rather of the Byzantine pattern (*uroro*), embroidered belt (*zunnoro*), cuffs (*zendo*), and a chasuble (*phaino*) like a cope without hood or orphreys. The deacon wears an ungirdled *kuthino* of any colour, with his stole falling back and front over the left shoulder.

A bishop adds to the sacerdotal garments an embroidered hood (*masnaphto*), rather like a Dominican amice, and the *omophorion*, which is like a large scapular embroidered with crosses falling back and front over the *phaino*. Catholic bishops affect the Roman mitre (the Jacobites have none) and crozier, but the patriarch carries a pastoral staff of the Byzantine pattern. The ordinary dress of the clergy is a black gown or cassock (violet for prelates), with a wide-sleeved open gown (*jubba*) and *kalemaukion* (sometimes with a polygonal brim) for outdoors and in church. Catholic bishops have adopted that headdress (over a small black hood, *eskhim*) in place of their traditional turban; they carry a hand-cross, wrapped in a silk veil, to bless with (even at the consecration), and wear a ring and pectoral cross. Out of doors they carry an ebony staff (the Byzantine *khazranion*), and sometimes wear a peculiar open cloak with a shoulder cape.

Altar-vessels and bread. Both chalice and large deep paten are either fitted with metal lids or covered with linen cloths; there is also a larger veil to go over both vessels. The purificator is now in use, but it is still called a "sponge." A spoon is needed for the priest's communion. The altar-bread is round, thick, and leavened, with a little salt added, and mixed with dough from the previous baking; it is stamped with twelve crosses. Syrian prescriptions about altar-bread are very exacting; e.g., it is supposed to be baked fresh for each Liturgy, and it must not be used if made by an infidel or non-Catholic, or if it has fallen to the ground. The reserved host, on which a few drops of the consecrated Wine are sprinkled, must be renewed every day. Cymbals, or similar things, are used during the Liturgy as the altar-bell is in the Latin rite.

Liturgical books. These have been printed from time to time at Rome, Bairut, Mosul, and elsewhere. The 1922 "missal" of Sharfeh was a reformed and improved edition. A new edition of the *Pontifical* has been in preparation at Rome and Sharfeh, and it will be in every way worthy of Syrian tradition.

Music. The Syrian chant has lately been the subject of a good deal of study, encouraged by the patriarch Rahmani. The Benedictines at the Jerusalem seminary have set it down in Western notation. As the native singers know it by tradition alone, it not having been written down, its variations are endless. It is strictly rhythmical and richer and more varied than the chant of the Maronites and Chaldeans.

Liturgical language. This is Syriac, i.e., the "Edessene" dialect of Aramaic (the language of Jesus Christ),[10] with the "western" pronunciation and characters. All the people speak Arabic (except a few in Irak and elsewhere, who still have a corrupt Syriac), and the scriptural lessons and certain pre-anaphoral prayers of the Liturgy are sung or read in that tongue. The rubrics in the older books are Arabic printed in Syrian characters (i.e., "Karshuni"). Syrians call the Liturgy *Kurobho,* "sacrifice," literally "approach."

THE EUCHARISTIC LITURGY

This represents the original rite of Antioch, which was modified for use in Jerusalem; this modified form then supplanted its parent at Antioch and throughout the patriarchate, and is known as the Liturgy of St. James. It was originally in Greek, but was soon translated into Syriac in various places, and after the monophysite schism the orthodox Catholics maintained its use in the first language, the Jacobites in the second; it was the source of the Byzantine, the Armenian, and perhaps the

---

[10] Such phrases of the Holy Scriptures as *Ethpatakh* (Mark 7:34), *Eli, eli, lamana shbktani* (Matt. 27:46), *Telitha kumi* (Mark 5:41), and *Maran-atha* (1 Cor. 16:22), and the words *korban, mammona, rabuni,* etc., are in this tongue.

Chaldean Liturgies, and the Maronite is simply a modified form of it.[11] There are now considerable discrepancies between the Greek and Syriac versions.

The Syrians may use their Liturgy of the Presanctified on ferias in Lent as well as on Good Friday. They never concelebrate, but on Maundy Thursday several separate Liturgies are celebrated at the same time on one improvised altar, the senior alone celebrating aloud and facing the people, the others on either side of him facing one another. There is now an approximation to "Low Mass."

An English version of the Syrian Liturgy, with the anaphora "of St. James the Brother of the Lord," can be found in the present writer's *Eastern Catholic Worship*. Other anaphoras in use are "of St. John the Evangelist," "of the Twelve Apostles," "of St. Mark the Evangelist," "of St. Eustace of Antioch," "of St. Basil of Caesarea," and "of St. Cyril of Jerusalem." There are sixty-four known Syrian anaphoras, but only these seven are printed in the Catholic books. The Liturgy is celebrated in the evening on the eve of Easter and of Christmas, and then entirely in Syriac (as also on the feast of St. Ephrem).

DIVINE OFFICE

The Syrian canonical prayers have seven "hours," which are recited in two parts: office of the Ninth hour, Vespers (*Ramsho*), and prayer of Protection (*Suttoro*) in the evening; Night Office (*Lilyo*) with three nocturns, Lauds (*Teshebhotho*), Morning Prayer (*Saphro*), and offices of the Third and Sixth hours before the Liturgy. The office is peculiarly rich in hymns and poetical compositions[12] but there are few psalms, in some hours none at all. Each hour begins with the *Trisagion* thrice and Our Father

---

[11] The local Orthodox, after they went into schism, entirely abandoned the Antiochene rite for its Byzantine daughter, as we have seen above (p. 40). The Catholics of the Syrian rite therefore represent the native church of our Lord's land in a rather special way. The dissident Orthodox have revived the use of the Greek St. James twice a year, at Zakynthos and Jerusalem.

[12] Many by, and still more attributed to, St. Ephrem the Deacon, doctor of the Church, whose feast both Latins and Syrians observe on June 18.

and always includes prayer for the dead; the *Te Deum* is sung
at Lauds. What psalms there are, are mostly invariable, according to whether it is a weekday or Sunday or great feast. The
version of the holy Scriptures used for liturgical purposes in all
the Syrian rites is the Peshitto. Daily recitation of the Office was
made obligatory on the clergy by the synod of Sharfeh in 1888.
Wherever there are two or more priests together they are directed
to sing all of it in church, but this is rarely observed except on
the eve of a Sunday or a feast.

THE SACRAMENTS

Baptism. The water is blessed for the occasion before each
baptism. After certain prayers the priest pronounces the exorcisms
and anoints the child with oil three times on the forehead. Then
he seats it in the font and pours water on its head three times,
saying, "N., is baptized in the name of the Father," etc. He at
once proceeds to

Confirmation, which consists essentially of anointing with
chrism the forehead, eyelids, nostrils, lips, ears, hands, chest,
back, and feet, with the words: "N., is sealed unto everlasting
life in the name of the Father, etc., with the holy chrism, the
sweet perfume of the divine Christ, sign and seal of true faith
and of the accomplishment of the gifts of the Holy Ghost."

Penance is administered with the Western formula, translated
into Syriac or Arabic.

Eucharist. The communicant stands, and the celebrant puts
a particle into his mouth; as each particle has, at the breaking
of the Bread, been anointed with the precious Blood, he thus
receives under both kinds. The words of administration are:
"The propitiatory coal of the body and blood of Christ our God
is given to his faithful servant for the forgiveness of sins and
the pardon of faults." The receiver replies, "Amen." "Coal," i.e.,
burning ember, is a common name for the Blessed Sacrament in
the East; also called "the pearl" (cf. Isa. 6:6). Deacons and
subdeacons are communicated with the spoon from the chalice.

Anointing is now administered according to the *Rituale*

Romanum in Syriac, as the proper rite requires the assistance of seven priests, as is usual in the East. The oil is consecrated as required by the priest.

Orders. The orders of the Syrian rite are singer, reader and acolyte, subdeacon; deacon, priest, bishop. All orders are conferred during the Liturgy by laying on of hands and delivery of instruments of office, without anointing. The formula resembles that of the eucharistic invocation of the Holy Ghost. The subdeacon is given a lighted candle, as his particular business is to care for the lights. Before ordination to the diaconate and upwards a profession of faith must be signed. There is no concelebration at the ordaining of bishops and priests.

Marriage. The wedding ceremony consists of two parts, the blessing of the rings and the crowning. A ring is given to each party and each is crowned with a wreath. The priest commits them to the care of one another, but there is no explicit contract, which is, however, implicit in the assurance that they have to give, that they are freely entering into matrimony.

Kalendar. The Gregorian reckoning is in use and the ecclesiastical year begins on the Sunday nearest to October 31. The kalendar is substantially the ancient one of the Church of Antioch; many of the feasts that we have in common are observed on different days. The seasons are Advent, Christmas, preparation for Lent, Lent, paschal-time, time after Pentecost, time after Holy Cross.

Feasts. Corpus Christi is adopted from the West, and the Immaculate Conception, All Saints, and St. Joseph transferred to our dates. In addition to Sundays there are twenty general holydays (not all of obligation) as well as local ones; they include the Praises of Our Lady (Dec. 26), St. Ephrem (June 18), the Praises of St. John the Forerunner (Jan. 7), and St. George (April 23).

Penitential season. During Lent (seven weeks) a complete fast from food and drink lasts till noon, with abstinence from certain foods for the rest of the day, except on Saturdays and Sundays. Nearly all Wednesdays and Fridays are days of abstinence, as well as three days three weeks before Lent (fast of Niniveh), four days before SS. Peter and Paul, seven days before the Assumption, and nine days before Christmas.

General observations. Catholic Syrians make the sign of the cross as in the West. Western devotions are in use, including Benediction of the Blessed Sacrament in a Syrian form. Holy Cross day (Sept. 14) is a great occasion, marked by the lighting of bonfires, and on the Assumption the Aleppines eat blessed grapes in memory of their dead. In the country parts the people are much attached to their own ways and customs; but in the towns they often try to approximate themselves to Western Catholics, in the words of a Benedictine monk working in Syria, "out of snobbery."

BIBLIOGRAPHY

Lammens, *La Syrie* (Bairut, 1921), 2 vols.

Khury, *Petit Manuel de la Messe Syrienne* (Paris, 1935).

Khayatte, *Manuel de Prières . . . selon le Rite Syrien* (Paris, 1926).

Jeannin, *Mélodies liturgiques Syriennes et Chaldéenes,* 2 vols. (Bairut, 1925–1928).

Codrington in *Eastern Churches Quarterly,* Vol. I, nos. 1–4 (Ramsgate, 1936).

2. THE MARONITES

The Maronites are Syrians, living chiefly in the Lebanon, and of the same race as the Catholic Syrians (described previously), Jacobites, and Melkites of both obediences (see pp. 104 ff.). Their existence as a separate "nation" is apparently entirely due to their ecclesiastical origins. There are no non-Catholic Maronites,[13] but the tradition (not found in writings previous to the sixteenth century) of their "perpetual orthodoxy" has now been abandoned by all except a few of the die-hards.[14]

The origins and early history of the Maronite Church have aroused controversy, not always conducted with urbanity. It would seem that after the Council of Chalcedon the monks of Bait-Marun, a monastery built around the shrine of St. Maro,[15] a fifth-century hermit, on the right bank of the river Orontes between Emesa (Homs) and Apamea, distinguished themselves by their strong opposition to the Monophysites. This conduct was naturally approved by the emperors, who greatly favoured the monastery in consequence, so that its influence spread throughout Syria Secunda.

But in the first half of the seventh century the Emperor Heraclius, seeking to unite his Syrian subjects against the

---

[13] Yet if you ask a Maronite if he is a Catholic he says, "No. I am a Maronite." To him "Catholic" means Catholic Melkite. Nevertheless, he does not object to frequenting Latin churches: some Catholic Orientals do, very much, as much as the average Latin would dislike having to frequent an Eastern church.

[14] Catholics are sometimes accused by their opponents of insinuating that the Catholics of Eastern rites have all been in uninterrupted communion with Rome. Yet it is "Roman" scholars who have maintained in the teeth of the Maronites that the Maronites were at one time in schism.

[15] He must not be confused with the seventh-century "St. John Maro, Patriarch of Antioch," who is known only from Maronite tradition. Grave doubts have been thrown on his existence.

invading Arabs, concocted with the patriarchs of Constantinople and Antioch a theological formula which they hoped would conciliate the Monophysites. Unfortunately it was heretical, and was promptly condemned by three successive popes and the patriarch of Jerusalem.[16] But Heraclius and his successor stuck to it, and the monks of Bait-Marun faithfully followed their patrons the emperors. After the Arab conquest and the third general council of Constantinople they and the people under their influence did not, for some unknown reason, return to orthodoxy, and it seems they continued to profess Monothelism long after it had died out everywhere else.[17] It is surmised that, while the patriarchs of Antioch were in exile at Constantinople during the first half of the eighth century, the monks decided to elect a primate for themselves and so began the separate line of Maronite patriarchs of Antioch; they certainly had a bishop in their monastery in the middle of the eighth century. After the destruction of Bait-Marun at the end of the ninth century the monks and their followers withdrew themselves entirely into the Lebanon mountains.

In the year 1182 almost the whole nation of the Maronites, 40,000 in number, moved, as the chronicler William of Tyre says, "by an inspiration from heaven," submitted to the Holy See through Amaury, the third of the Latin patriarchs whom the Crusaders had set up at Antioch. The Maronite patriarch Jeremias II al-Amshiti was present at the Lateran Council in 1215, and Rome had no doubt of their previous Monothelism then, for when Jeremias went home with a papal legate Pope Innocent III wrote insisting that he should make a solemn profession of faith in the two wills in Jesus Christ.

The Maronites who had emigrated to Cyprus were apparently heretical till after the Council of Florence, for they made

---

[16] And finally by the sixth oecumenical council (III Constantinople) in 680. The heresy was Monothelism, i.e., the denial that our Lord had a human as well as a divine will; it struck at His real humanity.

[17] The traditional Maronite explanation is that they denied the two wills (if they did) in error and in ignorance of the decisions of the oecumenical council. When they first heard of its teaching — from the Crusaders! — they at once embraced it.

an abjuration and submission in 1445, with their bishop at their head, and there seem to have been others disaffected here and there even during the late Middle Ages. But by the beginning of the sixteenth century the Maronites were stabilized, and since the fifth Lateran Council (1512–1517) they have been in close and uninterrupted contact with the Holy See. In 1584 Pope Gregory XIII founded the Maronite College in Rome. An outstanding figure was Germanos Farhat, Archbishop of Aleppo (1670–1732), founder at Ehden of the Aleppine Antonian monks. He was a great scholar, widely travelled in Europe, and of surpassing holiness of life.

By the eighteenth century ecclesiastical discipline had become very lax among the Maronites and the existence of abusive customs made reform difficult. The Holy See accordingly insisted on a plenary synod, which was eventually convened in 1736 at the monastery of Saidat al-Luaizeh, "our Lady of the Almond Trees." The famous scholar Joseph Assemani, himself a Maronite, was the papal delegate; and decrees were enacted aiming at the abolition of an excessive number of bishops, the sale of dispensations, the failure to reserve the Blessed Sacrament in rural churches, the neglect of the poor and of church buildings, the remarriage of widowed priests, and other abuses. To these were added certain liturgical prescriptions, some of which were necessary and some were not: e.g., *azyme* bread was imposed and communion in both kinds taken away from the laity. The acts of this synod were formally approved by Pope Benedict XIV but it took a century for them to be generally accepted and enforced. Their troubles were further aggravated by disputed patriarchal elections and by the activities of a nun of Aleppo named Anna Aggemi. In spite of the errors into which she fell (which culminated in her claiming to be hypostatically united to the Second Person of the Holy Trinity!) her reputation for holiness gained her the support of the patriarch, Joseph Stephani, and of a Lazarist father, Godez. The Holy See had to interfere in 1779, condemning her, censuring her partizans, and dissolving the sisterhood she had founded. But there were those who maintained

her sanctity fifty years afterwards. The great Maronite figure of
the nineteenth century was the patriarch Paul Massad, who ruled
for thirty-five difficult years. Four of his bishops assisted at the
Vatican Council, but Massad himself did not attend — it is said,
because he feared that pressure would be brought to bear on him
to abate some of his privileges.

After the Turkish conquest the people of the Lebanon, Maronites and Druzes,[18] were never governed directly by the Turks
but came under the control of the native emirs. The resulting
semi-independence caused the Lebanon to be the refuge of oppressed Catholics of Eastern rites, Melkites, Syrians, Armenians,
until they were emancipated from the civil control of the dissident patriarchs after 1829. But by the beginning of the nineteenth
century the feudal organization of the Lebanon was cracking;
after the abdication of the vigorous old emir Bashir II Shabab
and the evacuation of Syria by Mohammed Ali (1840), the political policies of the great powers precipitated a deadly struggle
between Maronites and Druzes, aggravated by the internal reforms imposed on Turkey by the Congress of Paris after the
Crimean war. The situation went out of control on May 30, 1860,
the occasion being a quarrel between a Druze and a Maronite
at Bait-Mari. The Druzes were armed and ready, but the Christians allowed themselves to be disarmed by the Turkish authorities on the pretence of maintaining order. In three weeks every
Maronite village of the main and southern Lebanon was pillaged
and burned, and six thousand Maronites were murdered, maimed,
or outraged; the abbot of Dair al-Kamar was flayed alive and his
twenty monks pole-axed. Khursud Pasha marched into the district
with a battalion of soldiers, fired a single gun, and then left his
troops to join in the massacre. On July 9 it broke out at Damascus,
where in three days the adult males alone numbered three thousand victims. Of these, eight Friars Minor and three Maronite
laymen were shown by the circumstances of their death to have
been martyrs of the faith, and were beatified by Pope Pius XI in

---

[18] A sect that broke away from Islam in the eleventh century; secular
rivals of the Maronites.

1926. The Maronites were brothers, Blessed Francis, Muti, and
Raphael Masabki. In all, 16,000 Maronites were slain and 100,000
rendered homeless.

France sent a military expedition to restore order, and the
Lebanon was given a constitution drawn up by a commission of
the European powers; it became an autonomous province of the
Turkish empire with a governor general, who was a Christian not
belonging to any of the chief local communions. This lasted till
1926, when the country was reorganized as the Republic of the
Lebanon, under French mandate: the district of Kasrawan, north-
east of Bairut, is almost exclusively Maronite.

The Maronites are properly proud of their devotion to the Holy
See; but they are an independent people and tenacious of their
rights and privileges: the more so that in the past Western
influence has sometimes tended to be coercive. The help they
gave to other oppressed Catholics in the seventeenth and eighteenth centuries, and the persecution they suffered themselves
from time to time, must not be forgotten.

PRESENT STATE

Patriarch. The Maronite patriarch of Antioch[19] is elected by
the bishops gathered in synod; the office is at once conferred by
the laying-on of hands of all the bishops present and the clergy
and people do homage. Notice is sent to Rome with a profession
of faith and obedience through the delegate apostolic in Syria,
and the Holy See confirms the election by sending a *pallium.* His
jurisdiction is over all the faithful of his rite in the old Turkish
empire in Asia and Egypt. Among his rights and privileges are
the ordination of all bishops, the nomination of titular bishops,
chorepiskopoi, and *barduts,* the convening of plenary synods, the
exclusive consecration of Chrism, the receiving of appeals from
lower courts, the absolution of certain reserved sins, the control
of the publication of catechisms and liturgical books and of trans-

[19] The concession of this title can only be looked on as an act of grace
on the part of the Holy See. It was first acknowledged by Pope Alexander
IV in 1254.

lations from Syriac into the vernacular. He is assisted by a curia of titular bishops, and is bound to send an account of his charge to Rome every ten years.

The patriarchal residence has been fixed in many places; for a long time now it has been at Bekerkeh in the winter and Gadaidat-Kannubin in the summer. The present patriarch is Mar Antony Arida, elected in 1932.

Bishops. The Maronite dioceses have been clearly delimited and their bishops permanently resident only since the synods of 1736 and 1818. The sees are all episcopal and dependent directly on the patriarch (but each holder is called archbishop); they are Gibail and Batrun (the patriarchal dioceses, each administered by a titular archbishop of the curia), Aleppo, Baalbek, Bairut, Cairo, Cyprus (practically all its subjects and their bishop live in the Lebanon), Damascus, Sidon, Tyre, and Tripoli. There is a vicariate patriarchal for Palestine. Vacant sees are filled by the patriarch and bishops in synod, the lower clergy and laity having an advisory voice. Among the bishops' means of support is a poll-tax on every adult in his diocese.

Parochial clergy. Parish priests are for the most part chosen by the faithful concerned (the bishop has a right of veto). Those in the rural parts are nearly all married and have often to support their families by working in the fields or plying a trade, as do the country clergy elsewhere. This class among the clergy is but poorly instructed, for though there were several diocesan seminaries only two were of any size. However, a general central seminary for the whole patriarchate was established in the autumn of 1934. It is situated at Ghazir and is directed by Jesuit fathers, the rector being of Maronite nationality. The Maronite College at Rome, first founded in 1584, was refounded in 1891, and is now also under the direction of the Jesuits,[20] but it can accommodate only twenty-four students. A considerable number of Maronite priests are trained in the Oriental seminary of the Society of Jesus at Bairut; some aspirants are sent to Latin semi-

---

[20] Its most famous alumnus is the Syriac scholar Joseph Assemani (al Sam'ani), (1687–1768).

naries. There are a thousand secular priests, but the number is insufficient, and so are vocations.

The offices of *chorepiskopos* and *bardut* (περιοδευτής, visitor), carry with them variable duties, e.g., to confirm and to confer minor orders for the bishop; archpriests and archdeacons are practically titular only.

Religious institutes. As is appropriate to a church that had its origins in a monastery, monasticism has always had many followers among the Maronites. Their monks of the Middle Ages led a rather go-as-you-please and unorganized life, and in 1700 the learned patriarch Stephen ad-Duwahi started a congregation modeled on Western lines, under the so-called Rule of St. Antony, the traditional patriarch of the solitary life. The enterprise prospered and spread, absorbing existing monasteries but, as in the case of the Melkite Basilians, the particularism of Aleppo caused trouble and in 1768 two distinct congregations were formed, the *Baladite* ("rural") *Antonians* and the *Aleppine Antonians*. During the same time a bishop, afterwards patriarch, Gabriel Blauzawi, united other monasteries into a congregation, which received the name of *Antonians of St. Isaias*, from its mother house.

The life and constitutions of all three congregations of Maronite Antonians closely resemble one another. They are primarily contemplative but about a third of the hieromonks serve parishes;[21] they are bound to perpetual abstinence from flesh-meat and tobacco. A few of them are definitely hermits, living alone in the neighbourhood of their monasteries. The habit is a black gown with a small round hood, leather belt, and sandals. All together there are about 750 of these monks, 520 of whom are priests. Each congregation has an abbot general at the head and is divided into provinces. There are seventy-two monasteries and forty-six residences, many of which have only one or two monks, who are dispensed from much of their rule and are engaged in looking after large landed estates. It is said that a third of the Lebanon belongs to the Antonians, and this excessive territorial

---

[21] The Baladites also do missionary work among the half-Moslem, half-pagan Nuzayris around Biadieh in the Alauite country.

wealth is still the cause of certain irregularities among them;[22] these have been much worse in the past, and the synod of 1818 and others had to take strong measures against monastic abuses.

The Aleppine congregation has a small college for its students in Rome. The causes of beatification of three nineteenth-century Antonians, two monks and a nun, are before the Congregation of Sacred Rites.[23]

The *Missionaries of Kraim* form an active congregation, preaching, giving retreats, and running a printing press. They were founded by Father John Habib in 1865, and have some thirty priest members.

The *Antonian nuns* are strictly enclosed and contemplative, with solemn office in choir. There are 160 of them, in thirteen convents. Other Maronite nuns are *Visitandines* and *Sisters of the Holy Family*, who are engaged in education. The Sisters of the Sacred Hearts of Jesus and Mary (*Maryamat*), an inter-ritual congregation originated by two Jesuit fathers in 1853 which does splendid educational work in Syria, has a large proportion of Maronite members.

The Faithful. The Maronites of the patriarchate, though reduced by emigration, still number 323,000 (10,000 in Egypt, 1000 in Cyprus, 2500 in Palestine, the rest in the Lebanon). By far the greater part of them are peasants and mountaineers, faithful to their religion and anxious to improve themselves; many a village has a catechism class and the Maryamat schools are eagerly sought. Unfortunately the influence of returned emigrants is corrupting: they have often lost the faith entirely, but their objection to the monks' large estates seems not without reason. Also "the influence of the Western press," says l'abbé Labourt, "is out-

---

[22] There are, for example, recognized "irregular monasteries" wherein the observance is relaxed and where the superior (*reis*) is sometimes to be found surrounded by his relatives or other lay people, who are supposed to assist him in the administration of the property of the monks.

[23] For an interesting account of a Maronite monastery, see Doughty's *Arabia Deserta*, Vol. II, cap. xiii, criticized in the *Dublin Review*, Jan., 1934. For the holy ones, see Attwater, *Eastern Saints*.

rageously bad." The Maronites owe an incalculable debt to the Jesuits, who have worked in Syria from 1625 till 1773 and from 1831 on; their university and its Oriental seminary at Bairut have been the door to intellectual and professional activities for many Maronites and others.

OTHER JURISDICTIONS

United States. Maronites are to be found in every large city of the United States and their number is difficult to estimate: but it seems to be well over 50,000. They are subject to the American bishops but there are *chorepiskopoi* empowered to confirm, consecrate churches and altars, etc. They have a score of churches and priests, and display some literary activity. Their first permanent priest was Father Peter Korkamas, who established a church in New York city; his nephew, Father Joseph Yasbak, founded the Maronite church in Boston.

Uruguay. There is a colony of 16,000 here, presided over by a monk at Montevideo, who is a titular abbot.

Elsewhere there are 5000 or so, with churches at Leghorn, Paris, Sydney, in Brazil, the Argentine, Canada, and other places; and 3000 in South Africa, where their centre is Johannesburg.

LITURGY AND CUSTOMS

The Antiochene usages of the Maronites have been very seriously modified, even before the synod of 1736, and their fundamental Orientalism is obscured by externals borrowed from the West. Their later *church buildings* tend to look exactly like those of the West; but there are ancient Maronite churches in the Lebanon retaining a screen before the sanctuary, and having the altar set in the apse, with the episcopal chair and seats for the other clergy behind it. The appointments of their churches and their *altar-vessels, etc.*, are entirely Latin, though blessings are given with a hand-cross and *ripidia* are carried in processions. Altarbreads are unleavened and just the same as ours. Their *music* is in origin that of the Syrians, with cymbals to mark the rhythm, but very different in detail.

Vestments. The eucharistic dress of a priest is purely modern

Roman,[24] except that he generally wears embroidered cuffs instead of a maniple. The lower clergy wears Syrian vestments (all with stoles worn in varying ways), and generally the bishops do too (with Roman mitre and crozier). Servers have cassock and cotta. A hieromonk celebrates with his hood (*schema*) drawn over his head.

The ordinary dress of the clergy is a black cassock (violet for prelates, red for the patriarch) with a round flat cap; wide-sleeved gown and low turban are for formal occasions. Bishops wear their turban over the Syrian *masnaphto* (hood).

Liturgical books. These were printed in Rome from 1594, and a definitive edition was drawn up and issued after the 1736 synod, reprinted at Rome, Kosayya, and Bairut. They include a "missal" and "breviary" arranged in the Roman way. Of the twenty-five alternative *anaphoras* only eight are printed and used; the most recent and common is "of the Holy Roman Church." A new and better edition of the Ritual was printed at the Jesuits' press in Bairut in 1942. The *Pontifical* is still in manuscript; but the new Syrian edition will be available for the use of Maronite bishops if they wish.

The *liturgical language* is Syriac, but the lessons and some other prayers are in Arabic, and the use of this vernacular tends to increase. Rubrics are in Karshuni.

THE EUCHARISTIC LITURGY

This is simply the "common parts" of the Syrian Liturgy of St. James (into which one or other of the *anaphoras* is inserted), subjected to "adaptation, often useless and servile, to Roman usages" (Labourt). Though in principle every Liturgy is sung, there is a uniform way of celebrating "Low Mass," but even at this the use of incense and some singing is normal. The people kneel throughout, women normally separate from men. Concele-

---

[24] When they borrow from the West, Orientals always choose the worst patterns. The first Maronite priest I ever saw, in a church at Cairo, had a chasuble of staring green, stiff as a board, with pink roses sprawling all over it. A very curious observance of some bishops is to change their *phaino* for a chasuble before the consecration.

bration often takes place in monasteries and big churches, and sometimes in smaller ones on certain occasions. The Liturgy of the Presanctified is confined to Good Friday.

In the anaphora "of St. Peter" the words of institution are expressed in the second person: "Thou didst take bread," "Thou didst lift up thine eyes," etc.

The Gospel is read in Syriac and other languages, as well as the usual Arabic, at Christmas. When the Liturgy has not been sung, the Western prayers for Russia are added at the end. The priest's private prayer before leaving the sanctuary is a manifestation of devotion to the altar of sacrifice, as in the pure Syrian rite. Blessed bread is distributed.

At least three translations of this Liturgy have been published in America: by Father Joseph Gorayeb at Buffalo, N. Y., in 1915, by Father Peter Sfeir at Detroit in 1936, and in Attwater's *Eastern Catholic Worship* (1945).

THE DIVINE OFFICE

This has been obligatory on the clergy since 1736. It is a recasting of the Syrian Office (see p. 161), with the same hours, except that it lacks Lauds.

THE SACRAMENTS

Baptism and *Penance* are administered according to translations from the Roman ritual, and *Confirmation* and *Anointing* very nearly so, all in Arabic. The synod of 1736 separated Confirmation from Baptism and assigned its administration to the bishops. There is now a movement to get rid of these anomalies, a process facilitated by the new edition of the Ritual published in 1942. *Holy Orders* are the same as those of the Syrians and conferred in similar fashion (p. 163); contrary both to common Eastern custom and to that of the Syrians, the subdeacon has the duty of singing the epistle. *Marriage* ceremonies also resemble those of the Syrians, carried out in Arabic, with added Western elements.

Since 1736 the *Eucharist* is given to lay people under the species of bread only, with the words: "The body of our Lord Jesus Christ is given to you for the pardon of faults, for the forgiveness of sins, and for life everlasting. Amen." When the Liturgy is sung solemnly the deacon receives Communion in both kinds.

Kalendar and feasts. These closely resemble those of the Syrians, with the same Western importations, and others, e.g., Rosary Sunday and the Name of Mary. There are twenty-three holydays, of which St. Maro (Feb. 9) is naturally one of the most important. Feasts of Old Testament saints are numerous. The Gregorian reckoning was adopted in 1606 at Tripoli and elsewhere.

Penitential periods. Lent lasts seven weeks (no fasting on Saturdays and Sundays); most Wednesdays and Fridays are days of abstinence, as well as four days before SS. Peter and Paul, eight before the Assumption, and twelve before Christmas.

General observations. In addition to all the principal Western "popular devotions" (especially those directed toward the Blessed Sacrament) the Maronites have adopted and adapted certain Roman liturgical observances, e.g., the blessing and imposition of ashes (first Monday in Lent), the covering of pictures and statues during passiontide, blessing of palms, and the washing of feet on Maundy Thursday, on which day, also, the patriarch must consecrate the chrism. These are all carried out with considerable dramatic effect and popular excitement, which are further displayed in their own special customs, such as the "Raising of Lazarus" (eve of Palm Sunday), and the "Burial" and "Resurrection of Christ." The Liturgy is celebrated at midnight on Christmas, the Epiphany, and Easter.

BIBLIOGRAPHY

Lammens, *La Syrie*, 2 vols. (Bairut, 1921).

Phares, *Les Maronites du Liban* (Paris, 1908).

Raphael, *Le Rôle des Maronites dans le Retour des Eglises orinentales* (Bairut, 1935).

Dib, *Etude sur la Liturgie maronite* (Paris, 1919).

—— *L'Eglise Maronite jusqu' à la fin du moyen âge* (Paris ,1930).

Sfeir, *The Language of Christ in America* (Buffalo, 1929).

A MARONITE MONK

A MARONITE MONASTERY
Qozhayya in the Lebanon

A BYZANTINE MONK

A BYZANTINE BISHOP
(Vested in the *Mandyas*)

COURTYARD OF A MELKITE MONASTERY

Pope Pius XI Presides

The Consecration
CONCELEBRATION OF THE BYZANTINE LITURGY
IN ST. PETER'S, 1925

CONCELEBRATION OF THE SLAV-BYZANTINE LITURGY

3. THE MALANKARESE

On pages 210–213 will be found a brief account of the Christians of Malabar in India and the events which led to their schism in 1653. Within ten years three quarters of them had returned to Catholic unity, but the rest remained obdurate under their leader the archdeacon Thomas Palakomatta (Parambil). He had received as commission only a sort of investiture by the imposition of hands of twelve priests, and he tried in vain to get episcopal orders from the Nestorians of Mesopotamia. Then he approached the Jacobite patriarch in the same country, who sent a bishop, Mar Gregory, to visit Malabar. He does not seem to have consecrated Thomas nor, in spite of Jacobite episcopal visitations from time to time, were any of his first four successors (all called Thomas) consecrated. However, the schismatics at last obtained a valid hierarchy in 1772, when the sixth Thomas was made bishop (as Dionysius I) by the episcopal delegates of the Jacobite patriarch. Dionysius presumably acknowledged some shadowy jurisdiction in that prelate, but the Malabar Jacobites claim that they never formally accepted monophysite errors. The Malabar schismatics began to abandon their Chaldean or East Syrian liturgy for that of the Jacobites, the West Syrian or Antiochene, but this substitution was not complete for another hundred years.

Throughout the eighteenth and nineteenth centuries the story of the Malabar Jacobites is a wearisome succession of squabbles, lawsuits, and sub-schisms, complicated since 1816 by Protestant missionary efforts. Four attempts were made at reunion with Rome during the eighteenth century and they were all abortive; the last two, by Mar Dionysius I, had direct encouragement from the Holy See but were frustrated by the policy of the local Western authorities.[25] So some of the Jacobites turned to the Anglicans (with more result) and, though there have been a number of individual reconciliations to the Chaldeo-Malabarese, there was no important reunion till our own day. In 1909 the Jacobite patriarch of Antioch, Abdullah Sattuf, came to Malabar, quarrelled with the metropolitan Dionysius V about church property and administration, and excommunicated him. Since then the "orthodox" Jacobites have been split into two litigious parties, those who want to depend on the Patriarch of Antioch and those who want to be independent.

Nevertheless, side by side with this deplorable state of affairs there has been a certain quickening of religious consciousness among some of the Malabar Jacobites; this became noticeable about 1868, when it was confidently expected that the Metropolitan Dionysius IV would lead a large number of his people back to the Catholic Church, though this did not in fact happen. In 1919 Father Givergis (George) Paniker-veettil, rector of the principal Jacobite seminary, founded at a place he called Bethany a religious brotherhood, "of the Imitation of Christ," for missionary and educational work, followed by a similar institute for nuns (for whom there was no provision among the Jacobites). In 1925 Father Givergis was consecrated bishop, taking the name of Ivanios (John).

At a synod of Jacobite bishops of the anti-patriarchal party held in the same year to consider measures for the spiritual regeneration of their church, Mar Ivanios was commissioned "to open correspondence with the Church of Rome with a view to explore the avenues for ending schisms so far as Malabar was concerned." In response to his overtures the Holy See replied that if the bishops abjured their errors and schism their Antiochene liturgy and customs would be maintained and, upon verifica-

---

[25] One bishop concerned, a Portugese Carmelite, Jacob Soledad, is referred to by the Carmelite historian Friar Paulinus as a "naturally rough man, who was kind to nobody and caused endless disturbance on the Travancore coast" (*India Orientalis Christiana*, p. 124).

tion of the validity of their baptism and ordination, the bishops would be confirmed in their offices and jurisdiction.

Of the five bishops concerned only two, Mar Ivanios and his suffragan Mar Theophilos, accepted the invitation. They were received into the visible communion of the Catholic Church on September 20, 1930, followed at once by two *rambans* (solitaries, who were also bishops designate) and other clergy, religious of the Imitation, and a thousand lay people (including the octogenarian parents of Mar Ivanios); there have been many more since then, including two more bishops. To distinguish them from their fellows of the Chaldean and Latin rites in Malabar, they are called the Malankara Catholics.

Unlike so many reunions with Rome in the course of history this movement is distinguished as an entirely religious one, without any element of political, social, or other temporal consideration in it. On the contrary, the new Catholics have to suffer a good deal of petty persecution sometimes, and they lose all their ecclesiastical property, churches, cemeteries, etc., upon leaving the Jacobite body. The Brothers of the Imitation set the admirable example of not going to law in order to try and retain their possessions; they were literally penniless and homeless till a generous and sympathetic Hindu came to the rescue with a small piece of land. The reunion is calculated to have far-reaching effects among the Jacobites, who can now become Catholics without having to abandon their familiar rites and customs, and, in the case of married priests, without giving up either their wives or their sacerdotal functions, as is their case in joining the Chaldeo-Malabar or the Latin rites.

PRESENT STATE

The Malankara province of Malabar consists of the archdiocese of Trivandrum (Mar Ivanios, metropolitan) and the diocese of Tiruvalla in Travancore. The faithful number 50,000 (several hundreds being new converts from Hinduism), and there are nearly one hundred and fifty priests, some of them married.

Priests who fill certain responsible offices (e.g., vicar general) rank as prelates and have the title *prodott*, "visitor."

Religious institutes. The members of the *Brotherhood of the Imitation of Christ* are definitely missionaries to India, primarily by prayer and contemplation; they wear the yellow gown of the Hindu holy man (*sanyasin*), they avoid all flesh-meat, and their monastery is called an *ashram*. In drawing up their rule the founder Mar Ivanios sought a synthesis of the prescriptions of St. Basil, St. Benedict, and St. Francis of Assisi. Their superior is called the *reesh*, "governor." The *Sisters of the Imitation* conduct schools, and the *Daughters of Mary* do social work.

LITURGY AND CUSTOMS

These are simply those of the West Syrian rite (see pp. 158–163), without most of the few modifications which the Catholics of that rite have introduced. Their *church appointments* are florid, and statues instead of pictures are sometimes to be seen. In the *Eucharistic Liturgy* the scriptural lessons and most of the prayers are read in the vernacular Malayalam; the priest's inaudible prayers are in Syriac. "And the Son" has not been added in the Creed. The *sacraments* are all administered according to the Syriac books. Concelebration is still in use.

The clergy wear the wide-sleeved gown, black or white, with a round flat cap, and bishops the turban over the small hood. They have on certain occasions the Western mitre and crozier, which the Malabar Jacobites use, and habitually carry the hand-cross.

Devotions in honour of the Blessed Sacrament have been introduced in the form of exposition and benediction. The last-named consists of an excerpt from the last part of the Liturgy, with a hymn and a blessing with the Holy Things added. Stations of the cross have been set up in some churches.

BIBLIOGRAPHY

Ivanios, "The Malabar Reunion," in *Pax*, No. 114 (Prinknash Priory, 1931).

Vattathara, *Le Mouvement de Bethanie* (Louvain, 1931). See also the bibliography on p. 219.

CHAPTER VII

THE ARMENIAN RITE

THE scattered people whom we call Armenians were formerly localized in the country which is bounded, roughly, by the Caucasus and Taurus Mountains, the Black Sea, and the Caspian Sea: Greater Armenia was to the east of the river Euphrates and Lesser Armenia to the west, later covering Cilicia to the Mediterranean. The Armenians are an Indo-European people, who call themselves Haikh and their country Hayastan, on account of a mythical descent from Haik, great-grandson of Noe. They have always been a very distinct people, with what we should now call a strong national sentiment, but their geographical situation was against their enjoying sovereignty for very long consecutive periods and they have been controlled and exploited in turn by the Medes, Romans, Persians, Byzantines, Arabs, Turks, and Russians.

The definitive conversion of the Armenians to Christianity was the work of St. Gregory the Enlightener,[1] a Parthian, who was made bishop by the Metropolitan of Caesarea in Cappadocia in 294. He baptized the king, Tiridates, and Armenia had the distinction of being the first nation to embrace Christianity officially and as a body. In 374 the new church repudiated its canonical dependence on the church of Caesarea, and became an isolated body under its own primate (the *katholikos*); he was, and admitted that he was, subject to the universal pontifical authority of the Holy See — but that meant in practice much less then than it does now.

---

[1] The non-Catholic Armenians are often distinguished as "Gregorians," they having evolved the theory that St. Gregory established a completely independent national church under his own rule.

During the first half of the fifth century St. Isaac (Sahak) the Great reformed the Armenian Church on Byzantine lines and, with St. Mesrop, translated the Bible and the liturgy into their vernacular. Owing to war with their Persian overlords the Armenians took no part in the monophysite troubles which culminated in the Council of Chalcedon (451); but some fifty years later, moved largely by political motives, a national synod repudiated that council. The Armenian Church thus cut itself off from the communion of the Catholic Church, and has ever since been reputed monophysite.[2]

For the next seven hundred years the story of Armenian Christianity was one of bloody persecution by Persians and Arabs from without and quarrels within. The people naturally welcomed and helped the Crusaders against their Mohammedan oppressors, and at the end of the twelfth century those who had fled westward and formed the kingdom of Little Armenia in Cilicia were reunited to Rome. Outside Cilicia the union was weak or non-existent, but the Western ritual and disciplinary practices adopted from the Crusaders affected the whole Armenian Church and have persisted to this day. The union was maintained till the Saracens took Akka in 1291, and in a weak and decayed form till the end of the kingdom of Little Armenia in 1375. After that, though individual katholikoi were in communion with Rome, the church as a whole was in schism again.

During the following centuries Latin missionaries were very active among the Armenians and before 1356 there appeared that curious phenomenon, the Friars of Unity of St. Gregory the Enlightener. These were under the protection of the Dominican Order on the one hand and of an Armenian abbot on the other, and they tried to combine Oriental monasticism with the Rule of the Friars Preachers. As often happens with such experiments the West crowded the East out, and it became

---

[2] It must be stated that many scholars, Armenian and other, Catholic and dissident, maintain that Chalcedon was repudiated under a misapprehension, and that the Armenians are not and never were monophysite heretics. But the dissidents are certainly in schism.

to all intents and purposes a Western order with an Armenian exterior. But these friars did a tremendous amount of work and are said at one time to have numbered 600 members. The congregation survived till the eighteenth century, when the remnant was absorbed in the ordinary Dominican Order.

Armenia sent four representatives to the Council of Florence and a decree of reunion was published, but nothing of importance came of it — except the famous instruction *pro Armenis*, on the sacraments, in the bull *"Exultate Deo."*

THE CATHOLIC ARMENIANS

Owing to the efforts of the Friars of Unity and others there were always groups of Catholics of the Armenian rite (for instance, in the Nakshevan province of Persia), and in the middle of the seventeenth century a Catholic was made patriarch of his nation in Constantinople. But an already troubled position was made worse by the shocking religio-political activity of the French ambassador, the Marquis Ferréol, who abducted a subsequent dissident patriarch, Avedik of Tokat, and sent him to be tried by the Inquisition in France. During the ensuing persecution there suffered, in 1707, Ter[3] Gomidas Keumurgian, who was beatified as a martyr in 1929.

The number of Armenian Catholics in the Near East continued to increase in spite of persecution,[4] and in 1742 Pope Benedict XIV established a patriarchal see in Asia Minor, at Kraim in the Lebanon, with the title of Cilicia. Its headquarters were moved to Bzommar a century later. The first patriarch was Abraham Artzivian. In 1830 French influence obtained the recognition by Turkey of the Catholic Armenians as a separate "nation" (*millah*), with a civil head and an archbishop as religious head at Constantinople. This dual authority caused grave difficulties till, in 1846, the two offices were united in the

---

[3] *Ter*, short for *terder*, the title of a married Armenian priest.

[4] So numerous were they a hundred years ago in Constantinople that the word "Catholic" in that city popularly meant one of the Armenian rite and nothing else.

person of Mgr. Hassun, and in 1867 his elevation to the patriarchal throne also unified the two ecclesiastical primacies of Constantinople and Cilicia.

In the same year Pope Pius IX issued the bull *Reversurus,* which regulated the election and powers of the Armenian patriarch and bishops and restrained the participation of the laity in ecclesiastical affairs. Many took this bull as an infringement of secular rights, and the commotion lasted for ten years, entailing the schism of several bishops, all the so-called Antonian monks, and a number of lay people. When peace was restored, the great Antony Hassun resigned his office and died, a cardinal, in Rome four years later (1884). He assisted at the Vatican Council.

But internal trouble continued, especially at Constantinople, a section of the lay people standing out for their old influence. The plenary synod of 1911 produced good results, but interested parties used the latent discontent for their own ends, and it became active again in 1927. A compromise was effected two years later.

During the massacres by Turks and Kurds in the war of 1914–1918 the Catholic Armenians lost seven bishops, over one hundred priests, forty-five nuns, and thirty thousand lay folk; over eight hundred ecclesiastical buildings and schools were pillaged and destroyed, and a dozen dioceses laid waste. Moreover, the formation of a soviet socialist republic in Russian Armenia cut off an indeterminate number of Catholics from their fellows.

A conference of Armenian bishops at Rome in 1928 reorganized their church in view of these events and of the conditions now obtaining.

PRESENT STATE

Patriarch. The "Patriarch of the Catholic Armenians and Katholikos of Cilicia" is the head of all the faithful of his rite except those referred to below. His see is now again at Bzommar, near Bairut (it was at Constantinople from 1867 to 1928);

a new residence has been built in the suburb of Ashrafieh as a gift from Pope Pius XI. He is elected by the bishops in synod and their choice must be confirmed by the Holy See, with the grant of the *pallium*. He has the right to consecrate the chrism for his whole patriarchate and to ordain its bishops, all of whom depend directly on him. He communicates with the Sacred Eastern Congregation through the delegate apostolic for Syria. All patriarchs take the name of Peter: the present, elected in 1937, is Gregory Peter XV Agagianian, who in 1945 was created cardinal (*cf.* pp. 72 and 156).

Bishops are chosen by the clergy of the diocese with the approval of the patriarch and the Holy See. The present sees are the patriarchal diocese of Bairut; the archdioceses (without suffragans) of Aleppo, Constantinople, and Mardin (residence at Bagdad); and the dioceses of Alexandria in Egypt and Isfahan in Persia; the other thirteen dioceses are in abeyance, mostly utterly destroyed in 1914–1918; the few Catholic Armenians of Palestine are in charge of a vicar patriarchal. The patriarch has a titular archbishop for vicar general, and there is an ordaining prelate attached to the Armenian College at Rome.

Parochial clergy. These are formed principally in the national college at Rome, founded 1883 and conducted by Armenian secular priests, in the patriarchal seminary at Bzommar, and in the Oriental seminary of the Jesuits at Bairut; some at the Capuchins' seminary in Constantinople and others abroad, but the Armenian bishops aim at a more unified arrangement. Married men may be ordained to the diaconate and priesthood, but the custom of voluntary celibacy is practically universal. The patriarchal clergy form a sort of religious congregation.

The office of *vartapet* is a rank peculiar to the Armenian hierarchy, conferred by a kind of ordination ceremony. They are celibate secular priests of superior learning and ability who are put in charge of responsible posts; they are divided into senior and junior classes and, in theory, are the only authorized preachers under the bishops. The *archpriest* is a sort of rural dean.

Religious institutes. Since the defection of the "Antonians" under Father Malachy Ormanian in 1871, monasticism has been represented, and most worthily, only by the *Mekhitarists.* These monks were founded by the Venerable Mekhitar of Sivas in 1701, with the Rule of St. Benedict as the basis of their constitutions. War drove them to Venice, where they settled on the island of San Lazzaro in 1717; later, a separate branch was established at Vienna. The good they have done for their countrymen by missionary and educational work and the printing and diffusion of books is incalculable. The catalogue of their publications is amazing. It ranges from the Bible to the pagan classics and from Buffon's *Birds* to *Uncle Tom's Cabin.* And in other languages besides Armenian — over twenty books in English are listed. Byron was a frequent (and welcome) visitor at San Lazzaro, and he even projected making a new translation of the Bible from the Armenian version. These monks have done more than anybody else for the religious and cultural welfare of their people during the disasters of the past two hundred years, and they are greatly respected by the dissidents. The Venice abbey has small houses and colleges at Padua, Rome, Budapest, Aleppo, Alexandria, and Sèvres, and the Vienna abbey others at Constantinople, Plovdiv, Cairo, and Piraeus. The order has over one hundred monks, of whom about eighty are priests. The two abbots were formerly always titular archbishops.

The *Sisters of the Immaculate Conception,* founded by Mgr. Hassun in 1852, conduct schools and orphanages in various places. Their mother house and novitiate is at Rome. The present superioress, Mother Elbis, is a woman of remarkable intellectual and literary attainments.

The Faithful. With the exception of the long-standing but now small disaffected party, the Armenian laity are on the whole good, observant Christians. It is curious that, while a non-Catholic Armenian is generally an adherent of his national church or of nothing, the Catholics are often quite ready to abandon their own rite; there is accordingly an unknown number of them who belong to the Western church, sometimes by a tradition dating back several generations.

The Catholic Armenians of the patriarchate number about 45,000, many of them refugees scattered among the villages of Syria. Bairut has 7000 and Aleppo 15,000.

OTHER JURISDICTIONS

U.S.S.R. Of the number and state of Catholic Armenians in Russian territory little certain information is available; they have been estimated at now 50,000 or less. An apostolic administrator, with residence at Tiflis, was appointed for them in 1921; he was Father James Bagaratian who died, a confessor of the faith, in the penal camp at Solovky in 1936.

Since 1939 the Catholics of Armenian rite in former Poland have been within the U.S.S.R. There were Armenians living in Galicia in the fourteenth century, and after great difficulties the majority of them, with their archbishop, were reconciled with Rome between 1630 and 1681. It is not surprising that, hemmed in by Poles and Ruthenians, they became very "hybridized" and many joined the Latin rite; today only about 5000 souls adhere to the local version of their proper rite. Their ecclesiastical superior is the Armenian archbishop of Lvov, immediately subject to and appointed by the Holy See. There is a convent of Armenian Benedictine nuns (founded 1680) at Lvov, who have (or had) a school. In 1934 the archbishop, Mgr. Joseph Teodorowicz, established a fine Armenian museum at Lvov.

Greece. In 1925 an ordinary, immediately subject to the Holy See, was appointed for the 3000 Catholic Armenian emigrants settled in Greece.

Rumania. Two-thirds (some 36,000) of the old Armenian colony in what is now the kingdom of Rumania have been Catholics since the later part of the seventeenth century, and are latinized beyond recognition. In accordance with the Rumanian concordat the Holy See has now appointed for them an administrator apostolic, with residence at Gherla (Armenierstadt) subject to the Latin bishop of Alba Julia; in due course they will probably form a diocese.

Elsewhere. There are 8675 Catholic Armenians in France and Belgium, with a few priests, subject to the French ordinaries, but at present in the immediate care of two bishops of their rite exiled from Turkey in Asia.

There are about 5000 in the United States, mostly in New York and New England. Their first priest was the Archpriest Mardires Mighirian, who worked in Boston and New York; other priests were sent later from Constantinople. Most, if not all, of these American Armenians hold their services in Latin churches or hired halls, being too poor to build churches of their own. They are directly subject to the American bishops. There were Armenians in New York as long ago as the days when it was New Amsterdam.

Western religious institutes working among the Armenians include the Augustinians of the Assumption (Bulgaria, Constantinople), Capuchins and Jesuits (Syria, Constantinople), and Lazarists (Persia).

LITURGY AND CUSTOMS

Church buildings. An Armenian church is usually rectangular in plan, and its typical characteristic is a central dome which outside forms a low round tower with a cone-shaped roof. Inside it rather resembles a Latin church; sometimes they are almost indistinguishable. The sanctuary is open, considerably raised from the nave, and approached by two lateral flights of four or five steps; the altar may stand in the middle, beneath a *ciborium,* but is usually nearer the east wall in the midst of a sort of open screen. The altar table (of stone) is narrow and has at the back three, four, or even five gradines; on it is a crucifix, an indeterminate (but large) number of candlesticks, a small hand-cross with which blessings are given, and a tabernacle containing the reserved Sacrament. On the north side is a credence table or niche in the wall. Numerous lamps burn before this and other altars, of which there are generally two simpler ones, one on either side.

In front of the sanctuary is a raised and enclosed space for the choir. The singers stand here in a semicircle, dressed in a long, wide-sleeved ungirdled garment with a short shoulder cape, varied in colour: I have seen them apple-green and heliotrope.

The nave now often has seats; properly, women are separated from men, sometimes in galleries, but this is passing out of use. There are a few pictures, e.g., behind the altars, and round statues and stations of the cross are now often found in Catholic churches.

Vestments. The vestments are the white *shapig* (equivalent to the alb, and sometimes replaced thereby), embroidered cuffs (*pazpan*), stole (*porurar*) in one piece hanging down in front with a loop for the head, over it an embroidered cincture (*koti*); then a tall, stiff, embroidered collar (*vagas*) which stands up around the neck — this is nothing but an adaptation of the mediaeval apparelled amice of the west, and a very handsome ornament; and over all the *shurtshar* (chasuble) which is like a full cope, without hood or orphreys; finally the priest wears on his head the *saghavard*, which is simply the episcopal crown of the Byzantine rite, adopted by Armenian priests when their bishops took to wearing Latin mitres in the twelfth century. Bishops add the *emiporon*, a big *pallium* worn over the shoulders, and the patriarch and archbishops have the *gonker* (the Byzantine *epigonation*), a lozenge-shaped ornament hanging at the right side. The deacon wears a coloured *shapig*, ungirdled, with wide sleeves, of silk or velvet and embroidered at wrists and shoulders, and a long stole (*urar*) over his left shoulder with the back end drawn round to come under his right arm and across his chest. When a bishop celebrates with six deacons, the protodeacon wears the sacerdotal crown. There are no liturgical colours; I have seen chasubles of golden brown silk with small black arabesques and another of plain saffron silk; black may be worn for funeral services.

Armenian bishops have used the Western mitre and crozier since the time of the Crusades. It is curious that the Latin ritual practices then borrowed (which non-Catholic Armenians claim to be customs of immemorial antiquity) were retained when the schism reopened, and in a few trifling matters Western influence continued to make itself felt; for example, the mitre worn by even dissident Armenian bishops is not the soft low cap of the twelfth century, but a towering curved affair copied from the worst Roman models of the eighteenth,[5] and their crozier likewise is of the baroque pattern.

Bishops wear the pectoral cross and ring, and for choir dress put on the *pilon*, a garment like a long very full cope, violet in colour, and a flat-topped cap covered with a veil. Vartapets have the right to a staff-of-office (*gavazan*) resembling a Byzantine pastoral staff, as well as to a veil over their caps and sometimes a pectoral cross. In processions the patriarch and archbishops carry a staff surmounted by a sort of heraldic emblem of their diocese and are preceded by ministers carrying the archiepiscopal cross, the crozier, and the vartapet's staff.

The ordinary dress of the Catholic Armenian clergy (who wear the beard) is the cassock and cincture, to which a long full-sleeved black gown, open down the front, is added on formal occasions; priests have a black cloak for choir and a veil over the flat cap if celibate. The traditional conical cap (*pakegh*) is no longer in use by Catholics.

Liturgical books. The nine Armenian liturgical books are analogous to those of the Byzantine rite and are well and clearly arranged, the best of all Eastern church-books. Four of them are required for the celebration of a solemn Liturgy, namely the *Donatzuitz*, a sort of perpetual *Ordo;* the *Badarakamaduitz*, containing the celebrant's part; the *Jiashotz*, containing the Epistles and Gospels and other parts for the deacon and minis-

---

[5] At the eucharistic congress in Jerusalem in 1893 Mgr. Terzian, bishop of Adana, said that, "I sometimes have to celebrate the holy Mysteries in the open air, for there is not always a room sufficiently high to hold me with a mitre on my head." He was, of course, referring to the poverty of his flock, but the statement provoked laughter.

ters; and the *Trebutiun,* which contains the hymns and chants of the choir. But "Low Mass" is common among the Catholics and in 1879 the patriarch Hassun provided for this by publishing an edition of the *Badarakamaduitz* arranged on the lines of the Roman Missal.

The principal other book is the *Mashdotz,* equivalent to our *Rituale.* It gets its name from the surname of St. Mesrop, who is traditionally but erroneously regarded as its compiler; actually, its contents belong to different ages and are drawn from several sources. The books have been printed at Rome, Venice, and Vienna (by the Mekhitarists at the last two places).

Altar-vessels and bread. The chalice and paten are similar to those used in the West, covered with a veil; the linen purificator is now used instead of the sponge. The bread is unleavened (even for the non-Catholics, who are the only Oriental dissidents to use *azyme*) and resembles Western altar-breads, but the disks are thicker and less crisp. A drop of water is added to the wine, but not by the dissidents, who, alone of all ancient Christians, have an "unmixed chalice."

Music. The very ancient Armenian ecclesiastical chant is of the usual Eastern enharmonic type: most beautiful really, but barbarous to those ears unable to listen with patience to anything outside the diatonic and chromatic scales. The singing is properly unaccompanied, except for the shaking of *ripidia* (*keshotz*) with little bells attached, cymbals being clashed to mark the rhythm; but organs are now sometimes found in the churches, and polyphony is occasionally heard.

The Eucharistic Liturgy

The Eucharistic Liturgy is essentially the Greek Liturgy of St. Basil, derived directly from Caesarea, translated into classical Armenian, but modified first by Syrian and Constantinopolitan and then by Latin influences till it has become *sui generis.*[6]

---

[6] The Armenians call it "The Liturgy of our Blessed Father the holy Gregory the Enlightener, revised and augmented by the holy patriarchs and teachers Isaac, Mesrop, Kut and John Mantaguni." This, of course, is not so. We of the West are not altogether free from a tendency to make patriotic flourishes of this sort.

The deacon's admonitions *"Orthi"* (ὀρθοί) and *"Proskhume"* (πρόσχωμεν) and *Amen* and *Alleluia* alone remain untranslated. It is remarkable among Eastern liturgies in that, like the Roman Mass, it has one fixed *anaphora*. The general "scheme" of the service is that the choir or people sing while the celebrant prays in a low voice, ending his prayers aloud, often at the invitation of the deacon ("Sir, bless!"). Solemn celebrations are carried out with very great magnificence. The Armenian Liturgy is never concelebrated by a number of celebrants nor is there a Liturgy of the Presanctified; according to the canons, the Liturgy should be celebrated only on Saturdays and Sundays during Lent.

A curtain is drawn across the sanctuary, or before the altar, at certain points in the service; during Lent the larger curtain cuts off the sanctuary throughout the Liturgy. In some Catholic churches elevations and genuflexions (instead of prostrations) have been introduced at the consecration; and many priests at "Low Mass" say even the words of consecration, as well as other parts, inaudibly. The people kneel from "Holy, holy, holy" until after the consecration. Blessed bread (*neshkar*) is usually no longer distributed among the Catholics.

Father James Issaverdentz's full translation of the Armenian Liturgy made at the San Lazzaro monastery in 1873 is long out of print;[7] but there is a version of it in Attwater's *Eastern Catholic Worship*.

In certain places the tendency to hybridize Armenian usages is very strong. The most astounding example — a veritable curiosity — is in Rumania. In the five Transylvanian parishes of these folk the churches are entirely Latin in appearance, Western vestments are worn, and the Liturgy used is that found in the 1728 edition of the missal of the Friars of Unity of St. Gregory — that is, the Dominican use of the Latin Mass translated into old Armenian. This is the more remarkable because these friars were never established in Transylvania.

---

[7] Father James dedicated his translation of the *Mashdotz* to the United States consul at Venice, Mr. F. Colton.

THE DIVINE OFFICE

The canonical prayer of the Armenian Church is divided into nine offices, namely, Midnight (in honour of God the Father), Matins (in honour of the risen Christ), Sunrise (in honour of the Holy Ghost), prayers of the Third, Sixth, and Ninth Hours (in honour of the descent of the Holy Ghost, of the passion, and of the death of our Lord respectively), Vespers (in honour of the entombment), Nightfall (invoking the peace of Christ), and Bedtime (for undisturbed repose). Sunrise and Nightfall are omitted on Saturdays and the eves of certain feasts, while "first Vespers" is supposed to be always celebrated in church.

These offices consist principally of psalms, variable hymns (*kanons;* several attributed to St. Nerses Glaietsi, who died in 1173), and prayers (several attributed to St. John Mantaguni, d. 490). The psalms are divided into seven groups, one for each day of the week.

The Song of the Three Children, *Magnificat, Benedictus, Nunc dimittis,* and a form of *Gloria in excelsis* are sung at Matins, and there are readings from the Gospels on Sundays and great feasts. The so-called Prayer of Manasses (which is printed at the end of the Vulgate) is recited on weekdays in Lent at Matins and Vespers. The last-named office should be preceded by readings from the lives of the saints or from homilies, and concluded by a procession through the church, but these observances are becoming more and more rare.

Since 1911 the daily recitation of the Divine Office has been obligatory upon all Catholic priests of this rite.

THE SACRAMENTS

Baptism is a long ceremony, which is begun outside the baptistery. The godfather renounces Satan and his powers, and makes a profession of faith for the child. The priest reads St. Matthew's Gospel (28:16–20), recites the Nicene creed with the godparent, and all go into the baptistery saying certain psalms. After four scriptural lessons and a litany the priest blesses the water and pours three drops of chrism into it. The actual baptism is performed by the priest sitting the child in the font, facing the east, and pouring water three times on its head, saying: "The servant of God N., coming by his own will to the state of a catechumen and thence to baptism, is baptized by me in the name of the Father . . . ," etc. Then the child is immersed thrice and held in the water (which is warmed) while Matt. 3:13–17 is read.

Confirmation is administered by the priest immediately after Baptism. He anoints the forehead, eyes, ears, nostrils, mouth, hands, breast, back, and feet of the child with chrism, accompanied by suitable words. Then he ties round its head a string of twisted red and white threads with a small cross attached; this has been blessed before the Baptism, and is removed ceremonially after eight days. He also clothes it in a white garment and offers it to God before the altar.

Penance. Confessional-boxes are in increasing use, and absolution is given by an indicative formula very similar to the Roman one.

Eucharist. The custom of Communion in both kinds has not been abrogated, but for the past hundred years or so it has not obtained in Catholic churches of this rite. Instead, the people receive a small particle, kneeling, with the words of administration translated from the Latin. The faithful are expected to go to confession and to Communion at least at Christmas (or Epiphany), Easter, the Assumption, the Transfiguration, and the Exaltation of the Cross; Easter only is obligatory.

Anointing. The proper Armenian form for the administration of this sacrament requires the presence of seven priests and is very long. It has been disused altogether by the dissidents since the fourteenth century, while the Catholics have substituted what is practically the rite in the *Rituale Romanum,* translated into their liturgical language.

Orders. With the exception of the romanized Malabarese, the Armenians, Catholic and dissident, are the only Christians of the East who have four minor and three major, or sacred, orders. Minor orders are conferred by the handing-over of the instruments of office; vesting in the distinctive vestments and laying-on of hands are added for the subdiaconate and diaconate, and anointing with chrism for the priesthood and episcopate.

Marriage is entered into by a long and admirable ceremony which, when carried out in its entirety, begins at the bride's home, includes a crowning of both parties with wreaths of flowers and celebration of the Liturgy in church, and ends with a blessed loving-cup at the house of the groom. The contract is effected by explicit declarations by the parties, unlike most Eastern wedding-services, in which they remain implicit.

Kalendar. The ecclesiastical kalendar of the Armenian rite is constructed on different principles from that of any other church. Strictly, there are only seven fixed feasts, all others falling on a day of the week following a certain Sunday which depends on the date of Easter; feasts may only be celebrated on Saturdays during penitential times and not at all in some others, e.g., Easter to Pentecost. These rules have been somewhat modified by the Catholics, who, moreover, gradually and unwillingly accepted the Gregorian reckoning between 1892 and 1912. Their national reckoning of years is from their eponymous ancestor Haik, who is put at 2492 B.C.

Feasts. The restrictions on the celebration of these reduces the number of saints' days to some 130 in the year, many of them of Armenian saints and several observed in groups, e.g., the Fathers of Nicaea, the Armenian Doctors, the Universal Doctors, the Egyptian Fathers, All Apostles. The chief fixed feasts observed by Catholics (and on the same dates as in the West) are Christmas, Circumcision, Epiphany, Purification, Annunciation, Birthday of Our Lady, her Presentation, and Immaculate Conception. Among the specifically Western feasts generally adopted are Corpus Christi, Christ the King, and Trinity Sunday; feasts special to the rite include that of the Ark of God (i.e., the Church). There are ten holydays, in addition to Sundays.

Penintential seasons. The canonical periods of fasting and absti-
nence or of abstinence alone are Lent (except Saturdays and
Sundays), six days before Christmas, five days before the As-
sumption, and five days "of Nineveh" or "of St. Gregory"; most
Wednesdays and Fridays of the year are days of abstinence.
The details of observance required vary in different dioceses.

General observations. Some of the Western traits referred to
above date from the time of the Crusades and are shared equally
by Catholics and dissidents. Others are due largely to the fact
that so many of the faithful have for so long looked to France for
protection and help, which has been generously forthcoming,
especially at the hands of certain religious congregations. In spite
of the fact that Armenians tend to regard their religious rites as
a concrete manifestation of their nationality, these same congregations have found many vocations to themselves among the
Armenians, which, whatever it may be for the individuals concerned, is not a good thing for the Catholics of the Armenian rite
as a whole, often depriving them of the direct services of very
capable men.

On the other hand, there has been for some time a movement,
in which the Mekhitarist monks are prominent, for maintaining
their orientalism, both of ritual and mind, in greater purity. Accordingly, canon 612 of the plenary Armenian council held at
Rome in 1911 declared that "devotions" are a supplementary cult
in Eastern worship and should conform to the liturgy both in
spirit and form. Nevertheless, such observances as the rosary,
way of the cross, benediction with the Blessed Sacrament, scapulars, etc., seem to grow in popularity, and the blessing of candles
on the feast of the Purification, of ashes, and of palms have been
adopted quasi-liturgically. All Armenians, whether Catholic or
not, make the sign of the cross from left to right.

BIBLIOGRAPHY

Issaverdentz, *Armenia and the Armenians* (Venice, 1886).
Lynch, *Armenia, Travels and Studies* (London, 1901).

Nurikhan, *The Life and Times of* . . . *Abbot Mekhitar* (Venice, 1915).

Tournebize, *Histoire politique et religieuse de l'Arménie* (Paris, 1910).

Weber, *Die Katholische Kirche in Armenien* (Freiburg, i.B., 1903).

Langlois, *Notice sur le Couvent Arménien* . . . *de Venise* (Venice, 1931).

Muyldermans, *Le costume liturgique arménien* (Louvain, 1926).

Issaverdentz, *The Armenian Ritual* (Venice, 1876).

Bianchini, *The Music of the Armenian Liturgy* [the melodies are made chromatic] (Venice, 1877).

CHAPTER VIII

THE CHALDEAN RITE

1. THE CHALDEANS

WHATEVER may have been the beginnings of Christianity in Mesopotamia and Persia there was a church in Edessa at the end of the second century; from that city the faith spread eastward and another greater centre was formed at Nisibis. At the beginning of the fourth century the Church in Persia was organized under his own direction by a bishop of Seleukia-Ctesiphon; and in 424 the synod of Markabta proclaimed the Persian church under its katholikos independent of the patriarch of Antioch and the "Western fathers" generally (the hierarchical bond with Antioch through Edessa had always been tenuous). During this early period the church of East Syria and Persia produced a doctor of the Universal Church, St. Ephrem (d. 373), and it was made illustrious by the theological schools of Nisibis and Edessa and by hosts of martyrs at the hands of the Persians.

In 431 the Council of Ephesus condemned the teaching of Nestorius, Patriarch of Constantinople (see p. 4). Many of the Persian Christians and a party of the East Syrians, considerably influenced by anti-imperialist political considerations, refused to accept the condemnation, which resulted by the year 500 in the development of an heretical Nestorian church under the protection of the sovereigns of Persia. They probably aimed at no more than a local autonomy like that of the recognized patriarchates and were moved toward Nestorianism by their strong antagonism to its opposite, Monophysism, but by the seventh century the schism had hardened and the Mohammedan conquest of Syria

and Persia confirmed their severance from the Catholic Church
and their profession of the condemned teaching.

For eight hundred years the Nestorian Church was, with fluc-
tuations of prosperity, a mighty organization, one whose missionary enterprise is unsurpassed in the history of Christianity. It had
twenty metropolitan sees with many bishoprics and monasteries,
extending to China and India; but the time of its greatest extension was soon succeeded by utter ruin. At the end of the fourteenth century the Mongol hordes of Timur Leng devastated
Asia, sweeping away the Nestorian Church in a cataclysm of
blood and apostasy. The remnants of the western part of his
church gathered round their katholikos in northern Mesopotamia;
of the eastern part, nothing remained (except in Malabar).

During the thirteenth century Dominican and Franciscan friars
were active among the Nestorians, and the katholikos Yaballaha
III had amiable relations with the Holy See,[1] several individual
bishops became Catholics, and in the following century a number
of Latin sees were erected, but they did not last long.

By the middle of the fifteenth century the office of Nestorian
katholikos had become hereditary in a family, passing from uncle
to nephew (it still does), and on the succession of Simon VIII
Denha in 1551 a disaffected party elected a rival, John Sulaka.
Sulaka at once turned to the Franciscans for help; they sent him
to Rome, where he made a profession of Catholic faith and was
appointed by Pope Julius III to be patriarch of those of his rite
who should follow his example.[2] It was at this time that the name
"Chaldean" began to be used to distinguish such people, as to
call them "Catholic Nestorians" was obviously impossible. From

---

[1] He was a Sino-Turk, born in Pekin. He sent another Mongol, the monk
Barsauma, on an embassy to Rome and the West. Barsauma received Holy
Communion from the hands of Pope Nicholas IV, and himself gave it to
King Edward I of England in Gascony. For all that, the profession of faith
he carried was only doutbfully orthodox.

[2] On this occasion Cardinal Maffei declared to the assembly that, "The
Chaldeans seem to have had the name of Nestorians without holding any
Nestorian errors." Whether or not this was true at that time, it displays a
striking difference of spirit from that of the Portugese in Malabar a few
years later (see p. 211).

now on there were two lines of patriarchs (or katholikoi), one Catholic, the other Nestorian.

THE CHALDEAN CATHOLICS

The successors of Sulaka all took the name of Simon (Shimun), and at times during the sixteenth century they made attempts (with the approval of the Holy See) to exercise their traditional jurisdiction over the Christians of their rite in India. But in the year 1692 Simon XIII apostatized, and from him the present line of Nestorian katholikoi is descended. They went to live in Kurdistan.

Meanwhile the line of Simon Denha had not been continuously in schism, for several of his successors (all of whom took the name of Elias) had been reconciled with Rome. Diarbekir particularly had become a Catholic centre, and in 1672 the metropolitan of this city, Mar Joseph, made his profession of faith and the Holy See allowed him to have the title of patriarch (but without specifying of where or of whom). He was succeeded by other "patriarchs" there, so that for twenty years, from 1672 till 1692, when Simon XIII lapsed, there were two Catholic patriarchs among the Chaldeans, and from 1692 till 1804 two Nestorian ones.

In 1778 Elias XIII succeeded his uncle as Nestorian patriarch at the same time that his young cousin John Hormizd, the metropolitan of Mosul, turned Catholic. In 1781 there was no Catholic patriarch in office, Diarbekir having become vacant by the resignation of Joseph IV, and in 1802 the administration of the see was confided to his nephew, the priest Augustine Hindi. There ensued a long and rather bitter rivalry between Hormizd and Hindi, both of whom wanted to be Catholic patriarch; the Holy See was not keen on either of them, and was hoping for the submission of Elias XIII. When the last-named died in 1804 without leaving a nephew to succeed him the rivalry became worse, and there was strong temptation for his cousin John Hormizd to apostatize (he was in fact under censure for a time).

At length Hindi also died, and in 1834 Rome appointed Hormizd to be patriarch at last.

The upshot of all this complication is that there has been a succession of Catholic Chaldean patriarchs ever since, who are in continuity with the original historical line of Simon Denha of the house of Mama. To avoid any chance of the assertion of the hereditary principle in the succession, the Holy See gave Hormizd a coadjutor with right of succession and the patriarchal family gracefully renounced its improper privilege.

The first successor of Hormizd, Nicholas Zaya, after eight years resigned his see, in 1846, and the next patriarch, Joseph VI Audo, had a long and stormy period of office. He was an energetic and competent prelate but ambitious, and very anxious to recover the ancient but abolished jurisdiction of his church over the Syrian Catholics of Malabar. Twice, in 1860 and 1874, he sent bishops (Mar Thomas Rokkos and Mar Elias Mellos) thither at the request of Malabarese malcontents and caused much trouble thereby. Meanwhile, in 1869, the Holy See decided to apply the bull *"Reversurus,"* governing the appointment of bishops,[3] to the Chaldeans. Audo asserted that this was an infringement of Eastern rights, and made a very temperate protest before the assembled Vatican Council. The advisers of Pope Pius IX, however, took a severe view of the patriarch's general policy, and he narrowly escaped excommunication. He was eventually reconciled with the Holy See and was highly spoken of by Pope Leo XIII; the troublesome bull was modified.

Such distressing events weakened the cause of Catholic unity among the Nestorians in the nineteenth century, but it nevertheless made good progress, which would have been even better but for the activities of Anglican and Russian missions. A great cultural work was done for his countrymen by Paul Bejan (1838–1920), a Chaldean born in Persia who became a Lazarist priest. He came to Europe and published magistral editions of their liturgical and other ecclesiastical books, as well as translations

---

[3] This was the bull that caused a schism among the Armenians (see p. 184).

into the spoken Syriac of the *Imitation of Christ*, lives of the saints, etc. An English translation of his text of the mystical treatises of Isaac the Syrian (of Nineveh) by A. E. Wensinck was published at Amsterdam in 1923.

The patriarch Mar Emmanuel II Thomas was in 1902 accorded the title of papal "delegate for the Nestorians," and he shortly after reconciled two bishops with several priests and their congregations, numbering altogether some 20,000 persons.

During the war of 1914–1918 the Chaldeans suffered equally with their neighbours from massacre and deportation. Six bishops (including the two ex-Nestorians), a score of priests, and thousands of their people were murdered by the Turks and Kurds, and four dioceses were destroyed.

PRESENT STATE

Patriarch. The Patriarch-Katholikos of Babylon of the Chaldeans lives at Mosul,[4] and he has jurisdiction over the faithful of his rite throughout the world. He is elected by a synod of all the bishops, the delegate apostolic for Mesopotamia presiding. The choice must be submitted to the Sacred Eastern Congregation for confirmation by the pope, who sends the *pallium*. He consecrates the chrism for his whole patriarchate and ordains and institutes all bishops. He is an *ex officio* member of the senate of Irak.

Bishops. The sees are that of Bagdad and Mosul (the patriarchal diocese, comprising nearly half the faithful), Kerkuk, Akra, Amadia, Zakho, Urmia, Sena, and Mardin (others are in abeyance). All the bishops depend directly on the patriarch but the two Persian sees of Urmia and Sena are called archiepiscopal.

A vacant see is filled by choice of the patriarch and bishops from a list of candidates recommended by the clergy and chief men of the diocese, or at will. The choice must be approved by the Sacred Eastern Congregation before the elect can be consecrated and enthroned.

---

[4] The title "of Babylon" seems to have been first given to Joseph II of the Diarbekir line by Pope Clement XI in 1701, from the erroneous identification of modern Bagdad with ancient Babylon.

There are patriarchal vicariates for Basra, Syria, Egypt, and Constantinople (13,850 faithful altogether); and there are colonies of Chaldeans, totaling about 800 members, in the United States, who have a church in Chicago.[5]

Parochial clergy. The principal seminary is the patriarchal college of St. Peter at Mosul, which has about fifty students. The Dominicans, who have worked among the Chaldeans without a break since 1750, established another seminary for them (and for the Antiochene Syrians) at Mosul in 1882. It is directed by the friars, with the help of secular priests of the rites concerned, but is rather French in its influence. A college for the Chaldeans of Persia was opened by French Lazarists at Khosrova in 1845; it was reconstituted after the war at Urmia (Rezaia). A few other students go to the Jesuit Oriental seminary at Bairut or elsewhere, but some of the clergy still make insufficient studies. They are not bound to celibacy and about a half of them are married; they mostly live in very poor circumstances. The rank of *chorepiskopos*, conferred as a title of honour by the patriarch, and that of *archdeacon* are given by a liturgical ceremony.

Religious institutes. The only Chaldean monks are a small congregation of *Antonians*, called "of St. Hormisdas," founded in 1808 by Gabriel Dambo, who for years was engaged in commerce at Mardin; after directing his foundation for twenty-four years he was murdered during a Kurdish insurrection. In all respects except corporate wealth the Chaldean monks resemble their Maronite brethren. They number about one hundred, a third of them priests (most of whom serve parishes), in three monasteries, one of which is very small. The most interesting, though no longer the mother house, is Rabban-Hormizd, near Alkosh. This was founded originally in the seventh century and was re-established by Father Dambo; some of its buildings are very old. These monks are steadily increasing in number; their life is one of hard work and considerable austerity, and they are an excellent influ-

---

[5] Father Gabriel Oussani, professor of ecclesiastical history and other subjects in the seminary at Dunwoodie, N. Y., was a Chaldean.

ence in their church. The habit is a black tunic and hood, though the ordinary clerical turban is commonly worn as well.

Sisters affiliated to the Dominican third order conduct village schools, and a recently formed congregation of other Chaldean nuns has two schools in Bagdad.

The Faithful throughout the world total over 96,000, nearly half of whom live in the great plain of Mesopotamia, north and northwest of Mosul.[6] Here a good deal of debased Syriac ("Sureth") is spoken by them; elsewhere Persian, Kurdish, or Turkish, according to the neighbourhood, and Arabic in the towns. So long ago as the middle of the past century a Protestant clergyman, G. P. Badger, commented on the superior civilization, intelligence, and order of the Chaldeans in Mesopotamia, in his book *The Nestorians and their Rituals* (London, 1852, Vol. I, p. 176). This praise is, of course, relative, the Chaldeans having for many centuries been part of a shamefully oppressed and exploited people. Their present encouraging state is due in a measure to the enlightened services of the Dominicans in Mesopotamia, of the Lazarists in Persia, and of other Western institutes both of men and women.

LITURGY AND CUSTOMS

Chaldean *church buildings* have their own plan. The sanctuary is raised above the nave and generally separated from it by a solid wall reaching to the roof. This wall is pierced by a door some six feet wide, covered by a curtain to be withdrawn during the Liturgy; before it is a low wall, broken in the middle, enclosing a space for the choir. Men and women are separated and there are usually no seats. In the more modern Catholic churches the altar is against the east wall of the sanctuary, and is now of western pattern, with gradines, numerous candlesticks, and artificial flowers; but the altar "stone" (*tablitha*) is of wood. The

---

[6] There were no Nestorians left in these regions until postwar persecution drove them toward Mosul from the mountains of Kurdistan. They are precisely the people who, under the name of "Assyrians," had to appeal to Europe for protection against their Mohammedan governors and neighbours in Irak. They are now considerably outnumbered by the Chaldeans.

Blessed Sacrament is reserved in a tabernacle. On the north side of the sanctuary there is an altarlike "credence-table," the *prothesis*, and in older churches the baptistery is on the south side of the sanctuary. Outside the church is a partly covered courtyard wherein the Divine Office is celebrated during the summer. There are pictures and sometimes even stations of the cross but no statues in these churches.

Vestments. These are similar to those of the Syrians: *kotina* (now generally an alb); *zande* ("cuffs"); *urara,* sometimes, but improperly, worn crossed like the Western stole; *zunara,* girdle; *paina* or *maapra,* a copelike chasuble; and embroidered shoes. Bishops have adopted the Western mitre, crozier, pectoral-cross, and ring, and have no *omophorion.* Deacons wear an ungirdled alblike garment, with a long stole disposed as a Western deacon wears it. The ordinary ecclesiastical dress is a round turban, wide, low, and flat, black cassock (violet for bishops), and over-mantle with wide sleeves.

Liturgical books. These were formerly sixteen in number, and some of them are still in manuscript. The most used ones, especially the *Takhsa,* priest's Mass-book with the addition of the variable parts of the Liturgy, and a pastor's manual have been accurately edited and beautifully printed by the Dominican press at Mosul, from which an Arabic Bible, Syriac dictionary, and other valuable works have been issued. A definitive edition of the four books of the Divine Office was published by Father Bejan in Paris in 1888. This last was republished for general use in 1938 at Rome; a new edition of the equivalent of the *Pontificale* is now ready for press at Mosul.

Altar-vessels and bread. Catholics make use of the same altar-vessels and accessories as in the West, with the hand-cross for episcopal blessings and *ripidia* for processions. The altar-breads are similar to Western ones in appearance but they are leavened and have a little salt added. The custom of baking them afresh for each celebration is almost extinct.

Music. The Chaldean enharmonic chant is traditional to the rite and is being studied by the Benedictines of Sharfeh and

Jerusalem, but they have not yet published any of it. The only instruments permitted are cymbals, triangles, and so forth, to mark the rhythm, and it is rather monotonous.

Liturgical language. This is pure Syriac, i.e., the Edessene dialect of Aramaic, with the Eastern pronunciation and characters, and with only the scriptural lessons in the vernacular.

THE EUCHARISTIC LITURGY

The Liturgy, derived from that of Edessa and perhaps a branch of the Antiochene, is called *Kurbana,* "the Offering," or *Kudasha,* "the Hallowing." The usual Liturgy is called "of the Holy Apostles" (i.e., Addai and Mari, reputed apostles of the East Syrians and Persians), and has two alternative *anaphoras* "of Theodore the Interpreter" (of Mopsuestia) and "of Nestorius." The Catholics naturally do not use these last names but call them "the Second," used on Sundays and feasts from Advent to Palm Sunday, and "the Third Hallowing," used only five times in the year.

The Liturgy is celebrated in the evening before Christmas, Epiphany, and Easter, and there is a form of Liturgy of the Presanctified for "Friday of Suffering." The Liturgy is not concelebrated but sometimes most of the pre-anaphoral part is carried out by a number of priests, each doing a part, and the presiding bishop then designates one of them to complete the sacrifice.

A translation of the Chaldean Liturgy, made by Father Dominic Dahane and Sister M. Loyola Hayde, was published at Chicago in 1939; there is another version in the present writer's *Eastern Catholic Worship.*

THE DIVINE OFFICE

This consists of only three "hours," Vespers (*Ramsha*), Night Office (*Lilya*), and Matins (*Sapra*), to which the Antonian monks add the "little hours," whose text they have borrowed from their Maronite brethren. The office is made up of a considerable number of psalms (the psalter is spread over a week), with hymns (many, of course, of St. Ephrem), prayers, and litanies. "Glory to God in the highest" is sung at Matins on Sundays and feasts. From the Ascension until the beginning of November choir-office is sung in the courtyard instead of in church.

THE SACRAMENTS

Baptism. The rite of baptism is very long, being modeled on the eucharistic Liturgy, with corresponding prayers, chants, litanies, and scriptural lessons. There is a preface leading to an "anaphora," wherein the font is blessed; the child is anointed twice, the second time all over. The baptism proper comes at the place of the communion. The child is set down in the water, which is poured thrice over its head with the words, "I baptize you, servant of God, N., in the name of the Father," etc.

Confirmation follows at once, the child being anointed with chrism between the eyes, the priest saying the Roman form of words.

Penance. This sacrament is administered practically as in the West. Confessional-boxes are now to be found in many churches.

Eucharist. Communion in both kinds for all is envisaged in the liturgical books. But nowadays the people receive it under the species of bread only, standing at the sanctuary door. The words are: "The body of our Lord is given to the devout believer for the forgiveness of sin." Priests not celebrating on Holy Thursday, and deacons on the anniversary of their ordination, are given Communion in both kinds, separately.

Anointing. The anointings are on the mouth, hands, and feet. Some prayers from the Roman office have been introduced, in Syriac.

Orders. The Chaldeans have five orders: reader, subdeacon, deacon, priest, bishop. They are conferred by the laying-on of hands, with a formula in each case analogous to the following: "O God the Father Almighty send down thy Holy Spirit for the ordination of N., to the office of the priesthood." The appropriate vestment is given. Archdeacons, *chorepiskopoi*, and archbishops are made in a similar way.

Marriage. The ceremony is called *Buraka*, "the Blessing," and includes the usual Eastern crowning of the couple (with a red, white, and blue fillet). It is very long and takes place entirely in the bride's home.

Kalendar. The Gregorian reckoning was adopted during the rule of Joseph Audo. The ecclesiastical year begins on Advent Sunday and is divided into ten periods: Advent, Epiphany, Lent, Easter, The Apostles, Summer, Elias, The Cross, Moses, and the Dedication. These periods are of unequal length.

Feasts. There are only some sixty feasts in the Chaldean kalendar, of which about a half are fixed and the remainder movable, many of them saints' days celebrated on certain Fridays. There are several collective feasts (e.g., the Four Evangelists, the Greek Doctors, the Syrian and Roman Doctors), and some less ancient celebrations from the West — Corpus Christi, the Sacred Heart, St. Joseph. Chrism is consecrated by the patriarch and there is a *mandatum* on Holy Thursday.

Penitential seasons. The fast of Lent lasts seven weeks, all food, drink, and tobacco being eschewed till noon; the fast before Christmas, nine days; before the feast of SS. Peter and Paul, two days; of our Lady, five days; and of the Ninivites, three days; all Wednesdays and Fridays are days of abstinence, except from Christmas to the Epiphany and in paschal-time. The Ninivite fast is observed with special rigour, and the whole of the psalter is recited in the office on each of its days; a Chaldean priest tells me he has known laypeople to go the whole of those three days without any food at all.

General observations. Despite his intransigence toward certain Roman legislation, it was the patriarch Joseph Audo who introduced several Western observances. In general, Latin influence has modified only accessories of the Chaldean rite, and encouraged private devotion by means of the rosary, scapulars, etc. The sign of the cross is made from left to right.

BIBLIOGRAPHY

Tfinkji, *L'Eglise chaldéene* (Paris, 1913).

Luke, *Mosul and its Minorities* (London, 1925).

Rabban, *La Messa Caldea detta "Degli Apostoli"* (Rome, 1935).

Hindo, *Primats d'Orient . . . et Maphriens syriens* (Rome, 1936).

Bello, *La Congregation de S. Hormisdas et l'Eglise chaldéene* (Rome, 1939).

Codrington, "The Chaldean Liturgy" in *Eastern Churches Quarterly*, Vol. II, nos. 2, 3, 4 (Ramsgate, 1937).

2. THE MALABARESE

Malabar is that part of the southwest coast of India which lies between Mangalore and Cape Comorin. Including the native states of Cochin and Travancore it has a large number of native Christians (Catholics of three rites, Jacobite dissidents, and Protestants of many sects), who are, however, greatly outnumbered by their pagan neighbours. They are Indo-Europeans of the Dravidian family, and speak a widely used dialect called Malayalam.

These Malabár Christians call themselves as a body "Christians of St. Thomas" and are quite sure they were evangelized by that apostle, whose alleged first shrine they show on the opposite coast, at Mylapore.[7] Nevertheless, their origins are a matter of very great uncertainty. It seems certain that there were Malabarese Christians before the sixth century and it is likely that they were a fruit of the missionary activity of the East Syrian Church (it does not follow that they were always, or ever, formally Nestorian); there is no doubt that their geographical position brought them into touch with the metropolitans of Revardashir and that their continued existence was due to their connection with the Nestorian Church: from the earliest times their liturgy was Chaldean and its language Syriac, and their traditions are unanimous that their bishops were sent to them from "Babylon" (Bagdad).

There are incidental references to these people in the earlier Middle Ages and in the records of the later mediaeval travellers, and the Holy See was aware of their existence. In 1122 an "arch-

---

[7] The *Anglo-Saxon Chronicle* states that in 883 King Alfred the Great sent Sighelm, bishop of Sherborne, with gifts to Rome and to "the church of the Apostles Bartholomew and Thomas" in India, in fulfillment of a vow.

bishop of India," one John, went to Rome *via* Constantinople and received the pallium from Pope Callixtus II; and in 1328 Pope John XXII consecrated a Dominican, Friar Jordan, bishop and sent him with a letter addressed to the head of the Christians at Quilon. Twenty years later a Franciscan bishop, John of Marignolli, visited India; he was well received by the Christians there, who declared their devotion to the Holy See. They had early received a grant of privileges from the Hindu kings, and at this time even had a ruler of their own, to whom Pope Eugenius IV addressed a letter as "My most beloved son in Christ, Thomas, the most illustrious Emperor of the Indians."

During the second half of the fifteenth century they were for a long time without a bishop, apparently on account of persecution by the Mohammedans of southern India, which prevented communication with the East Syrian katholikos. In 1490 Joseph the Indian made his way to Gazerta Bait Zabdai in Mesopotamia, with the result that two bishops were sent to Malabar; later on Father Joseph went to Rome, where he declared that both the East Syrians and Malabarese professed the Catholic faith and looked on the pope as their supreme pontiff.

But for practical purposes direct contact of the Malabarese with the West begins with the coming of the Portugese in 1498. It seems clear that the Malabarese religious leaders regarded the Portugese from the first as their brothers in religion, affirming their own communion with the Holy See and acknowledging its prerogatives. And at first the Portugese do not seem to have questioned their Catholicity (as St. Francis Xavier did not when he was at Cranganore in 1549), recognizing their bishop, Mar Jacob, and clearly holding religious communion with him. But almost at once they began to show anxiety to "latinize" the Indian Christians. In 1553 Pope Julius III recognized the jurisdiction of the Catholic Chaldean patriarch, John Sulaka (see p. 199), over India, and Paul IV confirmed the appointment of two Chaldean bishops for the Syro-Indians. But the Portugese, who had a Latin archiepiscopal see at Goa, were not familiar with the phenomenon of non-Latin Catholics and hardly believed it possible for right living and orthodoxy to flourish apart from specifically Roman observances; without adequate reason, they scented the Nestorian heresy everywhere among these strange native Christians.[8] There followed a period of clash and intrigue between Europeans and Indians, in which the conduct of the ecclesiastics on either side was not uniformly edifying. For example, there is extant a letter from Pope Gregory XIII to the king of Portugal, dated 1578, asking him to see that the viceroy in India gave fair play to one of the Chaldean bishops, Mar Abraham, "whom we hear has been greatly vexed by some." The other, Mar Joseph, was also accused of Nestorianism, but the root of his offence seems to be that he refused to ordain Indians who had been trained in a Portuguese seminary without being taught their liturgical language.[9]

When the last Chaldean bishop died, the archbishop of Goa, Alexis de Menezez, an Augustinian friar, made a visitation of the Syro-Indians and in 1599 convened a synod to deal with their affairs at Diamper (Udiamparur). The archbishop presided, assisted by Jesuit fathers, and they, together with 150 sacerdotal and 600 lay deputies of the Syro-Indians, made a profession of faith and anathematized the errors of Nestorius. Among the arbitrary changes brought about by the Portugese at this synod or about the same time were: the abolition of the jurisdiction of the Catholic Chaldean patriarch in India and the substitution of Portugese bishops for Syrians; a number of changes in the Eucharistic Liturgy, and the introduction of communion in one kind, Roman vestments, and other innovations; the abolition of

---

[8] The Indians had the Nestorian characteristic of not using holy images in their churches. "We are Christians," they said. "We do not worship idols." That attitude may be a proof of religious ignorance but it is no proof of heresy. Mar Jacob was one of the bishops consecrated by the katholikos of the Nestorians at Gazerta Bait Zabdai. Several of the katholikoi had relations with Rome around this time. Things were apparently complicated by the word Nestorian being used as a racial appellation, without theological significance.

[9] Among the Jesuits at Goa at this time was an Englishman, Father Thomas Stevens. He it was who helped the merchant-adventurers John Newbery and Ralph Fitch to escape when they had been imprisoned by the Portugese during their famous journey that began in 1583.

the Syrian Pontifical and Ritual; the imposition of clerical celibacy; and the setting up of the Inquisition.[10]

These measures caused grave discontent. There is no serious reason to suppose that the Indians secretly hankered after Nestorianism, and there is direct evidence that they respected papal supremacy; but they disliked their Portugese masters, with their domineering ways and innovations from Europe.[11] After several vain attempts to get redress of their grievances by lawful methods, almost the whole body of Syro-Indians went into schism in the year 1653. The occasion was the arrival of a Chaldean bishop, Ahathalla, from Bagdad at Mylapore, who had been sent for by the Indian leader, the archdeacon Thomas. The bishop was seized by the Portugese, and the Indians alleged (untruly, no doubt) that he was deliberately drowned in the sea off Cochin on the way to Goa. Ahathalla was certainly a Catholic.

Pope Alexander VII sent out Carmelite friars to deal with the trouble. One, Joseph Sebastiani, was made bishop and commissary apostolic and by 1662, 84 out of the 116 Indian "parishes" had returned to Catholic unity. The remainder became that schismatic body now known as the Malabar Jacobites (see Vol. II). In the following year the Dutch drove all other Europeans from Cochin. Before he went, Mgr. Sebastiani consecrated bishop, as administrator for the Indians, a native priest who had led the faithful remnants of Catholics in 1653. This

---

[10] "The Inquisition rarely succeeded in receiving hearty affection from its victims," observes Dr. Fortescue dryly. J. S. Assemani says roundly in his *Bibliotheca orientalis* that most of the acts of the Synod of Diamper were an outcome of misguided zeal, ignorance of Eastern Catholic usages, and undue attachment to those of the West. The synod has never been formally confirmed by Rome, nor could it be in its entirety for, as Mgr. Giamil notes in his *Genuinae Relationes*, p. 610, some of its acts ran clean contrary to the decrees of the Holy See. The fact is that, in addition to his "imperialism," Menezez was obsessed by his suspicion of latent Nestorianism: but some of his actions have been unjustly exaggerated or misunderstood.

[11] That Portugese policy in India was not actuated solely by concern for the good estate of the Catholic Church is shown by the history of the *Padroado* troubles, which culminated in flat defiance of the Holy See by them in 1838.

was Shandy Palliveetil (Alexander de Campo), and he ruled his church and consolidated the reunion for fourteen years. Before he died he welcomed the Carmelites (Italian this time) back to Malabar, but his request for a Syro-Indian successor was not granted.

Mar Shandy was followed by a succession of Carmelite vicars apostolic, who ruled till 1887, not without difficulties.[12] The Syro-Indians never ceased trying to get indigenous bishops, either by petitioning Rome or by negotiating with Catholic Chaldean prelates in Mesopotamia. One of these, Mar Elias Mellos, sent to Malabar in 1874 by the Chaldean patriarch Joseph VI Audo (who was involved in trouble with Rome) stirred up a schism which still exists: the "Mellusians" are a tiny nominally Nestorian sect in Trichur.[13]

In the words of a Belgian Jesuit, "For three centuries the European missionaries went on footling and blundering and worrying the poor Syrians with their Latin bishops, until Leo XIII got enough of it and, in the face of a strong opposition, appointed three Indian Syrian bishops" (Catholic Herald of India, Jan. 30, 1924). This was in 1896, when Malabar was divided anew into three vicariates apostolic; a fourth was made in 1911. Finally in 1923, Pope Pius XI restored to the Syro-Indians a regular hierarchy, consisting of one archbishop and three suffragans. During their fifty years of renewed home-rule the Malabarese have made considerable progress in every direction.

PRESENT STATE

Organization. The Syro-Indian province comprises the native

---

[12] One of them, Miles Prendergast, was an Irishman. His career was unfortunate. He expected the secular clergy to live as strictly as mendicant friars, and he got himself so disliked that in 1831 he was recalled to Rome and asked to resign.

[13] Both the Chaldeans and Indians wanted, and a few still want, the restoration of the Chaldean patriarch's jurisdiction over the Syro-Malabarese, but the differences of race, culture, and language are against it. Audo tried to bring the question before the Vatican Council. But as recently as 1831 the Holy See appears to have been less opposed to this arrangement; see Bello's *Congregation de St. Horimsdas . . . et l'Eglise chaldéene* (Rome, 1939), p. 85.

states of Travancore and Cochin, with British Cochin, and depends on the Sacred Eastern Congregation through the delegate apostolic of the East Indies. The hierarchy consists of the archbishop of Ernakulam, with the bishops of Changanacherry, Trichur, and Kottayam; they are appointed directly from Rome. The present archbishop and metropolitan is Mar Augustine Kandathil, appointed in 1923.

Parochial clergy. They are mostly formed at the seminary of Alwaye (founded *c.* 1675 at Verapoly), now an interritual establishment directed by Belgian Carmelites on almost exclusively European lines; others go to Latin seminaries at Kandy, Mangalore, or Rome. In addition to their vernacular Malayalam all Malabarese priests are taught Latin, English, and their liturgical Syriac. The sacerdotal standard is very high.

Subdeacons and upwards are strictly bound to celibacy. Priests are called *kathanar* (Lord's man) and the bishops *abuna* (our father); pastors are helped in their administrative duties by a council of lay people.

Religious institutes. Among the Syro-Indians there is a most remarkable number of vocations to the religious life. The congregation of men, *Tertiaries of our Lady of Mount Carmel,* was founded by Fathers Thomas Palakal and Thomas Parukara in 1831 at Mannanam. It was affiliated in 1860 to the Order of Discalced Carmelites, whose habit is worn. Its principal work is the giving of missions and retreats, both to Syrians and Latins, and by its pioneer efforts the Malabarese were the first postschism Catholic Orientals to do missionary work among the heathen (they were till recently the only ones who had the opportunity). The prior general resides at Thevara and there are fifteen other monasteries, with 135 priests, 107 clerics, and 55 brothers. Among their works they conduct twelve schools and have three printing and publishing establishments. There is a small "Southist" congregation, called the *Oblates of the Sacred Heart.*

The principal congregations of women, chiefly engaged in teaching, are the *Carmelite Tertiary Sisters* (630 members in

38 convents) and the *Franciscan Tertiary Sisters* (240 in 20
convents). There are six small "Southist" houses of Visitation
nuns, and 180 Sisters of Adoration of the Blessed Sacrament.

The Faithful. There are two social "castes" among Malabarese
Syrians, called "Northists" and "Southists." The last-named, a
small minority, are exclusively found in the diocese of Kottayam
and are supposed to be the descendants of some of the Syrians
who, according to local tradition, came to Malabar with one
Thomas Cana in the fourth (much later?) century.[14] The
Northists claim to be the superior race, and even among the
Catholics their mutual relations are not always what they should
be. The bishops discourage distinctions based on caste with
reference to low-caste converts from Hinduism.

The Malabarese have a strong taste for education; since the
restoration of native bishops schools of all grades have arisen
on every hand and the people have made good use of them.
Their religious temper is characterized by an addiction to
elaborate exterior observances and long prayers.[15] In the opinion
of an apostolic delegate, Mgr. Zaleski, they are "the noblest and
most intelligent race in the whole of India," but this can hardly
be seriously maintained. Their real piety is weakened by a
certain "flightiness" of character. Except for the Eucharistic
Liturgy they are hardly distinguishable in their formal religious
practices and outlook from Latin Catholics and their general
edifyingness and the success of their institutions have been used
as an argument for the latinization of Orientals — by those who
forget that the price of latinization in Malabar is represented
today by over 400,000 souls not in communion with Rome.

Early marriages are the rule, usually arranged by the parents.
Northists and Southists do not intermarry.

In addition to the 928,000 Syrians there are in Malabar 469,000
Catholics of the Latin rite, fruit of European missionary efforts

---

[14] A traditional local explanation is that they are respectively the descendants of the two wives of Thomas Cana — or even of St. Thomas the
Apostle.

[15] In some households evening prayers for the family last the greater part
of an hour.

since the fifteenth century, and the small body of Malankara Catholics (see p. 177).

LITURGY AND CUSTOMS

Church-buildings. These are plain aisleless rectangles, with the roof of choir and sanctuary sometimes higher than that of the nave. The bigger and older churches have, especially on the western façade, a good deal of applied ornament and architectural features that are a curious mixture of Indian fashions with European baroque. They are furnished with stations of the cross, statues, confessional-boxes, etc., just as in the West. The sexes are separated in church, men being in front.

Vestments and altar-vessels are in the Western forms and of the worst patterns, and the *liturgical books* correspond to the Roman ones; they are printed in Rome by the Propaganda press and also by the local Carmelites. Clerical dress is Western, even including the biretta and shaving the beard, but priests often wear a plain gown, white or black, for ordinary dress.

Music. The liturgical chant of the Malabarese rite is Chaldean in origin but it, too, has undergone much Western influence, with surprising results. It has more recognizable resemblances to the plainsong of the West than the music of any other Eastern rite. A system of notation is being worked out for the chant in order that it may be printed.

THE EUCHARISTIC LITURGY

This is simply the Chaldean Liturgy, with the sole anaphora "of the Holy Apostles" (SS. Addai and Mari), as revised by the Synod of Diamper; it is celebrated in Syriac. It is called *Kurbana,* the Offering, and there is a proper fixed form of "low" celebration. The moving of the book from one end to the other of the altar and the ringing of a "sanctus-bell," introduced into this Liturgy and sometimes found in others as well, are quite meaningless ceremonies, at any rate at a solemn Liturgy, for they have arisen from the particular history of the Roman Mass. After "Low Mass" the prayers for Russia are said as in the West, and before leaving the sanctuary the celebrant kisses the altar and says a prayer with reference to it similar to that in the Antiochene rite.

Concelebration is not used by the Malabarese (except at ordinations); they have a Liturgy of the Presanctified on Good Friday only. There is an English translation of the Malabar Liturgy in Attwater's *Eastern Catholic Worship*.

THE DIVINE OFFICE

This was the only rite of Malabarese worship left untouched by the Portugese; it was abridged and rearranged, and the recitation of the new edition made obligatory, in 1876. There are three "hours," *Ramsha* (Vespers), *Lilya* (Night-office), and *Sapra* (Day-office), consisting almost entirely of psalms (the psalter is spread over a fortnight), with a few hymns and prayers.

It is hoped that the new edition (Rome, 1938) of the Chaldean office will come into use in Malabar, and also that the Chaldean Pontifical, shortly to appear, will also be adopted (cf. next paragraph). This will be in accordance with the wish of the Sacred Eastern Congregation that the Malabar Church should return to its earlier and more appropriate usages.

THE SACRAMENTS

These are administered according to the forms in the Roman *Pontificale* and *Rituale* as edited at Goa and translated into Syriac. Confirmation is separated from Baptism, and conferred by a bishop. The rite of communicating the laity has been adopted complete from Roman usage. The name of St. Thomas the Apostle is added to Peter and Paul in the "I confess" and Communion is in one kind only: but the people kneel leaning back on their heels in the Indian manner, and the words of administration are: "May the body of our Lord Jesus Christ be to this devout believer for the forgiveness of sin and to everlasting life. Amen."

Kalendar and feasts. The Malabar kalendar is practically that

of the Western church. Besides Sundays there are thirteen holydays of obligation, including one of their special feasts of St.
Thomas, his martyrdom, on July 3.

Penitential seasons. Fasting and abstinence or abstinence only
is observed in Lent (fifty days, but excluding Sundays), Advent
(twenty-four days), "Ninive" (three days), Ember Days, the
Roman vigils, and every Friday and Saturday.

General observations. All the Western "popular devotions"
and observances, and in the same forms, are in great favour with
the Malabarese. They even have "methods of hearing Mass":
I have seen one taken from the works of St. Leonard of Port
Maurice. But there are those among them who hope that, under
the influence of the indigenous hierarchy, some of the more
unhappy effects of foreign domination will be undone, in such
matters as revision of the Liturgy, restoration of Oriental vestments, the encouragement of Indian studies, and so on.

BIBLIOGRAPHY

Mackenzie, *Christianity in Travancore* (Trivandrum, 1901).
Panjikaran, *The Syrian Church in Malabar* (Trichinopoly, 1914).
—— *Christianity in Malabar* (Rome, 1926).
Bernard, *Brief . . . History of the St. Thomas Christians*
    (Trichinopoly, 1924).
The Carmelite Congregation of Malabar (Trichinopoly, 1932).
Schurhammer, *The Malabar Church and Rome* (Trichinopoly,
    1934).

    See also the bibliography on page 180.

CHAPTER IX

EASTERN MONASTICISM

TO CATHOLICS in the West nowadays monastic life means the life of monks, of friars, of canons and even clerks regular, of enclosed nuns, and of active sisters. There are different orders, with different names, different rules, different ways of life, different aims and activities. So striking are the differences between some of them, that if we are suddenly challenged to say what it is they have in common (apart from the Catholic faith), we may unthinkingly fall back on some such reply as, "Oh, er . . . their monasticism." Of course that is quite wrong. Monasticism pertains to monks (and their female counterpart), and most of these people are not monks at all. The friars (e.g., Dominicans), though they retain certain monastic characteristics, or the clerks regular (e.g., Jesuits), are not monks; the Little Sisters of the Poor or the Sisters of Charity, though we may call them nuns for convenience, are not female monks. What these people have in common is that they are *regulars*, living under a rule (*regula*), or as we often say, *religious*, all following "a stable mode of life in community, whereby they undertake to observe not only the general precepts but also the evangelical counsels, by means of the vows of obedience, chastity, and poverty."

But even the monks properly so called are not homogeneous. There are great practical differences between life in a Benedictine monastery of the English or American congregations, with their educational and pastoral work, and in a monastery of the congregation of Solesmes, with its intense liturgical preoccupation and normal repudiation of activity outside the cloister walls; between the public prayer and organized agriculture of the

Cistercians and the eremitical solitude of the Carthusians. Yet these are certainly all monks, engaged in the various legitimate developments which have taken place within monastic life in the West during fourteen hundred years.

All this is strange and incomprehensible to the traditional monk of the East. Of the regular or religious life in its extended meaning he knows nothing;[1] and within monasticism itself he knows of no distinctions equivalent to "Benedictine," "Cistercian," "Carthusian." He does not belong to any "order"; he is just a monk. There is only one "rule" (except for the so-called Antonians), that of St. Basil, drawn up in the form of question and answer for the use of his monastery in Pontus, and that does not meet the requirements of a rule as understood in the West. We call these monks Basilians, but the label is inaccurate, and meaningless to those of whom we use it. There was no such thing as an Eastern "Order of St. Basil" until the Italo-Greek, Ruthenian, and Melkite monks were reformed and reorganized during the past three hundred and fifty years. St. Basil was not a legislator or maker of any systematic foundation and "his" monks do not regard him as such. "They do not belong to St. Basil's order but St. Basil belonged to theirs," as it has been well put. Although St. Pachomius made an experiment in federation sixteen hundred years ago and there is a monastic republic at Mount Athos today, with a governing council, a traditional Eastern monk still belongs to a certain monastery and to nothing else, and each monastery (*laura*) is independent of all the others.[2]

With us Latins, a monk, with due regard for St. Benedict's

---

[1] There have been experiments in some dissident Orthodox countries of recent years. I refer elsewhere to those Catholic Eastern organizations which have come about by way of development or by direct importation from the West.

[2] It is worth remembering that a Benedictine monk is professed not, like a friar, for the whole order, but for his own monastery, and the principle of individual self-governing monasteries still obtains to a considerable extent. There are even some Benedictine monks who will not make use of the expression Order of St. Benedict, but call themselves "monks of such and such an abbey."

prescription that nothing is to be preferred before the celebration of the Divine Office, may be engaged in many ways, in
teaching, in learned studies, in agriculture or the fine arts, even
in parochial work. Not so in the East. "These things," they would
say, "are the concern of schoolmasters, of laymen, of scholars,
of clergy; we are monks." As such, their business is to flee from
"the world," to practise penance, and to worship God. In a
word, to live as much as possible like the angels; and in fact
they call their life the "angelic life" and their dress the "angelic
habit." The conditions and means of attaining such a way of life
vary in detail, but one general result is that "an Eastern monastery is the most perfect relic of the fourth century left in the
world" (Fortescue). Theoretically the day is divided into three
parts: eight hours for liturgical worship, eight for work (almost
entirely manual), and eight for food, sleep, and recreation. The
whole of the Divine Office is sung and it takes every minute
of eight hours when it is celebrated properly. The principal
prescribed austerity is fasting, which in its strictness and fre-
quency outdoes anything prescribed by any rule in the West.
An American Catholic, paraphrasing Dr. Fortescue, wrote in a
publication of the Catholic Students' Mission Crusade that,
"Eastern monks sing very lengthy offices, pray incessantly, fast
incredibly, and *that is all*" (italics mine). It is therefore not
out of place to point out that these activities, without the quali-
fying epithets and with the addition of *manual* work (which
in fact Eastern monks commonly do), are precisely the occupa-
tions of monks as envisaged by St. Benedict. As an English
Benedictine abbot, the late Dom Cuthbert Butler, has written:
"The real use of a monastic house lies not in its activities and
usefulnesses. It lies rather in things that cannot be counted by
statistics or estimated by results." A monk of the East would
consider that so obvious as hardly to be worth saying.

There are no lay-brothers in an Eastern monastery, and just
as St. Benedict legislated for independent, self-governing families
of men not in holy orders, so it still is the exception for an
Eastern monk to be a priest. But no distinction is made between

the monk who is a priest (hieromonk) and the monk who is not.[3] The latter may be elected abbot and rule his ordained brethren, just as a monk of the lowest degree may be made abbot and rule over those of the higher degrees. The difference between the three monastic grades, *rasophore, stavrophore* and *megaloskhemos*, are personal, and affect the individual life; whatever the theory of beginner and proficient, imperfect and perfect monks, they are all in fact monks.[4] The *rasophore*, though he has taken no vows, is considered equally to have bound himself for life by entering upon the way of monastic perfection and assuming a part of the habit, and until a hundred years ago dispensations to leave the monastery were unheard of, though a monk could be expelled for misbehaviour. Even now the stricter non-Catholic canonists regard such a dispensation as opposed to the fundamental teaching of Eastern monasticism.

Monasticism in the past was even more influential in the East than in the West, and has left its imprint on every aspect of religious life, from the form of the Divine Office and the dress of bishops to the high ascetical standard and the fasts imposed on the laity.

The traditional Eastern monastic life is still the only form of monasticism, in various states of vigor or decadence, in the different dissident Orthodox churches today. In the Catholic Church, as has been shown elsewhere, it survived in an almost unrecognizable form at Grottaferrata (see p. 62), while among the Ukrainians and in Syria the monks became in varying degrees more like clerks regular, many of them serving parishes. Thus traditional Eastern monachism was practically non-existent among Catholics until it was revived in Galicia by the late Metropolitan Andrew Szepticky.

---

[3] Except that only a hieromonk may admit a man or woman to the monastic state, and then not to a degree higher than his own. For example, an abbot who is a priest and a monk of the second degree governs *megaloskhemoi*, but he cannot admit to that degree. Bishops who are monks have plenary powers in these matters.

[4] The respective vows of *stavrophore* and *megaloskhemos* are not at all equivalent to our simple and solemn profession. The whole thing is different from beginning to end.

This revival was due radically to half a dozen Ukrainian peasants who wished to undertake a more perfect way of life but were considered unsuitable for acceptance by the Ruthenian Basilians. So about 1900 they began to live a common life of their own, under the direction of the parish priest of Olesko, a village near Zloszov. Here they were found by the Metropolitan Szepticky (himself a monk), who transferred them first to Vulka, near Lvov, and then to Skynliv. In 1906 he gave them constitutions (*typikon*), in 1908 ordained the first hieromonk, and later appointed an abbot (*hegumenos*) in the person of his own brother, Father Clement (Count Casimir Szepticky), who had been trained under the Benedictines of Beuron. In 1914 there were forty of these monks, but a Polish officer denounced them as Russian partisans; so they were conscripted, interned, or deported to Hungary, and their monastery at Skynliv burned down in the Polish-Ukrainian war. After the war the metropolitan (who retained supreme authority over them as archimandrite) collected them together in his country-house at Univ and they began all over again.

These monks call themselves Studites, as emulating the life lived in the monastery of the Stoudion at Constantinople in the ninth century.[5] That observance simplified and systematized the customs of St. Basil and, so far from being a particular code, was an attempt to gather up and express the spirit of all Eastern monastic legislation; it had a profound effect particularly on the monasticism of Russia. The Ukrainian Studites aim at no particular task, and accept any vocation that is not at variance with Oriental ideas of monastic life. Most of the subjects were young peasants, used only to manual work, but even before 1914 Mgr. Szepticky had made the nucleus of a foundation in Lvov itself where those who were suitable could undertake intellectual pursuits. The Byzantine Liturgy is carried out with great care, and the morning office with the Eucharistic Liturgy lasts from

---

[5] There is a good article on Catholic Byzantine monasticism in *Pax*, No. 84 (Caldey Abbey, 1927). For the Stoudion, see Gardner, *Theodore of Studium* (London, 1905).

five in the morning till nine; but daily life is far less precise and ordered than in a monastery of the West, for spontaneity and freedom are among the notes of Eastern monachism. In general the life of these monks is passed in prayer and manual work, to which those engaged in intellectual work must also give some time daily. Apart from necessity, silence is broken only at recreation. There is no ordinary limit to the quantity of food taken, but it is very plain and meat is served only on Sundays and feast days (not at all in Lent). In accordance with Eastern custom, no distinction is made in way of life or otherwise between monks who are priests (hieromonks) and those who are not.

In 1939 the Studites had one principal *laura*, four lesser monasteries, and several other small establishments. There were about two hundred monks, of whom some eighty were *skhimniky* (the Slavonic equivalent of *stavrophore*, monks of the second grade, "professed"). Twenty were priests and six deacons. There were also three Studite houses of women, with about forty nuns; they were strictly enclosed and bound to choral office, but conducted an orphanage, etc., within their precincts. During the events of 1939–1945 these Studites were a special object of soviet violence, and there is every reason to fear that they are now completely broken up and dispersed.

So far I have referred only to monks of the Byzantine rite, but there are others of other rites, who are commonly called Antonians, as professing the so-called "rule of St. Antony." This was put together from the oral instructions and written apophthegms of the saint and was intended rather for those living a semi-eremitical life than for cenobites. It is professed by the non-Catholic Coptic monks of Egypt and Ethiopia and at the famous dissident Orthodox monastery of Mount Sinai, but the most important bodies of Antonians are among the Catholic Maronites in the Lebanon. They have preserved the Eastern prescription of three classes of monks, over and above a postulancy of one or two years, and are distinguished as "habit-wearers," "cross-bearers," and "great-habiters"; but they take the three vows of the West. Some of the Lebanese monasteries have hermitages in their neighbourhood, each occupied by two monks (one a priest); these do not normally receive visitors. keep an almost perpetual silence, fast daily, and are bound to a certain number of hours of manual work every day. The more recent Chaldean Antonians resemble the Maronites, on whom they were modelled.

Further particulars of other contemporary Catholic Eastern monks and "regular" clergy will be found in the account of each different church; but special mention must also be made here of the Armenian Mekhitarist monks, who in the Rule of St. Benedict have found inspiration for a monastic life admirably fitted to the needs of their church (see p. 186).

Since Pope Pius XI's letter to the Benedictine abbot-primate in 1924, several Benedictine monasteries have been accepting subjects of Eastern rite, and the international double-rite house of Amay (now at Chevetogne) was founded in Belgium in the same year. The Benedictines of the Greek College in Rome and the Syro-Benedictines have been referred to (pp. 116 and 157), as have the Ethiopian Cistercians (p. 147); in the United States, the Benedictine abbey of St. Procopius at Lisle, Illinois, has some Oriental monks, and there is a Slav-Byzantine monastery at Prague.

APPENDIX

DISTRIBUTION
OF THE CATHOLIC EASTERN CHURCHES

(Where no later figures are available, the numbers of the faithful are taken from the figures in the official Statistica *published in 1932).*

Alexandrian Rite:

i. Copts	63,000
ii. Ethiopians	30,500

Antiochene Rite:

i. Syrians in patriarchal territory	60,000	
in U. S. A.	6,800	
in other places	7,700	
		74,500
ii. Maronites in patriarchal territory..	323,000	
in U. S. A.	60,000?	
in other places ....c.	8,000	
		391,000
iii. Malankarese		50,000

Armenian Rite:

In patriarchal territory	45,000	
In Rumania	36,000	
Elsewhere in Europe	11,600	
In U. S. A. and other places	8,000	
In Russia	50,000?	
		150,600

Byzantine Rite:

Bulgars	5,500
Greeks	3,300

Italo-Greek-Albanians:

In Italy and Sicily	50,850	
In U. S. A.	10,000?	
		60,850
Yugoslavs		55,000
Melkites in patriarchal territory........	150,500	
in U. S. A.	20,000	
in other places .... *c.*	2,500	
		173,000
Rumanians in Rumania	1,426,000	
in U. S. A.	8,000	
		1,434,000
Russians in Eastern Europe	18,000?	
elsewhere .... *c.*	4,500	
		22,500
Ruthenians in Galicia	3,500,000	
in Podcarpathia	500,000	
in the Bukovina	69,000	
in Hungary	160,000	
in U. S. A. .... *c.*	625,000	
in Canada .... *c.*	300,000	
in South America	67,000	
"Displaced" .... *c.*	250,000	
		5,471,000

Chaldean Rite:

i. Chaldeans in patriarchal territory...	95,000	
in U. S. A.	800	
elsewhere .... *c.*	1,000	
		96,800
ii. Malabarese		928,000

The general total of the Catholics of the Eastern rites is therefore nearly 8¾ million souls, without taking into consideration the
results of recent events (see p. 76 ff.).

They have 6 patriarchal sees and 60 archiepiscopal and episcopal sees, and in 1932 there were in addition 34 titular bishops.

Secular clergy, in 1932, 8,250.

Regular clergy in 1932 (priests and deacons): *c.* 1,380.

CHART OF CATHOLIC EASTERN CHURCHES

Church	Where Found	Chief Bishop	His Residence	Total Number of Faithful (Round Numbers)	Liturgical Language	Vernacular Language	Date of Definitive Separation of Original Church	Date of Reunion of Present Catholic Body
ALEXANDRIAN RITE								
1. Copts	Egypt	Patriarch of Alexandria	Cairo	63,000	Coptic and Arabic	Arabic	451	1741
2. Ethiopians	Ethiopia, Eritrea	An episcopal ordinary	Asmara	30,500	Ge'ez	Amharic, etc.	c. 550	1839
ANTIOCHENE RITE								
1. Syrians	Syria, Irak, U. S. A.	Syrian Patriarch of Antioch	Bairut	74,500	Syriac and Arabic	Arabic, Syriac	543	1656
2. Maronites	Syria, U. S. A.	Maronite Patriarch of Antioch	Bekerkeh	391,000	Syriac and Arabic	Arabic	c. 650	1182
3. Malankarese	India	Archbishop of Trivandrum	Trivandrum	50,000	Syriac and Malayalam	Malayalam	1653	1930
ARMENIAN RITE								
1. Armenians under the patriarch	Syria, Near East	Patriarch of Cilicia	Bairut	45,000	Classical Armenian	Armenian	c. 525	1198: 1742
2. Other Armenians	Europe, Russia, U. S. A.			100,000(?)				
BYZANTINE RITE								
1. Bulgars	Bulgaria	An episcopal ordinary	Sofia	5,500	Church Slavonic	Bulgarian	c. 1472	1860
2. Greeks	Greece, Turkey, etc.	Two episcopal ordinaries	Athens; Istanbul	3,300	Greek	Greek	1472	1860
3. Hungarian-Ruthenians	Hungary	Bishop of Hajdudorog	Nyiregyhaza	c. 140,000	Magyar	Magyar	c. 1472	c. 1652
4. Italo-Greek-Albanians	Italy, Sicily, U. S. A.	Two Bishops	Lungro; Piana	c. 60,000	Greek	Italian, etc.	Never separated	
5. Melkites	Syria, Egypt, U. S. A.	Patriarch of Antioch	Damascus	173,000	Arabic	Arabic	c. 1517	1724
6. Rumanians	Rumania, U. S. A.	Archbishop of Fagaras	Blaj	1,434,000	Rumanian	Rumanian	1701	1701
7. Russians (a) in U.S.S.R.	U.S.S.R.	An episcopal visitor		18,000	Church Slavonic	Russian	c. 1472	1595: 1920
(b) elsewhere	Europe, Amer., Far East	An episcopal ordinary	Rome	c. 4,500	Church Slavonic	Russian	1472	1905
8. Ruthenians (a) in U.S.S.R.	Galicia	Archbishop of Lvov	Lvov	3,500,000	Church Slavonic	Ukrainian	c. 1472	1595
(b) Podcarpathian	U.S.S.R.	Bishop of Mukachevo	Mukachevo	500,000	Church Slavonic	Ukrainian	c. 1472	1652
(c) elsewhere in Europe	Bukovina, "displaced," etc.			c. 250,000	Church Slavonic	Ukrainian		
(d) in the Americas		Three episcopal ordinaries	Philadelphia; Homestead; Winnipeg	927,000	Church Slavonic	Ukrainian		
9. Yugoslavs	Yugoslavia	Bishop of Krizevci	Krizevci	55,000	Church Slavonic	Croat, etc.	c. 1472	1611
CHALDEAN RITE								
1. Chaldeans	Irak, Syria, U. S. A.	Patriarch of Babylon	Mosul	96,000	Syriac	Arabic, Syriac	c. 500	1551
2. Malabarese	India	Archbishop of Ernakulam	Ernakulam	632,000	Syriac	Malayalam	?	Before 1599

GENERAL BIBLIOGRAPHY

REFERENCE BOOKS

Statistica con Cenni Storici della Gerarchia e dei Fedeli di Rito Orientale (Sacra Congregatione Orientale, Roma, 1932).

Alès, *Dictionnaire apologetique de la Foi catholique.*

Vacant, etc., *Dictionnaire de théologie catholique.*

Baudrillart, etc., *Dictionnaire d'histoire et de géographie ecclésiastiques.*

Cabrol, *Dictionnaire d'archéologie et de liturgie.*

Viller, *Dictionnaire de spiritualité ascétique et mystique.*

Herbermann, etc., *The Catholic Encyclopaedia.*

GENERAL

Attwater, *The Book of Eastern Saints* (Milwaukee, 1938).

Batiffol, *Catholicism and Papacy* (London, 1926).

Baynes, *The Byzantine Empire* (London, 1925).

Bréhier, *L'Eglise et l'Orient au moyen âge: les Croisades* (Paris, 1928).

Byron, *The Byzantine Achievement* (London, 1929).

de Clercq, *Les Eglises unies d'Orient* (Paris, 1935).

Congrès eucharistique international à Jérusalem, 1893. Full text of the papers read (Paris, 1896).

Davis, *A Short History of the Near East* (New York, 1923).

Dawson, *The Making of Europe* (London, 1932).

Diehl, *Histoire de l'Empire byzantin* (Paris, 1920).

Duskie, *The Canonical Status of Orientals in the United States* (Washington, D. C., 1928).

Dvornik, *Les Slaves, Byzance et Rome* (Paris, 1925).

—— *National Churches and the Church Universal* (London, 1944).

Every, *The Byzantine Patriarchate 451–1204* (London, 1947).

Fortescue, *The Greek Fathers* (London, 1908).

—— *The Lesser Eastern Churches* (London, 1913).

Hughes, *A History of the Church*, Vols. I, II, and III (London, 1934–1946)

Hussey, *Church and Learning in the Byzantine Empire* (Oxford, 1937).

Janin, *Les Eglises orientales et les Rites orientaux*, 3rd ed. (Paris, 1935).

Kolarz, *Myths and Realities in Eastern Europe* (London, 1946).

Lagier, *L'Orient chrétien des Apôtres jusqu'à Photius* (Paris, 1935).

McGarrigle, et al., *The Eastern Branches of the Catholic Church* (New York, 1938).

Runciman, *The Byzantine Civilization* (London, 1933).

Scott, *The Eastern Churches and the Papacy* (London, 1928).

Sesostris Sidaruss, *Les Patriarchats dans l'Empire Ottoman* (Paris, 1907).

Vasilyev, *Histoire de l'Empire byzantin*, 2 vols. (Paris, 1932).

Various hands, *The Pre-Nicene Church* (London, 1935).

LITURGY AND ART

Attwater, *Prayers From the Eastern Liturgies* (London, 1931).

Bayet, *L'Art byzantin* (Paris, 1924).

Dalton, *Eastern Christian Art* (Oxford, 1925).

Dirks, *Les Saintes Icones* (Amay, 1929).

Glück, *Die Christliche Kunst des Ostens* (Berlin, 1923).

Hanssens, *Institutiones liturgicae de ritibus orientalibus* (Rome, 1930).

———— *De Missa rituum orientalium* (Rome, 1932).

King, *Notes on the Catholic Liturgies*, Vol. I (London, 1930).

Monneret, *Le Chiese della Mesopotamia* (Rome, 1940).

Nilles, *Kalendarium manuale utriusque Ecclesiae orientalis et occidentalis*, 2 vols. (Innsbruck, 1896–1897).

Rahmani, *Les Liturgies orientales et occidentales* (Bairut, 1929).

Rice, *Byzantine Art* (Oxford, 1936).

Salaville, *An Introduction to . . . Eastern Liturgies* (London, 1938).

PERIODICALS

The Eastern Churches Quarterly (Catholic Near East Welfare Association, New York).

The Voice of the Church, monthly, in Russian and English (Lisle Abbey, Illinois).

The Chrysostom, monthly, published from 1935 to 1938 (McKeesport, Pa.).

Irénikon, quarterly (Prieuré d'Amay-Chevetogne, Belgium).

Echos d'Orient, quarterly (5 rue Bayard, Paris).

L'Unité de l'Eglise, published every two months from 1922 to 1938 (same address).

Stoudion, a most valuable publication in six volumes, ending in 1930 (12 via Vespasiana, Rome).

Roma e l'Oriente, quarterly (Grottaferrata, Italy).

Der Christliche Orient, quarterly (St. Andrew's College, Munich).

Orientalia Christiana, a double series, of articles and monographs, beginning in 1923 (Instituto per gli Studi orientali, Rome).

The Ark, Ukrainian monthly (111 West North Street, Stamford, Conn.).

GLOSSARY

Most of the terms noted are used and explained in the text, but are repeated and briefly defined here for convenience of reference. Liturgical terms mostly apply to the Byzantine rite. *Ar.* = Arabic, *Gk.* = Greek, *Lat.* = Latin, *Sl.* = Slavonic, *Syr.* = Syriac.

ABA, ABBA (*Syr.*, father). The title of an Ethiopian priest, bishop, or saint.

ABUNA (*Ar.*, our father). The title of the head of the dissident Ethiopic Church, and the ordinary form of address to clergy in Arabic.

AER (*Gk.*, air. *Sl.*, *vozdukh*). Large veil covering the chalice and paten.

ALEPPINES. Maronite and Melkite congregations of monks, centred at Aleppo.

AMBO (*Gk.*, a raised place). A sort of pulpit in front and to one side of the *eikonostasis* in some churches.

AMNOS (*Gk.*, lamb. *Sl.*, *agnetz*). The first and principal part cut from the *prosphora* for consecration.

ANALOGION (*Gk.*). A lectern or small table.

ANAPHORA (*Gk.*, offering). Equivalent term to "canon of the Mass," sometimes used for the whole Liturgy. Most Eastern Liturgies have several alternative *anaphoras*.

ANBA, AMBA (*Coptic*, father). The title of a Coptic priest, bishop, or saint.

ANOINTING (*Gk.*, *eukhelaion*. *Sl.*, *eleosvyaschenie*). The sacrament called Extreme Unction in the West.

ANTIDORON (*Gk.*, a gift instead of [Holy Communion]). Blessed bread.

ANTIMENSION (*Gk.*, instead of a table). A cloth with relics laid on the altar for the Liturgy to be celebrated on.

ANTONIANS. Monks of the Maronite and Chaldean rites.

APOCRISIARIUS (*Lat.*, from *Gk.*, *apokrisis*, answer). A legate or nuncio.

APODEIPNON (*Gk.*, after-supper. *Sl.*, *povecherie*). Compline.

APOLYSIS (*Gk.*, dismissal. *Sl.*, *otpust*). The conclusion of a liturgical office.

APOSTOLOS (*Gk.*). The lesson from the Epistles or Acts; the book containing them.

ARCHBISHOP. In strict Byzantine usage the head of a series of metropolitan provinces. No longer so used.

ARCHIEREUS (*Gk.*, high priest). A bishop. The pope is *Ho tes Romes Archiereus.*

ARCHIMANDRITE (*Gk.*, chief of a fold). The superior of a large monastery or of a congregation; also a titular dignitary.

ARTOKLASIA (*Gk.*, breaking of bread). Blessing of bread, wine, and oil at Vespers on a vigil.

ARTOPHORION (*Gk.*, bread-carrier. *Sl.*, *kovtcheg*). The tabernacle of an altar.

ASTERISKOS (*Gk.*, star). A metal frame to keep the veil off the host.

AZYME (*Gk.*, unleavened). Unleavened altar-bread.

BALADITES (*Ar.*, rustics). Maronite and Melkite congregations of monks.

BASILIANS. Improperly, Eastern monks in general; properly, certain Catholic congregations.

BEATITUDE, HIS, YOUR, or BLESSEDNESS. The style of address and reference given to an Eastern patriarch.

BEMA (*Gk.*, step). The sanctuary of a church.

BYZANTINE. Primarily, appertaining to Byzantium (Constantinople); by extension, appertaining to all those churches using the Liturgy, etc., of Constantinople.

"CANONS, THE." Canon law.

CHARTOPHYLAX (*Gk.*, keeper of records). A diocesan chancellor.

CHERUBIKON (*Gk.*). The "hymn of the Cherubim," intoned just before the great entrance in the Byzantine Liturgy.

CHIROTONY (*Gk.*, stretching forth of hands). The sacrament of Holy Orders; ordination or consecration.

CHOREPISKOPOS (*Gk.*, rural overseer). A title of honour in several rites, sometimes with duties attached. It is occasionally rendered into the horrid word "chor-bishop."

CIBORIUM (*Lat.*, from *Gk.*, a cup). A canopy of wood or stone, supported by pillars, covering an altar.

CONCELEBRATION. The celebration of the Liturgy by several priests at one altar at the same time.

CREED. The creed of Nicaea-Constantinople is the only one used liturgically in any Eastern rite.

CROSS. The "Russian cross" has three bars, the top one representing the title and the bottom one (sloped from left to right) representing the footrest. The "Greek cross" is equilateral.

CROWN. The Byzantine episcopal mitre, worn also by Armenian priests.

CROWNING. The marriage rite, from its chief ceremony.

DIAKONIKON (*Gk.*, of the deacon). The part of the sanctuary to the south of the altar; a liturgical book for the deacon's use.

DIKERION (*Gk.*). A two-branched candlestick.

DIPTYCHS (*Gk.*, twice-folded). The commemoration of the living and the dead in the Liturgy, whose names were formerly written on two conjoined tablets.

DISKOS (*Gk.*, quoit). The Byzantine paten.

DISSIDENT. Non-Catholic Christian, especially of an Eastern church.

DOORS. "Holy," the central doors of the *eikonostasis;* "royal," the central doors from the narthex into the nave. The "holy doors" are sometimes called "royal."

EIKON (*Gk.*, image). A flat painted sacred picture, often covered with embossed metal except over the faces and hands.

EIKONOSTASIS (*Gk.*, picture-stand). The screen separating the nave from the sanctuary, and adorned with pictures.

EILETON (*Gk.*). A linen corporal.

EKPHONESIS (*Gk.*). A "lifting of the voice" at the last words of an inaudible prayer.

ENKOLPION (*Gk.*, that worn on the breast). An oval medallion worn on a chain round the neck.

ENTRANCE, LITTLE, GREAT. Processions, with the Gospel-book and the bread and wine respectively, in the Byzantine and Armenian Liturgies.

EPARCHY (*Gk.*, province). Any episcopal diocese.

EPIGONATION (*Gk.*, *epigounis*, thigh. *Sl.*, *palitsa*). A lozenge-shaped episcopal vestment, worn above the right knee. Peculiar to the pope in the West.

EPIKLESIS (*Gk.*, invocation). A prayer that the Holy Ghost may come down upon the bread and wine and turn it into Christ's body and blood, and imploring the grace of the sacrament for the recipients. It comes in fact after the consecration.

EPIMANIKIA (*Gk.*, upon the sleeves. *Sl.*, *narukavniki*). Liturgical cuffs.

EPITRAKHELION (*Gk.*, upon the neck). The sacerdotal stole.

EUKHELAION. *See* Anointing.

EUKHOLOGION (*Gk.*, prayer-book. *Sl.*, *Sluzebnik*). A book containing the texts of the Liturgies and other offices.

EXARCH (*Gk.*, ruler). The primate of an independent church, between a patriarch and an archbishop; but more usually now a priest or bishop with a special charge. Also a title of honour.

FILIOQUE (*Lat.*, and from the Son. *Gk.*, *kai ek tou Huiou*). The phrase added to the Nicene Creed in the West which Photius in 863 declared to be a "corruption of the faith."

GE'EZ. Classical Ethiopic, the liturgical language of that rite.

GYNAECEUM (*Lat. Gk.*, *gynaikites*). The part of a church reserved for women.

HAGIA (*Gk.*, holy things). The sacred elements after consecration.

HAIKAL (*Ar.*, temple). The sanctuary of a Coptic church.

HEGUMENOS (*Gk.*, leader). An abbot.

HESPERINOS (*Gk. Sl.*, *vechernya*). Vespers.

HEXAPTERYGON (*Gk.*, six-winged). Another name for the *ripidion*.

HIERARCH (*Gk.*, sacred ruler). Any high member of a hierarchy, but especially an archbishop or patriarch.

HIERATIKON (*Gk.*). A book containing the prayers most used by a priest, a variable compilation. Also called the *Leitourgikon* or Little Eukhologion.

HIERODEACON. A monk who is a deacon.

HIEROMONK. A monk who is a priest.

HOROLOGION (*Gk. Sl.*, *Chasoslov*, book of the hours). A book containing the common prayers of the Divine Office, etc.

ICONOCLASM (*Gk.*, image-breaking). The campaign against the veneration of holy images and the accompanying persecution, centred at Constantinople, from *c.* 726 till 787 and from 814 till 842.

JULIAN KALENDAR. Issued by Julius Caesar in 45 B.C., corrected under Pope Gregory XIII in 1582. The Julian reckoning is now 13 days behind the Gregorian.

KAMELAUKION (*Gk.*, *kamelos*, camel, *aukhen*, nape of the neck). The clerical hat of the Byzantine rite, at first made of camel-hair cloth.

Kamision. The long ungirdled vestment proper to minor clerics.

Kanon. A rhythmical hymn.

Karshuni. Arabic written in Syriac characters.

Katholikos (Gk., universal delegate). The title of the heads of the Nestorian, Armenian, and Georgian churches, now equivalent to patriarch.

Koimesis (Gk., falling asleep. Sl., Uspenie). The feast of the Assumption of our Lady.

Kontakion (Gk.). A hymn referring to the day's feast.

Kummus. A Coptic abbot; also a title of honour for any priest of that rite.

Lance, The Holy (Gk., lonkhe. Sl., kopyo). The Byzantine liturgical knife.

Laura (Gk., alley). Formerly a monastery consisting of rows of cells or huts; now any sizeable monastery.

Lector (Gk., anagnostes. Sl., chtets). The lower of the two lesser orders normal in the East. His chief office is to read the Epistle.

Liturgy, The (Gk., leitourgia, a public duty or work). The Eucharistic Sacrifice, i.e., "Mass."

Mandyas (Gk.). 1. A short cloak, part of the monastic habit. 2. A sort of cope, worn by bishops.

Mar (Syr., lord). Title given to saints and bishops in the Syriac rites; fem., mart.

Masnaphto (Syr.). A small hood worn by bishops of the Antiochene rite.

Megaloskhemos (Gk., great habiter). The highest grade of Eastern monk.

Melkites (Syr., malok, king). Name given to the Catholic and Orthodox Byzantines of Syria, Palestine, and Egypt.

Menaion (Gk., men, month). A liturgical book in six or twelve volumes, containing the proper parts of the Divine Office for fixed feasts.

Mesonyktikon (Gk., midnight. Sl., Polunoschnitsa). The night-office.

Metany (Gk., penance). Great, a complete prostration; ordinary or little, a profound bow, taking the place of the Western genuflection.

Metokhion (Gk.). An estate or cell belonging to a monastery.

Metropolitan. In strict Byzantine usage, equivalent to a Western archbishop. Catholics now use the title almost indifferently with archbishop.

MOLEBEN (*Sl.*). An occasional service of thanksgiving or petition.

MYRON (*Gk.*, sweet oil). The Holy Chrism, which may be blessed only by patriarchs or other primates; Confirmation therewith.

MYSTERY (*Gk.*, something hidden). The ordinary word for a sacrament in the East.

NARTHEX. The western vestibule of a church.

OLD BELIEVERS OR OLD RITUALISTS. Russian sectaries who refused the reforms of the Patriarch Nikon of Moscow in the seventeenth century. Before the revolution they numbered, with other sects, over 30 millions, but are commonly reckoned by Westerners as members of the dissident Orthodox Church.

OMOPHORION (*Gk.*, borne on the shoulders). The large Byzantine *pallium*, worn by all bishops when celebrating the Liturgy; a smaller one is used for convenience at certain parts.

ORARION (*Gk.*). The deacon's long stole.

ORTHODOX (*Gk.*, *orthodoxos*, *Sl.*, *pravoslav*, right believer). The name for all those who accepted the Council of Chalcedon; now usually confined as a title to the non-Catholic Eastern Orthodox Church.

ORTHROS (*Gk.*, daybreak. *Sl.*, *utrenya*). The office equivalent to Matins and Lauds.

PANAGIA (*Gk.*). "All-holy," used for the Mother of God as we say "our Lady." Also another name for the *enkolpion*.

PANNYKHIDIA (*Gk.*, all night). An office for the dead.

PANTOKRATOR (*Gk.*, all mighty). An image of our Lord ruling from heaven, i.e., Christ the King.

PAPPAS (*Gk.*, father, i.e., pope). All Greek-speaking priests are called *pappas*, and the equivalent (*pop*) is common among the Slavs but is considered wanting in respect; they say *batyushka* "little father." "Pope" is one of the official titles of the Orthodox patriarch of Alexandria.

PAREKKLESIA (*Gk.*, beside church). A side chapel or addition to a church.

PATRIARCH (*Gk.*, ruler of a family). A bishop who holds the highest rank after the pope in the hierarchy of jurisdiction. A patriarch can be subject to no other prelate except the pope. In the West the title is honorary, except for the pope himself, who is "Patriarch of the West" or "of Rome."

PERIODEUTES (*Gk.*, visitor. *Syr.*, *bardut,* Malayalam, *prodott*). A title of honour given to priests holding positions of responsibility in the three churches of Antiochene rite.

PHENOLION (*Gk.*). The Byzantine chasuble.

PRESANCTIFIED, LITURGY OF THE. A Liturgy in which there is no consecration; a Host consecrated at a previous Liturgy is consumed at the Communion.

PROSKOMIDE (*Gk.*, preparation). The preparatory part of the Liturgy, at which the ministers vest and the bread and wine are prepared.

PROSPHORA (*Gk.*, oblation). The Byzantine altar-bread, like a small loaf or cake.

PROTHESIS (*Gk.*, ante-deposition). The part of the sanctuary to the north of the altar, where the bread and wine are made ready.

PROTODEACON. Archdeacon or senior deacon. Archdeacons are generally deacons, i.e., not priests, in the East.

PROTOPOPE — PRESBYTER — PRIEST. An archpriest, "rural dean" (distinguish from *archiereus*). In some churches protopresbyters are different from archpriests.

PROTOPSALTES (*Gk. Sl., regent khora*). The chief cantor.

PROTOTHRONE. The first see of a patriarchate, after the patriarch's; e.g., Tyre is the protothrone of Antioch; or a primatial see, e.g., the see of Rome is the protothrone of the world, Constantinople of the East.

RABBAN (*Syr.,* our father). The Syrian term corresponding to hieromonk, a monk who is also a priest.

RASON (*Gk.*). The wide-sleeved gown proper to the Eastern clergy.

RASOPHORE (*Gk.*, rason-wearer. *Sl., ryasonosets*). The lowest grade of Eastern monk.

RIPIDION (*Gk.*, fan). A metal liturgical fan affixed to a pole.

ROSARY (*Gk., konbologion. Sl., chotky*). The Eastern rosary usually consists of one hundred beads at each of which a metany is made and an ejaculatory prayer said. It is a purely monastic practice. Most Eastern Catholics use the Western rosary.

"SAINT SOPHIA." A barbarous name often given in English to the church of the Holy Wisdom at Constantinople.

SAKKOS (*Gk.*, a sack). The principal eucharistic vestment proper to Byzantine bishops.

SKOUPHOS. The cap worn by monks under their veil and by minor clerics.

SOLEA. The step before the holy doors at which Communion is given.

STAROSLAV. A rather barbarous name, given first by French writers, to Church Slavonic.

STAROVERY (*Russ.*). *See* Old Believers.

STASIDIA (*Gk.*, standing-places). The fixed seats behind the altar, in front of the *eikonostasis*, and around the walls of a Byzantine church: usually stood at rather than sat upon.

STAVROPHORE (*Gk.*, cross-bearer, *Sl.*, *skhimnik*). The middle grade of Eastern monk.

STIKHARION (*Gk.*). A vestment equivalent to an alb.

SUBDEACON. A lesser order in the Eastern church, and properly having no liturgical office.

SYNAXARION (*Gk.*). A kalendar or martyrology with brief notices of the saints; a passage from the same read in the office.

SYNAXIS (*Gk.*, assembly). 1. A feast on which are commemorated saints connected with the mystery of the previous day. 2. The council of seniors in a monastery.

SYNKELLOS. 1. A bishop's secretary. 2. An auxiliary or titular bishop.

SYNOD (*Gk.*, meeting). 1. Any ecclesiastical council. 2. The governing assembly of an Orthodox church.

SYNTHRONON (*Gk.*). The bishop's seat and stalls for clergy behind the altar in a cathedral.

TEMPLON (*Gk.*). Another name for the *eikonostasis*.

THEOTOKOS (*Gk.*, *tokos*, childbirth). The Mother of God. *Theotokion:* a hymn in her honour.

THRONE. An expression used in the East equivalently with the Western "see" (episcopal).

TREBNIK (*Sl.*). A Slavonic book of the Byzantine rite, the Ritual of the Sacraments.

TRIKERION (*Gk.*). A three-branched candlestick.

TRISAGION, THE. The thrice-holy hymn: "Holy God, holy strong One, holy deathless One, have mercy on us."

TROPARION (*Gk.*). A generic name for the short hymns of the Byzantine rite.

TYPIKON (*Gk.*). 1. A book of the kalendar and rubrics; each chief church of the Byzantine rite has one of its own. 2. A charter of monastic constitutions.

VARTAPET. A rank in the Armenian hierarchy, below the episcopate.

VICAR PATRIARCHAL. A local representative appointed by a patriarch.

VLADYKA (*Sl.*, lord, master). The Slavonic form of address to a bishop.

XEROPHAGY (*Gk.*, dry food). The stricter form of Eastern fast.

ZEON (*Gk.*, boiling). Warm water poured into the chalice before Communion.

ZONE (*Gk.*). Girdle.

INDEX